The United States Army Second Division
Northwest of Chateau Thierry
in World War I

The United States Army Second Division Northwest of Chateau Thierry in World War I

JOHN W. THOMASON, JR.

Edited by George B. Clark

McFarland & Company, Inc., Publishers
Jefferson, North Carolina, and London

LIBRARY OF CONGRESS CATALOGUING-IN-PUBLICATION DATA

Thomason, John W. (John William), 1893–1944.
    The United States Army Second Division Northwest of Château Thierry in World War I / John W. Thomason, Jr. ; edited by George B. Clark.
        p.   cm.
    Includes bibliographical references and index.

    ISBN-13: 978-0-7864-2523-5
    ISBN-10: 0-7864-2523-7 (softcover : 50# alkaline paper)

    1. United States. Army. Division, 2nd.   2. World War, 1914–1918 — Regimental histories — United States.   3. World War, 1914–1918 — Campaigns — France.   4. Château-Thierry, Battle of, Château-Therry, France, 1918.   I. Clark, George B., 1926–   II. Title.
D570.32nd .T56   2006
940.4'34 — dc22   2006010762
British Library cataloguing data are available

©2006 George B. Clark. All rights reserved

No part of this book may be reproduced or transmitted in any form or by any means, electronic or mechanical, including photocopying or recording, or by any information storage and retrieval system, without permission in writing from the publisher.

On the cover: Major John W. Thomason, Jr.; background image ©2004 Brand X Pictures

Manufactured in the United States of America

McFarland & Company, Inc., Publishers
  Box 611, Jefferson, North Carolina 28640
    www.mcfarlandpub.com

Contents

Preface	1
Editor's Introduction	5
Some German Divisional Records	9
ONE Robert d'Espagne to Chaumont-en-Vexin	11
TWO Chemin des Dames	14
THREE Chaumont-en-Vexin to Montreuil: 27 May–1 June	23
FOUR 1 June — Deployment	33
FIVE Plan of Employment, 31 May–1 June	43
Chateau Thierry	45
Belleau — Belleau Wood — Physical	45
Torcy — Bussiares — Tactical	49
SIX IV Reserve Corps (German): Movements, 27 May–1 June	51
23rd Infantry — 2 June	55
SEVEN IV Reserve Corps (German): 2 June	61
EIGHT 2nd Division and French XXI Corps d'Armée: 3–5 June	66
3 June	66
5 June	71
2nd Division — Midnight, 5–6 June	73
NINE IV Reserve Corps (German)	74
4 June	74
5 June; Condition of 10th Division	75

TEN 4th Brigade Field Order #1— Hill 142 79
  French XXI C.A. 81/P.C. 79
  Attack on Hill 142, 6 June 82
  45th Company — 7 June 91

ELEVEN First Attack on the Bois de Belleau 93
  pm 6 June 93
  7 June 109

TWELVE 3rd Brigade — 6 June 111
  23rd Infantry 111
  9th Infantry 120

THIRTEEN Relief of 10th and 197th Divisions, 7–9 June 122

FOURTEEN Bouresches and Bois de Belleau 125
  2nd Attack on Bois de Belleau by 3/6 on 8 June 125
  3rd Attack on Bois de Belleau 127
  4th Attack on Bois de Belleau — 2/5 Marines 130

FIFTEEN 237th and 28th Divisions (German): 10–11 June 145

SIXTEEN 5th Attack on the Bois de Belleau, 12 June — 2/5 149
  Attack on Bouresches, 12–13 June 153
  Gas Attack, 13 June 156
  13 June 159
  17th Company of 1/5 in the Bois de Belleau: 13–16 June 160

SEVENTEEN Relief of the 4th Brigade by the 7th Infantry 165
  7th Infantry Regiment in Bois de Belleau 166

EIGHTEEN Final Attacks in the Bois de Belleau by 3/5 175
  Note on Attack of 25 June 181
  Note on 87th Division Prior to 23 June 182
  Gassing of 3rd Brigade 183
  Regimental Sectors, 4th Brigade 183

NINETEEN 4th Brigade, 25 June–5 July 186

TWENTY Vaux: XXI CA, 12 June 189
  Notes on 5th M. G. Bn. in Vaux Operation 201
  2nd Trench Mortar Battery 206
  4th Machine Gun Battalion 207
  3rd Brigade Regimental Sectors 208

TWENTY-ONE Relief of Second Division, 3–10 July 211
  Casualties 215
  He Takes the War Too Seriously 218

Appendix I: Biography of John W. Thomason, Jr. 221

Appendix II: Brief History of the 2nd Division, 1917–1919 228

Suggested Reading 237

Index 241

Preface

Some years ago a book dealer offered me an original copy of the proposed chapter to be included in the U.S. Army's semi-official history of the Second Division during the World War. I purchased the bound manuscript at a price unheard of for anything but the most desirable and rarest of published books, primarily because it was written by Captain John W. Thomason, Jr., USMC. (He will sometimes be referred to as JWT; when necessary I will refer to myself as GBC.) Many aficionados of that author, artist, historian and full-time Marine had heard of it but none, or not many, certainly not myself, had ever seen it. People in the 2nd Division "business" have spoken of its detail; believe me, it is as meticulous and possibly more so than has generally been known.

When it arrived and was read, it assumed a very important place within my collection of material about the division's part in the war. It was used extensively in my research and writing of the book *Devil Dogs: Fighting Marines of World War I*.

In fact, besides its microscopic description, it was in fact possibly the only thing written by John W. Thomason, Jr., that remained unpublished. I also believed that it would be a very desirable product if allowed to circulate among the many Thomason admirers, members of the U.S. Marine Corps and the U.S. Army, and demanding historians of America's part in World War I, especially in France in June, 1918.

After many years of transferring the original typed material to my word processor I finally decided to offer a finished product to McFarland & Company, Inc., Publishers. They were interested but made the important suggestion that I obtain support for the project from members of the Thomason family, which I did. I insisted that it was the final unpublished work of a famous writer and artist and as such, should be presented in his style, as much as was possible. McFarland agreed and made valuable suggestions, most of which I have accepted and which you will find in the final text. We also agreed to leave the references and footnotes as they were and not gathered at the back of the book. I have effected the chapter titles in order to have a more easily useable Table of Contents. Overall, as editor, I was guided by the fact that what Thomason wrote was just a draft and I'm positive that the editors of the entire project would have modified the presentation somewhat in any case.

It was not a finished work by any standard but is presented much as it appears in my own copy, though my additional comments (usually in brackets and in italics) have, I hope, been of value. I have kept them to a minimum and only where I thought they should be included to clarify certain factual situations. My own copy has numerous original margin entries written by some of the "players" and I have included most in italics. My corrections are few. Thomason was not the finest speller (he seemed not to know that his aide in the project, Mathews, did not spell his name with two "t's" or that 1st Lt. Elliott Cooke, USA, a splendid company officer, had the letter "e" attached to his name). Nor was he always aware of the correct French spelling of town names. That has been helped by several friends in France who have provided corrected information. They are gratefully mentioned by name in the section on Acknowledgments. His use of the British version of certain words (like "defence" and "metre/kilometre") might indicate affectation but more likely lack of a Maxwell Perkins editing.[1] It appears that not just one person was involved in typing the manuscript; abbreviations vary considerably, as do military designations. I have endeavored to modify a few and have provided them with a relative consistency. The notes were especially a problem. The word "division" in the foreign units has usually been modified to "DI" meaning Division of Infantry" in keeping with most of the entries. Additionally, JWT began the unit designation, battalions and below, as III/5, or II/6, as examples. I have changed all to read "3/5" or "2/6." He also thought nothing of beginning a sentence with "III/5," which I have changed to "Three/5." The foregoing are all just examples.

Additionally, I have redone all the maps, very much in the manner of the person who executed them originally. They may have been done by Thomason himself or by someone else. Their final original appearance is nearly impossible to read, mainly because the hand-lettering was all rather poorly done, and because of their age. I have added several, not highly

---

1. Perkins, of Charles Scribner & Sons, was once the most famous editor in the publishing business in the United States, and he saw Thomason's value from the very first, adding much value to the first and final works of JWT published by that firm.

detailed, maps of the entire area of France in which this action took place. Those are to just place the action and are not definitive except by scale.

Illustrations by Thomason are not scarce, but selecting those of World War I, and those not too common, has taken some effort and time. In her will, Leda Thomason left all of JWT's original art work, much of which you will find in the book, to Sam Houston State University. I can well thank several persons there and especially those responsible in maintaining the Thomason Collection at the highest degree. The curator in charge, Paul Culp, has been extremely helpful as has his assistant, Cheryl S. Patton. I especially recommend them for catering to a near helpless neophyte. When all seemed lost, they were there to help bring the transfer of illustrations from their large collection to this edition. Many of the illustrations were selected because they have not been seen in previous publications. Each has a caption. Captions appearing in italics are my own interpretation of what the artist was saying. The other captions were taken from titles utilized in previous JWT books.

I also wish to thank Mr. Culp for putting me in personal contact with Margaret Thomason Cole, John W. Thomason's sister and the last surviving family member of that era. Her son, Dr. Thomas C. Cole, Jr., was gracious and supportive, expressing gratitude that "Uncle John's last project will be published." Which they, like most of you, have never seen.

Thomason's errors are mild, his accusations minimal, and though he had the "goods" on several less than adequate officers, Marine and Army, he was not too hard on them. Regardless, his effort, using U.S., French and especially German records, has produced a singular treatment of the bloody fight "northwest of Chateau Thierry." I don't know of any other effort on this particular time period of U.S. history that is so well developed.

I have added a brief biography of Thomason because he was, after all, the main constituent in this part of the project. It isn't highly detailed nor original but has been derived, primarily, from the excellent Roger Willock publication with a few helpful additions provided by Martha Anne Turner, his other biographer. I know that people are desirous of knowing something about the author of a piece and though our subject was once very famous, amongst Marines especially, he may not, unfortunately, now be so well known. I have, however, checked the internet and have found more than 500 hits, many of which are providing the opportunity to buy books by him.

A "biography" of the 2nd Division is also added simply to place the actions within this period and should not be misconstrued as an official history. That is my next project. The same holds true for the first two maps. I did those to place the action in France for persons not well acquainted with the division in World War I "northwest of Chateau Thierry." This was a great division. It was held to a high expectation and never failed to produce. Each sub-unit was continually trying to outdo the opposite unit, especially between the Marines and Army. Consequently, they were the very best. Each set a maximum standard below which they refused to go. When it came time to move, off they went. For that and other reasons, the rest of the A.E.F. called it the "Race-Horse Division." They, all of them, were the real "Goods."

George B. Clark
Pike, New Hampshire
May 2006

Editor's Introduction

The 2nd Division, Regular Army was officially authorized by the U.S. Army War Department Chief of Staff, Major General Tasker H. Bliss on 22 September 1917. The order further stated:

> ... the War Department directs the organization of the 2d Div, Regular Army. The Div includes troops of the United States Marine Corps which are at Quantico or already in France, and units of the Regular Army stationed at Chickamauga Park, El Paso, Gettysburg, Governors Island, Philadelphia, Syracuse, Fts Benjamin Harrison, Ethan Allen, Myer, Oglethorpe, Riley, Sam Houston, and Camps Robinson and Vail as well as others en route to, or already in, Europe.[1]

The division organized was to become, arguably, perhaps, the finest organization the United States Army sent to France. It would register a record "Second to None" and superior to most. The details suggest that they spent more time in actual combat, gained more ground, suffered many more losses, and captured material and personnel to a degree dominating the American Expeditionary Forces. It was, with few arguments, the best of the best. It deserved a written record for posterity. This is partly the story of that attempt. The failure of completion is another story.

In 1927 the U.S. Marine Corps Major General Commandant, John A. Lejeune, selected Captain John W. Thomason, Jr., to join with a group of U.S. Army officers at Fort Humphrey, now Fort McNair, in Washington, D.C., for the purpose of writing a history of the service of the 2nd Division, Regular, while in France and Germany. Thomason had just been

---

[1] Order of Battle of the United States Land Forces in the World War. American Expeditionary Forces: Divisions. *Volume 2, Washington, D.C.: Center of Military History, United States Army, 1988. p. 25.*

released off the Special Service Squadron flagship, *Rochester*, cruising off Latin America. Lejeune gave the project the highest priority and selected the man he believed could best represent the Marine Corps in this endeavor.

If you have read his brief biographical sketch, you will be aware that Thomason had served notably in the 5th Marines in France. He was also from a very interesting and varied background before deciding to become a professional sea soldier. Among other attributes, he had graduated from the Sam Houston Normal School (now the Sam Houston State University) in Huntsville, Texas. He had first become a school teacher in his native state, went to art school in New York City for a year and served briefly as a "cub reporter" for a Houston, Texas newspaper. He had an extremely well-received first book which he illustrated and wrote, concerning the activities of the Marine Brigade in the bloody conflicts of France. His second book, also mainly about Marines, was well on its way toward success when he was selected by Lejeune to represent the Corps in the project.

Thomason's first thoughts were toward complete coverage of the war and he asked permission to be allowed to go to Europe, at his own expense, to peruse the records of Germany and France, whose units served alongside or opposed to the 2nd Division. This was granted and Thomason, and his wife Leda, spent several months in Berlin and Paris, among other choice "watering holes" gathering factual data for the project. Upon his return he set to work and began writing, from all available records, the part played by the division in the bloody month of June, 1918, Northwest of Chateau Thierry.[2]

Major John W. Thomason, Jr.

However, according to his interpretation of what the records suggested, he realized that all was not well during that month. Using official records as a basis he began to visualize that major mistakes were made by senior officers of the division and therefore his writing of the history encompassed those errors. It wasn't long before several now senior officers, some still on active duty, began making serious complaints about his writing and "suggesting" that records be modified

---

2   It is my understanding that he had an "aide" in the project. Captain William Mathews, formerly of the 2nd Battalion, Fifth Marines, former Battalion Intelligence Officer and later platoon leader and "skipper" of the 55th Company, had served well and added valuable personal knowledge to much of the scenario. He was very obviously biased but honest.

to more correctly reflect what those men wished to be seen as the final record. This, evidently, and from comments made to others, annoyed Thomason and before the project was finished in its entirety, in 1929 he was relieved of the assignment, probably at his own request. At the time, Lejeune was no longer commandant; his successor was Major General Wendell C. Neville. Neville's commitment to the project may not have been as acute as had been Lejeune's. There were too many other pressing needs for Marine officers, the Corps being badly understaffed at the time.

In letters, especially to his parents in Huntsville, he stated that "he had no intention of submitting a whitewashed account of what had transpired," for in his opinion "an unbiased investigation of source materials had revealed that in certain instances some of the Division officers had not exercised proper judgement; moreover, the evidence had shown that on occasion others were professionally incapable of coping with the situation."[3] He added that because of the circumstances he was reluctant to continue and that he had provided a draft copy as ordered and that those selected to provide the finished copy could resolve the issue. In other words, "if it will be altered, it wont be by me."

There has been, among Army and Marines interested in the work, much conjecture as to why the complete history met a dead end. It is my opinion that other men involved in producing the various parts were coming up with interpretations much as Thomason had. At any rate, a couple

Self-portrait sketch by Thomason

---

3   Willock, Roger. *Lone Star Marine. Princeton, NJ.: private publication, 1961.*

of years after Thomason stepped aside, one senior Army officer, who was somewhat of a target of the factual interpretation, requested that he be reassigned to the task. Thomason was then very happily located with the Peiping Legation Guard and refused to return to the project.

Army officers could have been selected to complete the section Thomason had been working on, but, since the major 2nd Division unit involved in the sector was the 4th Marine Brigade, it was probably deemed essential that a Marine do the job. At any rate, the entire project lay dormant for a decade and then a version, much less in extent and, in the present editor's opinion, not worthy of the undertaking, was eventually produced in 1937, without events as previously described. That version had no details to speak of, was "vanilla" in all its aspects, and possibly, pleased no one. There is no comment of record from Thomason concerning the latter work, which, undoubtedly, he saw and probably read.— *GBC.*

Some German Divisional Records

by Captain John W. Thomason, Jr., U.S.M.C.

During this past summer [1927] it was the privilege of the writer to examine certain divisional records of the German units which were on the front of the 2nd United States Division in the World War. Some observations on them may be of interest to the Service.

The records of the German Army are preserved in the *Reichsarkiv* at Potsdam, the old seat of the court, about forty kilometers from Berlin. The *Reichsarkiv* is under the Department of the Interior, and not, as might be supposed, under the Ministry of War. The Reich asserts that no active officer of the present Army is in any way connected with it, and administratively and technically it has no liaison with the existing *Reichswehr*. The officials of the *Arkiv* are retired officers of the old Imperial Forces, and you address them by the civil title in correspondence and in official contact.

The records themselves are of absorbing interest, both as to contents and as to method of compilation.

Each division kept a war diary—*Kriegstagebuch*—with annexes—*Analgen*. These were written up and bound by months in heavy cardboard folders. Each folder has its serial number, fixing its period, and its general divisional number. The first folder for the month contains the diary. This gives, from day to day, all events concerning the division: location of headquarters and subordinate organizations, movement of troops with the division area, occupation of troops—marching, training, combat, as the case may be; air activity, artillery activity, and the weather, and the health of personnel and animals. In battle, the front lines are given, with all the information of the enemy, changes in the location of all units, movement of support and reserve bodies, and incidents of the fighting. Concise estimates of the situation in the light of changing events are included. Where the occasion calls for it, entries are made by the hour and half-hour. Casualties for the day are noted. All orders received and issued by Division are referred to at the time they come in or go out, and such orders are referenced in their proper file. These entries are models of compact writing, reflecting vividly the competence of the staff.

The striking thing about them is that every statement made can be proved or verified by the references given in the text. Where an order or a report or a sketch is mentioned, you can go to the annex indicated and check the entry by the original paper, which facility is of the utmost value to the military student, who is not allowed to accept any statement, but must examine himself the evidence.

The annexes, of course, form the bulk of the records. They consist of the file of orders, incoming and outgoing; of the operations reports of Brigade, Regiment, and Battalion; of the maps; the Artillery reports and orders, and all field messages, down to and including platoons; and intelligence data, the examination of prisoners, the reports of avions and observation balloons, and the reports of patrols and scouting parties. These are arranged by period and by organization, and may be readily found.

The basic system followed may vary in its details.

ONE

Robert d' Espagne to Chaumont-en-Vixen

(Sources, War Diary, 2nd Div., 9 May–23 May)

The Second Division was relieved in the Toulon–Troyon sector by the 2nd French Colonial Corps, and concentrated behind the Verdun front in the camps of the Robert Espagne area. The movement began by battalions on the 9th of May and each element was relieved by a corresponding unit of French troops. Each proceeded back by marching, motor, or by rail. Since the distribution of the Division was wide, and some organizations were at a great distance from the designated concentration area, reconcentrating was lengthy. The 12th Field Artillery was the last regiment to come out, and it arrived near Sommedieu on 17 May.

On 18 May the 2nd Division started for the Gisors–Chaumont-en-Vixen area, in the department of the Oise, Normandy. The Division was destined for the on-going battle in the north. Men and animals were routed by rail, a train to each battalion and each battery and division motor transport was ordered overland. On 19 May the advance echelon of Division Headquarters was opened at Chaumont-en-Vixen. The length of the journey by rail was two days, and on the 20th the first elements arrived at their detraining points. They continued to come up through the 21st and 22nd, when the last unit left its train. Hikes of varying lengths brought the troops to their final billets, which were, in some cases, more than a days march from the railheads at l'Isle Adam and Marines.[1] The weather had turned clear and warm, and regimental diaries mentioned that the men suffered from the heat during these marches, burdened as they were with overcoats,

1   [Marines, as identified, is a town, east of Paris.— GBC.]

Doughboys marching

jerkins, and the heavy gear of trench warfare. Also, they were stiff from the cramped box cars, and the May sun developed powerful heat in small enclosures. Headquarters closed in the Robert Espagne area on 21 May, and all organizations were reported in their final billets in the new area on 23 May. After the briefest interval for cleaning up, the Division embarked upon a period of intensive training.

Chaumont-en-Vixen lies about 60 kilometres north of Paris, as you go towards Rouen. The Division Headquarters were in Chaumont, and the 2nd Field Artillery Brigade, the 3rd Brigade of Infantry, the 2nd Engineers, and the 4th Machine Gun Battalion were distributed in villages and farms north and east of the town. Artillery Headquarters was also in Chaumont; the 17th Field Artillery Regiment lay at Chambors and Lavinville; the 15th Field Artillery was around Delincourt; and the other artillery regiment, the 12th, was to the west near Trie Chateau. The 3rd Infantry Brigade established Headquarters in Chateau Ferme le Betz. The 9th Infantry had Headquarters and its 3rd Battalion at Liancourt, the 1st Battalion at Loconville, and the 2nd at Fay. The 23rd Infantry Regimental Headquarters was in Chateau Berticheres, Headquarters Company at Gomarfontain, the Supply Company at Vivray, the Machine Gun Company at St. Brice Ferme, and the three rifle battalions around Trie La Ville. The Fifth Machine Gun Battalion was billeted at Bouconvillers.

A few miles west of Chaumont-en-Vexin, out the Rouens road, was Gisors, and in this vicinity was billeted the 4th Brigade of Marines. Brigade Headquarters were at Le Bout du Bois. The Colonel of the 5th Regiment of Marines with his Headquarters Company, Supply Company, and the 8th (regimental) Machine Gun Company, and the 1st Battalion, was at Boury. The 2nd and 3rd battalions of the 5th were at Courcelles and Vaudancourt. The entire 6th Regiment was in and around Serans, and the 6th Machine

Gun Battalion was at Montjavoult. The Field Signal Battalion, the Medical Detachments, Trains, Military Police, and other small units centered on Chaumont-en-Vexin, with Division Headquarters. It may be noted that the Division Postal Detachment first functioned under military control in this area, setting up Army Field Postoffice 710 in Liancourt–St. Pierre, on 29 May.

TWO

Chemin des Dames

These are the events which brought the 2nd Division into the Marne Salient.

Early in April—about the time it became apparent that the Bavarian Crown Prince would achieve nothing decisive in the second drive against the British, on the Lys,—the Army Group of the German Crown Prince was directed to submit a plan for an attack between Pinon and Reims, to be carried out by the 7th and 1st Armies.[2] The plan was drawn up and approved by Great Headquarters. It contemplated a drive across the Chemin des Dames plateau to the Aisne, with exploitation to the Vesle, and perhaps Soissons and Reims as prizes. "How far the attack could take us," Ludendorff writes, "could not be foretold. I hoped that it would lead to such a heavy drain on the reserves of the enemy as would enable us to resume the attack in Flanders."[3] For Flanders remained, in the view of the Great Headquarters, the theater in which the decision would be reached. The enemy's masses had, in April, become too dense behind the threatened junction of the French and British armies: the thrust to the south would divert them and use them up.

In the meantime, Ludendorff's mass of manoeuvre, his fresh divisions and rested divisions, lay through the rest areas of the valley of the Oise, so situated as to move either east or west with facility, while the French reserves were known to be collected west of Compiegne and were somewhat committed to the northern theater. The Army Group of the German Crown Prince was groomed for the approaching effort. The lessons of the March Drive were studied and applied: the quota of light machine guns per company was increased: machine guns were issued to supply and transport columns for protection against enemy aircraft. Equipment was checked

2 "Ludendorff's Own Story" 2, pg. 615.
3 Ibid.

and renewed, and training in the art of open warfare went forward in all organizations. Colonel Brockmüller, Ludendorff's Chief of Artillery in the March Drive,[4] was ordered to Headquarters of the 7th Army.

The sector called the Chemin des Dames, on the front of the 6th French Army, was held by the German 7th Army, Colonel-General Max von Boehn. On 14 May, von Boehn had in line three corps, the 54th, the XIII Reserve, and the 65th, with seven divisions in line and two in reserve.[5] None of these divisions were of the attack order: they were either second-raters, sector-holding formations, or divisions exhausted in the recent offensives in the north and now recuperating. The situation gave the French no uneasiness. But about the middle of May, the troop concentration for the 7th Army began.[6]

On 22 May the headquarters of three new corps were located in the 7th Army area, the IV Reserve, the XXV Reserve, and the VII. The order of battle on the front, however, remained the same. No new divisions had been inserted, and none had been moved into the area. Preparations went forward with the most careful secrecy. From the valley of the Oise the divisions destined for the attack approached the 7th Army area by night marches, lying in the woods through the day. Accumulation of material was also carried out by night. During the daylight hours, French observers saw nothing unusual. As late as the 25 May the French Sixth Army noted nothing alarming on its front.[7] The routine raids of the French gathered no information. They even failed to make any contacts with the Germans. As a matter of fact, the German 7th Army had taken precautions against losing prisoners who might talk. The front line was ordered to avoid any contacts, and forward details were withdrawn into their back areas each night,[8] so that the French found the front lines deserted where they entered them. This very circumstance seems to have given the 6th Army command a hint of what was coming.

During the night 25–26 May, a raiding party of the 22nd French Division, spurred to extraordinary exertions by the insistence of the Army Commander, Duchêsne, went deep into the lines of the VIII Reserve Corps. At about the center of the 7th Army, they captured two prisoners, an aspirant-officer and an enlisted man, of the German 197th Division.[9] Examined, the

    4   Ibid, pg. 628
    5   *War Diary Army Group German Crown Prince — April–May/18* also *War Diary German 7th Army, April–May–June 18.*
    6   *Situation Map 1233A German Crown Prince Army Group.*
    7   *Pétain Report: Aisne Defensive 1918,* War College.
    8   *War Diary German 7th Army: also,* Ludendorff's Own Story.
    9   *War Diary, German 7th Army* says a sergeant of the IIIrd Bn., 7th Saxon Regiment of 197th Division.

officer said he knew nothing of any projected movements. He was voluble in his assurances of German inaction. The private however, talked. He said that it was believed among the troops that an offensive was immediately to take place. That much material had been moved into the division sector, and that troops of the Guard Divisions and other shock formations were billeted close behind the front. The officer was then recalled, and told that, that while he would not be forced to give information by any procedure contrary to the laws of war, he had made certain statements, and if those statements proved to be misleading he would be held strictly responsible for falsehood. Under this pressure, the aspirant-officer broke down and communicated everything he knew, which was considerable.

His information embraced the main points of the German plan, and some of the details.[10] It was, however, after noon of the 26th when he was gotten back to Headquarters of the French Sixth Army, and then it was too late to do anything except to notify Great Headquarters and alert the meager divisions on the front.[11] The last preparations of the Germans were complete. It is related that, in the afternoon of 26 May, they abandoned secrecy. French observers saw battalions openly coming up behind the German line.[12] That night, seventeen divisions, including some of the best attack formations, were on the German front, with twelve divisions in close support.[13]

At dawn on 27 May the German 7th Army left its trenches and fell upon the line of the Chemin des Dames. The order of battle, from the German right to left, was VII Corps, 54th Corps, VIII Reserve Corps, XXV Reserve Corps, XVII Reserve Corps and 65th Corps—six corps, of seventeen line divisions, with twelve supporting—a total of twenty-nine in all.

The French Sixth Army held a line of about 85 kilometres, between Reims and Soissons. It had, on 27 May, eleven divisions, composed of eight French and three British. There were available seven divisions in line and four in reserve. Of the total, seven divisions, including those of General Alexander Hamilton-Gordon's British IX Corps, had been engaged in the battles in the North, on the Oise and Scarpe. The British formations were originally of Gough's V Army which was decimated in the March drive on the Somme. They were sent to the Lys River for rest and there, in April, sustained the shock of the Bavarian Crown Prince's blow. The Chemin des Dames had been designated in May as a tranquil sector where they might

10   *GQG 1915–1918 — Jean de Pierrefeu*, also *Pétain Report: Aisne Defensive.*
11   *Pétain Report.*
12   Ibid.
13   *War Diary, German Crown Prince Army Group. Situation Map GCP — AG 27 of May.*

recuperate. They were far under strength, as were the French divisions which had been through the same ordeal. The remaining French formations were not first-class troops.[14]

On 26 May, the French mass of manoeuver was west of Compiegne, where Foch expected either the next German drive, or an opportunity to make a counter attack. It would be possible to reinforce the 6th Army at the rate of two divisions a day but it was not possible to pass troops into its line for 48 hours after the alarm was received.[15] The distance being too great, and available transport being too limited.

Being unable to relieve the 6th Army, Pierrefeu has described the distress at GHQ, through the 26th and 27th while the French staff waited for the blow to fall.[16] Divisions were ordered forward, but it was certain that the line of the Chemin des Dames would be inundated before they could arrive. The German 7th Army had achieved a thing rare in this war, a perfect strategic surprised, and in effect, a tactical surprise. Of all Ludendorff"s tactical achievements, the concentration of the May drive was the most ably handled.

The following five days were terrible upon the French. The battle eventually absorbed thirty-seven divisions from Foch's carefully hoarded forces. Of these, by 1 June, seventeen were exhausted, and two were so cut to pieces that they were never reconstituted. A number of these formations, like the 43rd Division of the French XXI Corps which was later relieved by the American 2nd Division, were engaged twice.[17]

It appears to have been Pétain's idea to throw formations into the fight as they could be brought up — anywhere in the breach the Germans had made. At first they would be swept away. Then some of them would stand, and presently more of them would stand, and finally the breach would be welded.[18] It is evident, however, that the weight of the French reserves were sent, not to the crumbling center of the 6th Army, but to the flanks before Reims and south of Soissons. There the great Foret de Retz offered a natural barrier to the German advance, and a holding ground for the defense. And before Reims, and in the east face of the Foret de Retz, the French held firm. The Germans pressed between, to be increasingly cramped as the center went forward and the flanks were refused. The resulting salient was too deep for its base. A salient is subject to strict rules. When its depth exceeds

---

14   War Diary, German Crown Prince Army Group, Situation Map GCP AG 27 May, 7th Army War Diary and Pétain — report Aisne defensive. 1918, War College.
15   Pétain Report.
16   Pierrefeu GQG 1915–1918.
17   Pétain report Aisne defensive, 1918, War College.
18   War Diary, German 7th Army, 27 May/18

a certain proportion of its breadth, it becomes dangerous for the aggressor. The vast Marne pocket into which the 7th German Army rushed, with elements of the 1st and 18th Armies, brought them to disaster.

    The French reports from the Sixth Army for the next five days, are not coherent. The 6th Army was broken into pieces and hurled southward and the Germans advanced with a terrifying swiftness. Their center went ahead at peace-time manoeuver speed. We must turn to the records of the German Crown Prince Army Group, and of the German 7th Army, to plot the day-by-day stages of the drive.

    At 2:00 am., on 27 May (3:00 am French time), the German artillery opened overwhelming with HE and shrapnel on the French forward zones and approaches, from Soissons to Reims.[19] At 4:40 am. (3:40 French time) the German infantry left its trenches and went forward from the Wood of Mortier, northwest of Soissons, to Conde-sur-Suippes, just north of Reims. Two factors favored them. First, the marshes of the Aillette covering the western end of the 6th Army front, and which had been calculated upon in the French defensive plan, offered no obstacle to the advance, for the spring had been unusually dry. Secondly, a dense mist had covered the entire terrain, and the French machine gun and artillery defense had been blinded in the fog. Only to the northeast of Soissons, on the line Chavigny Pargny and Filain-Malval Farm was effective resistance encountered, and the right Corps of the German 7th Army held up. Elsewhere the attack went forward, and the Chemin des Dames plateau was crossed as early as 6:30 am, by the 1st Guards Division of the XXV Reserve Corps. With this start, the German center, particularly the IV Reserve Corps, to the left of the XXV, began to lead the movement. At 11:30 am, the 2nd Battalion of the 109th Body Grenadier Regiment of the 28th Division crossed the Aisne. So swiftly did the waves of the Germans inundate the river line that the Aisne bridges were not destroyed, and the French formations passing the river to the front, were caught astride of it and cut to pieces. By noon the length of the Aisne, from Vailly to Berry-au-bac, was all in German hands. In Vailly a railroad gun with its locomotive was captured by German infantry before it could be moved out of danger. At 9:00 pm, in the evening the Grenadier Guards Regiment [*German Queen Elizabeth*] of the 5th Guards Division, IV Reserve Corps, crossed the Vesle, and at 9:45 pm, was established on Hill 179 south of Cour Magneuse. From the parallel of departure of the IV Reserve Corps to Hill 179, south of the Vesle, is 22 kilometres. The 5th Guards had come that far against resistance in 17 hours.

    The Vesle had been the tentative objective of the German thrust,

---

    19   [*This was German time; French time was one hour earlier.— GBC.*]

although it would seem from Ludendorff's statements that the primary object was to bring to battle and use up the French reserves. With reports of success on the night of the 27th beyond the most sanguine hopes of the German staff—with the tale of prisoners and booty increasing and their own losses light, the Headquarters of the 7th Army ordered that the advance be pressed.

On the 28th the advance continued. The center of the 7th Army passed the Vesle everywhere, but Reims held, and the French fought hard in front of Soissons. Great Headquarters ordered that the weight of the offensive be shifted to the plateau south of Soissons. In the evening the Germans were in the edge of Soissons and drawing past it in the south and east and at the center, and the IV Reserve Corps continued to set the pace. There were more than 20,000 prisoners, and the captured material extended beyond calculation. That night, Great Headquarters ordered the capture of the hills southwest of Soissons, Fere-en-Tardenois, and the fortress belt south of Reims. The German 18th Army on the right and the 1st Army on the left moved to conform by advancing their inner flanks. The first divisions of the French Reserve were now identified by the Germans.

On 29 May the pace was slower, but very steady in the center. The French, evidently reinforced, counterattacked in the Soissons region, and the French and British, pressed sharply back on Reims, held their ground on the wooded hills south of the city. Great Headquarters gave the line Compiegne-Dormans-Epernay as a tentative objective. The Germans counted 29,000 prisoners and identified three new French Divisions—one of cavalry. The attack was directed along the Aisne to its confluence with the Oise at Berneuil, on the hills north of Neuilly-St. Front, and against the hills north of Chateau Thierry. At the close of the day, the French still barred the approaches to Villers Cotterets forest south of Soissons. They held the road to Reims but noticeably had given way in the center between the Vesle and Chateau Thierry.

The fighting continued through the night of 29–30 May. Soissons was lost to the French, and were forced across the plateau south of Soissons and back on the Foret de Retz, losing the Soissons-Chateau Thierry road, Tigny, and the Vierzy region. No impression was made on the Reims front, where the remnants of the British IX Corps continued in the fight. But the French IV Reserve Corps reached the Marne at Courtmont, between the Brasles and Passy, and crossed elements of the 28th Division to the south bank. The details on the south bank were later withdrawn, but the course of the Marne as far as Verneuil was occupied. Thence the line angled northeast, by Vandieres and Jonchery, towards the Mountain of Reims. The right of the IV Reserve Corps invested Chateau Thierry and pushed past the curve of

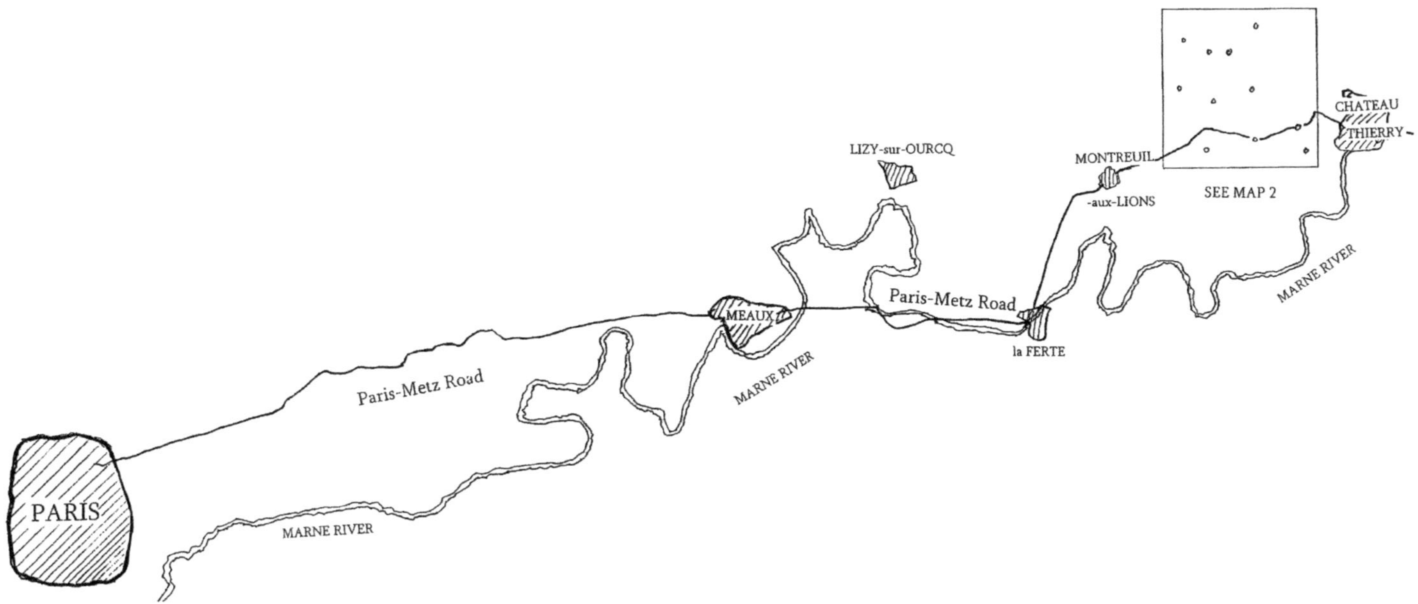

Map 1. Area of the second battle of the 2d Division Marines June 1918

Chemin des Dames 21

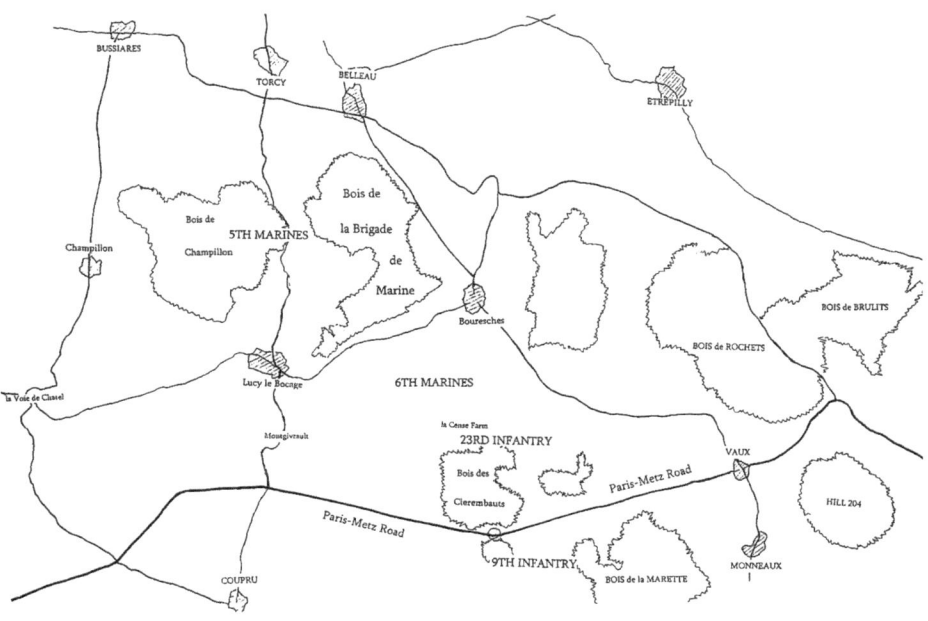

Map 2

the Marne towards Etrépilly. On 31 May the Germans were on the outskirts of Chateau Thierry, and fought with elements of the French XXI Corps, reinforced by machine gunners of the American 3rd Division, for the Marne bridges.[20] Elsewhere, south of Soissons, the 7th Army directed forces towards Villers-Cotterets. By 1 June Vierzy and Chaudun were cleared of the French, and the advance reached the edge of the Villers–Cotterets Forest, or, the Foret de Retz. West of Chateau Thierry, the Germans took Hill 204, flanked the town of Vaux and the town itself was taken by the 231st Division in a wild street fight. Now, on the left front of the 7th Army, the German possibilities were about exhausted. Their divisions lay along the Marne from Chateau Thierry to Verneuil, where the Marne valley curves southwestward towards Epernay. Additionally the Foret de Reims and the Mountain of Reims blocked their way, and were tenaciously held. There was also the Reims fortress belt, unshaken. Epernay, up the Marne, was a tempting prize, but the Mountain of Reims was too much of an obstacle, and the Marne was hard to cross, with the French gathering on the south bank.

20 [It was the 7th Motorized Machine Gun Battalion.— GBC.]

Great Headquarters turned to the right. Their prisoners were more than 30,000, and they had identified nineteen French divisions, in addition to the original 6th Army formations. There might still be something towards Meaux, in the direction of Paris.

At Chateau Thierry the Marne loops sharply south, and then flows west to Meaux. Above Meaux about 5 kilometres, at Lizy-sur-Ourcq, the Ourcq River joins the Marne, coming down from the north besides the Meaux-Soissons Highway. Some 15 kilometres north of its confluence with the Marne a stream called the Clignon joins from the east. Clignon rises just west and north of Etrépilly, and flows through a deep, narrow valley, parallel to the Marne and from 7 to 10 kilometres north of its course. To the Clignon junction, the Ourcq runs south from Troesnes, and comes to Troesnes from the east, where it rises near Fere-en-Tardenois. On 1 June the Germans were astride the Ourcq at Noroy, and nearly as far west as Troesnes, where the stream turns south. Thence their line curved back through Etrépilly to Chateau Thierry. It appeared feasible for the right of the 7th Army to push west and south from the line Troesnes-Etrépilly and occupy the Ourcq valley, with the Clignon covering the left flank of the advancing corps. Accordingly, orders were issued, shifting the weight of the advance from the IV Reserve Corps in the center to the XXV Reserve Corps on its right. With the 33rd and the 1st Guards, two strong attack divisions, Winckler's XXV Reserve Corps drove on the Ourcq. The IV Reserve Corps, replacing all but one of its battle-worn shock formations with second-rate troops, swung southwestward to build a defensive flank for the Ourcq thrust.

This was sound tactical disposition. With the line of the Ourcq taken, as far as the Clignon junction, Allied forces between the Clignon and the Marne were in a dangerous corner, their line of communication parallel to the front, and an un-fordable river at their backs. The country north of the Marne, between Chateau Thierry and Meaux, would be rendered untenable, whenever the German wanted it — provided always that their defensive flank along the Clignon was secure. A glance at the map makes the situation plain. The Ourcq movement began at daylight on 1 June. That morning, the first infantry regiment of the 2nd Division had arrived in the area of the French XXI Corps, and the remainder of the division was coming.[21]

---

21 Source: *War Diary, German 7th Army*. Note: *The foregoing is largely from official German Sources, particularly the War Diary of the German Crown Prince Army Group, and the War Diary of the 7th Army, with attached annexes and maps. They agree substantially with the Pétain Report of the Aisne Defensive Battle in 1918, and are in more detail. The French Sixth Army reports for the period are incomplete and incoherent.*

Three

Chaumont-en-Vexin to Montreuil: 27 May–1 June

Map: Meaux-1/80,000

Around Chaumont-en-Vexin the last days of May spun out pleasantly. While the storm troops of von Boehn were breaking the line of the French Sixth Army along the Chemin des Dames, and mounting the heights of the Aisne, on the 27th, the 2nd Division held terrain exercises. They were practicing mimic warfare over a somnolent countryside directed by umpires upon theoretical positions. Sweating files of men might, if the opportunity afforded itself, fall out and take refreshment in French farmhouses.[22] On 29 May, at morning formations, companies were advised that the American 1st Division had attacked at Cantigny with good success, and the companies cheered wildly.[23] Also on the 29th, Brigade maneuvers were held where Marines and infantry worked out problems in open warfare.[24]

The 30th was Memorial Day, and there were no drills.[25] Regimental Bands played "Departed Days" at noon formation.[26] Appropriate exercises commemorating the dead of other wars, were promulgated.[27] The men were free to amuse themselves when the parades were dismissed, but Headquar-

---

22 *War Diary, 2nd Div.*, 27 May, Vol. 6.
23 *Regt. Hist. 23rd Inf.*
24 *War Diary, 2nd Div.*, 29 May 1918.
25 *War Diary, 2nd Div.*, 30 May 1918.
26 *G.O. 38/2nd Div.*, 28 May-Vol. 9.
27 *War Diary 2nd Div.*, 30 May 1918.

ters found much to do. Orders were received from the Commanding General of the French Group of Reserve Armies of the North, to which the 2nd Division was attached, for the 2nd Division to move by marching into the area Beauvais, behind Cantigny. It was understood that the 2nd was to relieve the 1st, now somewhat mauled.[28] The movement would begin on 31 May, and would consume two days. March tables and directives were drawn up and issued from Division Headquarters. Billeting parties from each organization were ordered to assemble in Chaumont-en-Vixen, then to proceed by truck into the Beauvais area and make preliminary arrangements. Some of these billeting parties reported in the afternoon of 30 May, and some of them started toward Beauvais, but they were all recalled.[29]

At 5 o'clock in the afternoon of 30 May, a dusty automobile hooted up to Division Headquarters and a French staff officer got out. He brought news of disaster close at hand. The French Sixth Army was broken and the Germans were on the Marne. The American 2nd Division would go quickly to the Meaux area.[30] Meaux is on the Marne, between Chateau Thierry and Paris, about 90 kilometres on the airline from Chaumont-en-Vixen. Camions would be provided for the infantry, but there was no word as to transportation for the artillery and the horse-drawn services. Movement would begin by 5 o'clock the following morning, 31 May.[31]

Into discard went Division Field Order 3 regarding the Beauvais area with its march tables and station lists and the brigade, regimental, and battalion elaborations of the same. Division Headquarters settled down to work all night, and em bussing schedules for the troops who were to proceed by truck were hastily drawn up. Directions were sent to the elements of the division by courier and by telephone, and there was no time for formal orders. About midnight, another French staff officer brought word that trains would be provided for the artillery and the animal transport with motor vehicles, of course, proceeding overland.[32]

During the night camion trains began to roll into the area, driven by yellow Tonquinese and Anamites, and men from Madagascar, small weary heathen in Khaki uniforms and crested helmets. The infantry and engineer battalions formed at dawn, gulped breakfast[33] by their rolling kitchens—it was the last hot meal many of them were to have in this world—and got aboard as ordered. The artillery regiments loaded their guns and horses as

28   Ibid.
29   Ibid.
30   Ibid.
31   *War Diary, 2nd Div., 31 May 1918, Vol. 6.*
32   Ibid.
33   Ibid.

they received their trains, the first of which left at 5:30 am. The 4th (Divisional) Machine Gun Battalion was also entrained, while the 5th and 6th Machine Gun Battalions, with their guns, were em-bussed. The motor transportation of the Division set out under its own power. By sun-up the leading elements were in motion towards the east.[34]

The Division Commander, Major General Omar Bundy, and his personal staff proceeded to Paris.[35] Officers for the advanced echelon of Division headquarters were dispatched to Meaux, and the necessary quota was detailed to remain in Chaumont-en-Vexin until the area was cleared.[36] Following the departure of the first infantry camions, the Divisional Chief of Staff, Colonel Preston Brown, motored to Paris and went to the office of the American Provost Marshal in the Rue Ste Anne. From which place he called the Chief of Staff of the American I Corps, Colonel [Malin] Craig, at Neufchateau informing him of the movement in progress and of the projected dispositions of the 2nd Division. And he arranged for the immediate forwarding to Meaux of all available ammunition[37] and for the placing there of medical supplies sufficient for the care of at least 5000 wounded. This done, Colonel Brown then drove to Meaux where he located the leading camion trains. From Meaux proceeded some ten kilometres eastward to Trilport, where the Headquarters of the French Sixth Army were located, arriving about noon.[38]

The 2nd Division had been ordered to the 6th Army, but Colonel Brown found the headquarters of the 6th in a state of complete confusion. They knew nothing of the Americans, and they had no definite plans for their employment. "Let the Division concentrate at Meaux, and they would see." Colonel Brown was unable to get anything beyond this from the Army staff, and he went to Duchêsne, the General commanding. They had been driven back, said Duchêsne, and things were very bad, and he could give no orders. Colonel Brown pointed out to him that two brigades of infantry were behind him, and something must be done with them — they were routed through Meaux, and having just come from that place, he was sure that the laden camions would never get through the traffic congestion pre-

---

34 See War Diary, 2nd Field Artillery Brigade, 3rd-4th Brigades and Unit Histories, 31 May 1918. (War Diaries Vol. 6.)
35 Notes on Chateau Thierry, Maj. Gen. Preston Brown, 2nd Div. File.
36 War Diary, 2nd Div., 31 May, Vol. 6.
37 The 2nd Division was armed with the French automatic rifle (Chaut-Chaut) and French machine gun (Hotchkiss): ammunition for these could be obtained [only] from the French. But the infantry carried the American Springfield rifle, and .30 caliber and .45 caliber ammunition had to be found by the Americans. There was with the rifle brigades 100 rounds for each man that day.
38 Brown notes, ibid.

vailing there. For the narrow streets of the old city, and all the roads leading into and out of Meaux, were choked with refugees and their vehicles, and the transport of the retreating French. Transport coming from the west would be hopelessly blocked.[39]

There followed some consideration of the map. As far as Meaux, the Paris-Metz highway was the best road, and the camions were now upon it. There was required a place not to far from Meaux, to which they could be diverted, and where they could assemble after de bussing. Fifteen kilometres northeast, the town of May-en-Multien stood out on the map sheet. The route Nationale from Meaux to Soissons passed through it, and secondary roads provided a detour to the highway from the west of Meaux. From May-en-Multien the camions could circle back on another road to the west. As the contours ran, there was open country around the village where the regiments might form, and the Ourcq River was a short distance to the east. Colonel Brown suggested that the Division infantry be directed upon May-en-Multien, and General Duchêsne acquiesced. Let the 2nd Division go into that area, concentrating on the towns Lizy-sur-Ourcq, Crouy-sur-Ourcq, and Vendrest with Division headquarters at Crouy-sur-Ourcq, he said, and orders would be forth-coming. It was apparent that, at May-en-Multien, the Division would be astride the Soissons-Meaux highway, along which the enemy might advance. Accordingly, Colonel Brown dispatched couriers to meet and redirect the camions, and himself returned to Meaux, where the advanced echelon of Division Headquarters was established.[40] General Duchêsne and his chief of staff, with a diversion of American regulars coming into their hands, began to formulate a plan to properly utilize them.

At Meaux, about 2:30 pm, the advanced echelon of the Division staff at Meaux had news of the Divisional artillery. The first train leaving Chaumont-en-Vexin at 5:30 that morning passed the regulating station Mitry-Mory, on the Paris-Crepy en Valois line, and the French communicated the detraining points for the elements moving by rail. They were Danmartin-en-Goele, Nateuil-le-Hadouin, and Ormay-Villers,[41] which stations centered about 25 kilometres west of the area designated for assembly. But in the meantime, something else had happened at Chaumont-en-Vexin. Colonel C.[harles] H. Bridges, the Division entraining officer, was advised by the French at about 2:00 pm, that no more trains could be furnished. The Artillery Brigade and the 4th (Divisional) Machine Gun Battalion had received trains, loaded, and gotten out with dispatch — the motorized ele-

---

39   Ibid.
40   Ibid.
41   *War Diary, 2nd Div., Vol. 6 and Op 2nd F.A. Brigade, Chamberlaine, Vol. 9.*

ments had left early, under their own power. It was now necessary for the animal-drawn transport to march overland, and it included the regimental and battalion trains, and the field kitchens of the troops. During the afternoon these details were formed in three columns and took up the march. With their departure, the last elements of the 2nd Division, 27000 officers and men, were in motion for the front.[42]

The camions trains, one to each battalion, had come down from the Chaumont-en-Vexin area through Marines, Pontoise, and St. Denis, that suburb of Paris where the kings of France and the children of the Blood Royal are buried. They swept eastward on the Paris-Metz highway, along the same road by which, in September 1914, Gallieni passed his 7th Division in taxi-cabs to the battle at La Ferte on the Marne. As the battalions went eastward, beyond Paris, they began to meet the drift of refugees from the lost country between Soissons and Reims and Chateau Thierry — and the men who saw the fleeing host remember it as the most pitiful sight of all the war.[43]

The weather was clear and the sun hot and merciless on this last day of May. The hard Rue Nationale and the lessor roads bore a top-dressing of dust, as fine and white as talcum powder. The dust rose and hung thick in the still air, so that each motor column went in a cloud of its own making. The camions went up the right of the road and on the other side, coming down, was the melancholy flow of refugees. There were old men and old women, and children of all ages. They rode in farm wagons and carts, in old barouches and pony-traps, in quaint high shouldered vehicles of another generation, drawn by oxen and cows and old raw-boned horses rejected by the army, or they went on foot, trudging heavily through the dust. Some of them trundled wheel-barrows — an old bent woman pushed one, in which, atop a pile of household odds and ends, rode an ancient of many days, clad in a blue smock, sucking with toothless gums at a cold pipe. Every conveyance was loaded with gear — unnecessary and strange things, assorted and precious to householders, not to be left behind and things as absurd as people snatch when they run from burning houses. There were featherbeds and quilts and tall clocks, and ducks and chickens tied by the legs, and rabbits in crates, and chairs and birdcages and strings of garlic.

42   Ibid. *On 31 May there were present for duty 1064 officers and 25,614 men.*
43   Unit Histories, 2nd Div. File.
     [In my copy, Capt. William R. Mathews, JWT's aide in writing this project, and member of 2/5, 4th Brigade, hand noted "I was an eyewitness to the flight of the refugees and can confirm Thomason's graphic description." Perhaps the reason for Mathews addition was because Thomason was not actually on the scene. In fact it would be another week before he arrived in the vicinity, being a replacement officer on 7 June 1918. For some reason JWT always, throughout, spelled Mathews with two t's and "H." as the middle initial. I have corrected them. GBC].

The Mayor of a village passed: he limped in tight shoes and wore the high hat, the frock coat and the tri-color sash of ceremony. In the throng there were sheep and goats, herded anxiously. Men remember a flock of sheep at the crossroads, which went inescapably under the wheels of a battery of French artillery turning into the highway there. And they also remembered the lamentable cries of the shepherds.

It was a countryside in flight. After 1914, the population of the rich farming lands of the Marne Valley had returned to their homes, and for three years the war had kept away from them. Now the Boche had broken through again, as suddenly as thunder, and they fled. They went with a dazed look, compounded of weariness and terror. Mixed with them came the debris of the French Sixth Army, walking wounded, and unwounded men whose organizations had disappeared. There were malingerers and there were brave men who had fought to exhaustion. There were artillerymen without guns, and infantry without rifles, and demoralized machine gunners, riding on the gun-cart mules. The 2nd Division had not before happened upon this side of war. It was apparent to every man there that they proceeded to a serious front, as fast as the lumbering camions could take them.[44]

Camions make from ten to fifteen miles an hour, according to the roads and the temperaments of the drivers. By noon the 2nd Division infantry was widely extended, and shortly after noon, the leading battalions were in the vicinity of Meaux, and turned northward to the Soissons highway, on the orders sent by the Chief of Staff; and the Brigade commanders, motoring in advance, had from Colonel Brown what information there was. About 4:30 pm, two battalions of the 9th Infantry, 1/9 and 2/9, with Colonel Leroy S. Upton commanding the regiment, arrived at May-en-Multien and de-bussed. The third battalion had been delayed somewhere, but Colonel Upton was not allowed to wait for it. He was dispatched at once toward Crouy-sur-Ourcq, and marched, leaving Lieutenant Colonel [*Edward R.*] Stone to meet and bring up 3/9.[45] Headquarters of the 3rd Brigade had been established in Meaux at 4:00 pm: later, [*Brigadier*] General [*Edward M.*] Lewis moved his headquarters to Crouy-sur-Ourcq, where he remained overnight.[46] At this time, Colonel Brown still at May-en-Multien, received an order from the French Army.[47]

The order was not numbered, nor was the time of issue entered upon it. It was penciled, presumably written by the Army Chief of Staff, and

---

44   *Unit Histories-See 9th Infantry 31 May.*
45   *Ibid. 31 May, Vols. 6 & 7.*
46   *History 3rd Brigade, Hall, 2nd Div. file.*
47   *Brown and War Diary, 31 May, Vol. 6.*

signed in pencil by General Duchêsne. First, it noted the assignment of the 2nd Division to the French Sixth Army. And that the infantry of the 2nd Division was arriving in the vicinity of May-en-Multien-Neufchelles-Rouvres at about 3:00 pm: the Divisional artillery was expected the night of 31 May–1 June. Second, the infantry of the 2nd Division would be placed in position in rear of the valley of the Clignon, between Montigny d'Allier and Gandelu, and an advanced guard pushed to the line Chezy-en-Orxois-St. Quentin. Liaison would be established to the west with the French 2nd Cavalry Corps, which was in the region Bois de Bournville-Marolles, and to the east with the French 73rd Division near Priez. There would be further orders for the artillery. Third, the 2nd Division U.S. was placed under the orders of the French VII Corps—which would use it for closing the break in the French lines along the Ru d'Alland, and for counter-attacking as soon as possible in the direction of Pass en Valois and Marizy-St. Mard.[48]

Up to the late afternoon of 31 May, all the information gathered by the French Sixth Army and by the Staff of the 2nd Division—from units in combat, from retreating French elements, and from refugees—indicated that the German intention was to advance down the Soissons-Meaux highway. And the Duchêsne order placed the 2nd Division in position to meet the enemy. Nor was it necessary, on receipt of the order, to re-route the troops. They could continue to arrive on May-en-Multien, but they must proceed an average of 10 kilometres northeast of the Lizy-Crouy-Vendrest region, with a lessened chance of assembly before coming in contact with the enemy. The average march from the detraining points was also increased by 10 kilometres. In the meantime, elements of the 3rd Brigade already debussed moved on Crouy-sur-Ourcq, where they arrived about dark. There was no sign of the enemy in that region. Most of the refugees had cleared, and the villages were deserted. General Lewis, commanding the 3rd Brigade, was in Crouy-sur-Ourcq when the dusty columns of the 9th Infantry arrived, Colonel Upton leading them. While the battalions assembled in a field northwest of the village, General Lewis took the Colonel into his car. They set out for St. Quentin and Gandelu to find the French elements with which they were to make contact. But they found nowhere any organized line, nor could they get any information regarding the French dispositions from the officers they met. Late in the afternoon they were told by stragglers that the Boche had taken St. Quentin at 3 o'clock that afternoon. Returning to the 9th Infantry at Crouy-sur-Ourcq, about 2200, they found that once again the orders had been changed.[49] Later information indicated

48   Field Order Duchênse to C.G. 2nd Div. U.S. by 31 May, Vol. 4.
49   2nd Div. File at Chateau Thierry, Maj. Gen. E.M. Lewis notes.

that pressure was developing at and just west of Chateau Thierry. At 7:40 pm, the Chief of Staff, following further conferences with the French, issued Field Order 5.[50] The order was dictated by Colonel Brown to the Brigade Adjutant on the Soissons road just north of Beauval, west of Montigny.

Field Order 5 directed the 2nd Division to move into the area Montreuil-aux-Lions. In the course of the conversation between Colonel Brown and General Duchêsne at Trilport, earlier in the day, the line of the Clignon Brook had been discussed as a probable position of resistance. It was to the lower end of the Clignon Valley, where the little stream approached the Ourcq River, that the 6th Army had first ordered the Division. There they would be in readiness to fill the break on the Ru d'Alland, which was a stream parallel to the Clignon and five or six kilometres north of it. But during the afternoon, a strong German attack had developed on the line Epieds–Etrépilly–Bouresches. With this information at hand, the 2nd Division was passed from the French VII Corps to the French XXI Corps, as reserve. Field Order 5 designated the area Montreuil-Dhuisy-Coupru for concentration, and in effect placed the Division astride the Paris-Metz highway, between Montreuil-aux-Lions and Chateau Thierry. To the 3rd Brigade was allotted the zone Montreuil-Dhuisy-Marigny-La Ferte-Chateau Thierry road,[51] with Headquarters at Montreuil. And to the 4th Brigade the zone La Ferte-Chateau Thierry road-Coupru-Bezu-Charmost, with headquarters at Bezu. The Artillery Brigade would assemble on Cocherel, and take positions in support. Division Headquarters, with the Engineer Regiment and the trains and auxiliary services, would locate in and around Montreuil.[52] These dispositions were communicated to the troops already arrived by Colonel Brown. He found elements of them on the march between May-en-Multien and Crouy-sur-Ourcq. After dark he stopped by the road, and turned on his motor lights to mark a map for [*Lieut.*] Colonel [*William F.*] Herrinshaw of the Division trains. Boche planes saw the light and bombed the neighborhood, with effect.[53] Some of the troops were preparing to bivouac and others were still de bussing.[54] All were turned southeast from May-en-Multien and the Soissons road towards Montreuil and the Marne River.

Colonel Herrinshaw's existing map graphically show the proposed dispositions. They were as follows: North of the Paris-Metz highway, facing the Bois de Belleau and the Clignon line, was to be located the 3rd Brigade

50   2nd Div. File at Chateau Thierry, Maj. Gen. Preston Brown notes.
51   *Chateau Thierry Road refers to the Paris-Metz Highway.*
52   *F.O. 5, 2nd Div., 7:40 pm, 31 May, Vol. 1.*
53   Brown, notes.
54   See *Hist. 9th Infantry*, 31 May.

Marine officer issuing orders

and south of the highway and facing Vaux and Hill 204, was the 4th Brigade of Marines.[55] But the detailed movements detailed by Field Order 5 were never carried out — it only brought the Division into the area where it was to fight.[56]

Later in the evening of 31 May another order was received from the French Sixth Army. The 2nd Division would retrace its steps across the Ourcq and go into position north of May-en-Multien and west of the Ourcq canal, in the area Neufchelles-Rouvres. That order was completely disregarded. It was now plain that the enemy advanced from the east and northeast and the 2nd Division would not march away from the fighting.[57] The

55   Col. Herrinshaw's war map: Meaux 1/80000, 2nd Div. File.
56   [As will be seen, the formations would be entirely reversed. GBC].
57   Brown's notes.

movement from Montreuil continued, and the Divisional chief of staff got in communication with the French XXI Corps command regarding details.[58]

In the twelve hours between noon 31 May, and midnight, the 2nd Division had received four sets of orders from the French command. The first, verbally delivered to the chief of staff, directed the infantry to assemble in the Lizy-Crouy-Vendrest area. The second, in writing from the French Sixth Army, allotted it to the VII Corps on the line Gandelu-Montigny d'Allier. The third was embodied in Division Field Order 5 at 7:40 pm, diverting it to the area Montreuil under the French XXI Corps. The fourth, delivered late at night, ordered it west of the Ourcq again, to the Neufchelles–Rouvres area. By midnight, 31 May–1 June, the intention of the enemy was by now too evident for any further changes to be entertained.

Of these orders, the first was acted upon — May-en-Multien remained the assembly point of the regiments. The second was partially carried out, certain units moving well up the Soissons road north of May-en-Multien, and between Crouy-sur-Ourcq and Gandelu. The third was the order which brought the Division to its battlefield. The fourth was not acted upon nor even seriously considered.[59]

---

58   Ibid. [another hand written note by Mathews that reads "We went a mile or more till we could see French cavalry on the Clignon."-GBC].
59   War Diary, 2nd Div., 31 May, Vol. 6 and Brown notes, 2nd Div. File.

Four

1 June — Deployment

The 9th Infantry, Colonel Leroy S. Upton, was the first regiment of the 2nd Division to arrive in the Meaux area. It was embussed at Loconville, the most easterly point in the Chaumont-en-Vexin billeting area. They made an early start, and followed fairly direct roads. As the 9th rushed eastward, individual camions fell out, from engine trouble and the mishaps of the route, and its Third Battalion dropped behind. But at 4:30 pm, the First and Second Battalions were de bussing at May-en-Multien, in the midst of a vast traffic congestion of fleeing refugees and disorganized French troops—for May-en-Multien was an important road junction, and the backwash from the battle zone was ebbing through it. It is related that among the military details moving backward, was a French corps headquarters from which Colonel Upton was unable to extract information about anything. The Germans were coming, but of their own troops and of the enemy dispositions they had nothing further to say and the Americans were extremely irritated with them.[60] Colonel Upton's scanty information indicated that his regiment was to bivouac near May-en-Multien, and on the following day to take up a defensive position to the east. Accordingly, he sent out billeting parties to dispose his battalions in the adjoining villages. But before any movement could be made, he received orders to march to Crouy-sur-Ourcq, pursuant to the instructions given by the French Sixth Army at Trilport to Colonel Preston Brown at noon.[61]

Colonel Upton had a map, taken arbitrarily from an unsuspecting French officer who passed by,[62] and from it he learned that Crouy-sur-Ourcq

---

60   History 9th Infantry.
61   War Diary, 31 May, Vol. 6.
62   Capt. C.O. Mattfeldt, HQ 9th Inf., 2nd Div. File. [This officer would later work with JWT on the development of this 2nd Division history. GBC].

was five kilometres of hilly road east of May-en-Multien. The camions with the Third Battalion had not yet come up, and Lieutenant Colonel Stone was detached to wait for them and direct them when they arrived. The battalions 1/9 and 2/9 took the road and marched to Crouy-sur-Ourcq, where the General Lewis, the brigade commander, met them and took Colonel Upton on a reconnaissance towards Gandelu.[63] The troops bivouacked in the fields, and the battalions rested where they were until midnight.[64]

In the meantime, it will be remembered, subsequent orders had been issued by the French — the Duchêsne order, directing the Division to the line Gandelu-Montigny d'Allier, had come out in the afternoon. During the evening Colonel Brown, in the vicinity of Crouy-sur-Ourcq, had an order from the French Sixth Army to form on the line Neufchelles-Rouveres, back to the west. But these orders exacted no consequent move from the 9th Infantry, and May-en-Multien continued to be the assembly point for the incoming elements of the Division.[65] Field Order 5 of the 2nd Division was issued at 7:40 pm, which called for the deployment of the infantry east of Montreuil-aux-Lions, on the line Marigny-en-Orxois-Coupru-Bezu-Charmost, the 3rd Brigade of Infantry north of the Paris-Metz highway and the 4th Brigade of Marines south of the highway.[66] Except that the Division eventually moved into the area east of Montreuil, no provisions of Field Order 5 was carried out. About midnight an order, urgent and final, came in. The infantry would proceed to the area Montreuil, under the orders of General [*Jean M. J.*] Degoutte of the French XXI Corps d'Armee.[67]

The tired soldiers of the 9th were roused at once and set out for the new objective, Colonel Upton marching on foot at their head.[68] A regimental staff officer, Captain [*Clyburn O.*] Mattfeldt, was sent on to report to the French Corps Headquarters, then at Coupru, for detailed instructions. There he was told that the infantry would take up ground between Montreuil and Chateau Thierry, astride the Paris-Metz Highway. Between midnight and morning he returned to the Ventelet Farm Cross-roads and being very tired, he lay down to sleep in the road where the sound of the marching 9th Infantrymen would awaken him.[69] In the meantime, the two bat-

63   *Hist. 3rd Brigade, Hall, 2nd Div. File.*
64   *Hist. 9th Infantry.*
65   *War Diary, 31 May, Vol. 6.*
66   *F.O. 5, 2nd Div., 7:40 pm, 31 May, Vol. 1.*
67   *War Diary, 31 May, Vol. 6.*
68   *History 9th Infantry.*
69   *Ibid.*
     Confirmed by Capt. Mattfeldt. Mathew's own hand-written notation speaks otherwise. "One thing wrong about this I personally reported to Degoutte at Trilport with my aide at 6 and we were the first Americans he had seen." GBC].

talions of the 9th, well closed up with no stragglers, marched by way of Coulombs, Duhisy, and Montreuil-aux-Lions, fifteen kilometres to the crossroads. Where, about 7:00 o'clock,[70] they woke up Mattfeldt and received the orders transmitted through him. There arrived at this point also Colonel Preston Brown, and some officers of the French XXI Corps who had seen the marching column from a distance and were much relieved to find that it was American infantry and not the Boche. From them the final orders were communicated. The noise of the fighting came down from the heights north of the Clignon Brook, on which desperate small bodies of Frenchmen were fighting rear-guard actions against the Germans. During the day before, the German 231st Division had encircled Chateau Thierry, and on this morning they were mounting Hill 204, immediately to the west of the town. They were almost in sight of XXI Corps headquarters at Coupru, and in the judgment of the French staff the menace from the east was more pressing than from the north. The 9th Infantry would deploy south of the Paris-Metz highway — not across it.[71] The left flank would rest on Le Thiolet, five kilometres east of the Ventelet cross-roads, "if," added the French, "you can get there in time."[72] No one knew how fast the Germans were advancing but the French said the highway, along which the column of the 9th was halted, lay under the observation of the enemy from the heights to the east and north. Consequently, the regiment was moved off to the south into low ground, and prepared to go into position.[73] Colonel Upton did not hurry. The French thought that their forces still maintained something of a line in front of them so he moved his battalions forward deliberately, taking advantage of cover and dead space where he could find it.[74] The Germans had largely outrun their artillery, and although this reinforcement along the highway was observed and reported, they did not fire upon it during the morning.[75] The men of the 9th, whose last ordered meal had been at Loconville the day before, were able to forage what scraps they found in deserted farm houses as they went along.[76]

The 1/9, Major [*Franklin L.*] Whitley, placed its left on Le Thiolet, the farm on the highway at the southeast corner of the Bois de Clerembauts.

70   Ibid.
Confirmed by Capt. Mattfeldt and General P. Brown. Mathews adds "After the arrival of the 9th near the Ferme [farm] Paris they [Germans] would not engage the 2nd Div. that day. [The rest is impossible to read, GBC].
71   War Diary, 1 June, Vol. 6.
72   History 9th Infantry.
73   Ibid.
74   War Diary, 1 June, Vol. 6.
75   War Diaries, German 10th, 231st and 237th Divisions.
76   Captain C.O. Mattfeldt, 9th Infantry.

From there they formed a line southward along the western face of the Bois de la Marette, through Tafournay and the Bois de Tafournay. Major [*Arthur E.*] Bouton and 2/9, prolonged the line through La Nouette Farm to Bonneil, a kilometre north of the Marne at Azy. By noon both battalions were deployed and organizing their positions. About noon 3/9 reached the field, and was distributed as reserve — two companies going to Hill 201 on the highway where they began the construction of a redoubt, and two companies being located in the woods near Les Aulnois Bontemps, where Colonel Upton established regimental headquarters. It is related that as these battalions marched to position they met, retiring from the eastern face of the Bois de la Marette, files of French dismounted cavalry. Seeing the Americans, the dragoons returned to their lines and remained on the regimental front until they were relieved by the 9th on 5 June.[77]

Shortly after noon, all three battalions of the 9th were in place, one in reserve, and two holding a line of about five kilometres from Le Thiolet to Bonneil. They had come on the field with only the ammunition in their belts — 100 rounds per man — and lacked the regimental machine gun company and all animal-drawn transport, which was marching overland. The Divisional services, however, were getting up as the day drew on. Two days' rations were placed in dumps behind the troops, and the combat trains established small arms ammunition dumps. Those for the artillery were located at Lizy-sur-Ourcq. Meaux was designated as the railhead. A staff officer brought information from the French that 18 trains allotted to the Division had been canceled and the units assigned to them were obliged to march overland. Among these were the regimental machine gun companies. Arrangements were made to transport as many elements as possible in the Division motor trucks, and to hurry the others forward by forced marches.[78]

The other rifle regiments of the 2nd Division followed the 9th, suffering delays and checks from the increasing confusion that prevailed as the battlefront rolled down from the north and east towards the Meaux area.

The 23rd Infantry, Colonel Paul B. Malone, had embussed and cleared its billeting area by 5:30 am, on the 31st.[79] It passed through Meaux, not having been diverted to the north as planned by the Divisional chief of staff, and it was late afternoon before its camions threaded their way through the congestion in the town. Scattered and much extended on the road, its trains moved north on the Soissons highway, passed through May-en-Multien, and

77   *War Diary, 1 June, Vol. 6; History 9th Infantry; History 3rd Brigade: Hall: 2nd Div. file. [Bois de Clerembauts was actually Bois La Cense. One more mistaken identification, undoubtedly taken from old French maps that way. GBC].*
78   *Ibid.*
79   *History 23rd Infantry.*

de-bussed south of Marieul-sur-Ourcq about nightfall. Re-assembling, it marched back through May-en-Multien, encountering there some of the 5th Marines, filling the road as they debarked from their camions. To avoid further complications, the 23rd left the road and turned into the fields. Here they were later found by General Bundy, who was just returning from Paris. He directed Colonel Malone to fall out and bivouac, so that the 23rd made no further move that night.[80]

The 5th Regiment of Marines departed its billeting area about 6:00 am, and arrived at May-en-Multien about 5:00 pm. There it was ordered to proceed north on the Soissons road — the Duchêsne order forming the Division on the Gandelu-Montigny d'Allier line was then controlling dispositions— and one battalion, at least, moved north for some distance towards Marieul-sur-Ourcq. About 6:00 pm, a French staff officer advised the column of 2/5 that the Germans had entered the town on which it was directed.[81] The regiment left its camions and assembled on the road, then ascertained that the country immediately to its front was deserted and stood by to see what would happen. Further orders came from the French to proceed to the rear. All elements of the 5th then passed through May-en-Multien, halted and bivouacked very near the 23rd Infantry just east of the town.[82]

Thus, at midnight 31 May—1 June, before the 9th took up its march on Montreuil, the 9th, 23rd and 5th Marines were closely concentrated between May-en-Multien and Crouy-sur-Ourcq.

The 6th Marines, the last regiment to leave the Chaumont-en-Vexin area, started at about 9:00 am, and remained in its camions all day and all night. The regiment passed through Meaux and about daylight on 1 June the battalions were set down west of Montreuil-aux-Lions. The men were ordered to get out of sight in the houses along the road, and to keep covered against Boche planes. Trucks of the 2nd Division Trains unloaded some iron rations for them, and they were able to forage for fowls and rabbits and eggs in the deserted French farms and dwellings. The regiment remained near Montreuil until afternoon, awaiting orders. Three/nine marched through Montreuil about noon, and between 1:00 pm, and 2:30 pm, it took up the march for the front along the highway.[83]

At daylight on 1 June, the units of the Division were more scattered than the day before. By that time two battalions of the 9th Infantry had cov-

---

80   Ibid; Brown notes; Lewis notes; History 3rd Brigade.
81   Battle Belleau Woods, Lt. E.C. Cooke, 2/5, 2nd Div.
82   History 5th Regiment, Marines. [What wasn't mentioned was that Lt. Col. Frederick M. Wise told a senior French office to "go to H-1" when told to retrace his steps. However, after a suitable dressing down, he soon after managed to accept that order. GBC].
83   History 6th Regiment Marines; History 2/6 and History 3/6, 2nd Div. files.

ered eighteen kilometres and were near the Marigny-Coupru crossroads on the highway in readiness for deployment. The 5th Marines and 23rd Infantry were rising from their bivouacs east of May-en-Multien, with twenty-five kilometres to march and the 6th Marines were ten kilometres west of the 9th Infantry in Montreuil. The 5th and 6th Machine Gun Battalions were still in their camions,[84] back somewhere around Meaux where traffic conditions grew worse instead of better.

At noon on 1 June, all three battalions of the 9th were up, and the first two were deployed between Le Thiolet and Bonneil. The 5th Marines and the 23rd Infantry were on the road from May-en-Multien, marching down through Crouy-sur-Ourcq, Venderest and Cocherel, to Montreuil. The 5th Marines were ahead and while the Marines continued to march the 23rd Infantry had been delayed by conflicting orders and by the authorization of the Division commander.[85] In the meantime, Division headquarters were set up in Montreuil: the supply trains were up, the infantry Brigadiers, Generals [James G.] Harbord and Lewis, had moved ahead through Montreuil and examined the terrain they were to occupy[86] and Colonel [William] Chamberlaine, had received orders from the Division commander in Meaux at 8:30 am, to march his artillery units from their detraining points to Cocherel for assembly.[87] But no more troops arrived in the battle area until mid-afternoon.[88]

As the day drew on, General Harbord who was located at the front, heard the rattle of small arms where the Germans and the French fought for the heights just north of the Clignon Brook. Trucks of the 2nd Supply Trains were in the area, depositing field rations and small arms ammunition along the highway. Seizing a section of these trucks, the General riding in the leading one, went back along the highway towards Montreuil-aux-Lions and picked up the rearmost marching battalion of the 6th Marines.[89] It was 2/6, Major Thomas Holcomb in command. The trucks transported 2/6 up to Le Thiolet where, behind the Bois des Clerembauts, the battalion got out and deployed. Thereby extending the line of the 9th Infantry north of the highway, along the eastern face of the Bois des Clerembauts, through Triangle Farm and the west end of the Bois de Tri-

84   *War Diary, 1 June, Vol. 6.*
85   Brown notes.
86   History 3rd Brigade: Hall: 2nd Div. File.
[Also have pencilled comment by Harbord which states "I had passed through Montreuil before 6:00 pm June 1 and found General Degoutte at Coupru but had no chance to examine the terrain." GBC].
87   *Journal of Operations, 2nd F.A., Brig. Chamberlaine.*
88   *War Diary, 1 June.*
89   *War Diary, 4th Brigade, 1 June, Vol. 6.*

angle, to Lucy-le-Bocage. Major Holcomb was reported in position at 5:05 pm.[90]

While 2/6 was deploying, the 6th Machine Gun Battalion, Major [Edward B.] Cole, arrived in camions and de-bussed near Hill 201. They established headquarters at Montgivarault-le-Grande and then sent guns forward to support the line of 2/6. Two of its guns were emplaced on the highway at Le Thiolet.[91]

The leading battalion of the 6th, Major [John A.] Hughes, marched up behind the machine gunners, turned north off the highway, and prolonged the line of 2/6 to the west, from Lucy-le-Bocage through the Bois de Champillon[92] to Hill 142. Colonel Catlin, commanding the 6th, led Sibley off the highway and placed it in reserve in the woods north of La Voie du Chatel. Colonel Catlin established headquarters in La Voie du Chatel,[93] reporting the regiment in position at 6:50 pm.[94] The 6th Marines now occupied a line of about six kilometres, with two battalions deployed, and one in reserve.

The 5th Marines, Colonel Neville, arrived, and was directed to Pyramide Farm, where it bivouacked in the fields. Regimental headquarters being located after dark at Carrieres, 300 meters northwest of Marigny.[95] The 5th Machine Gun Battalion of the 3rd Brigade entered the area and strengthened the line of the 9th Infantry.[96] At 8:00 pm, the 23rd Infantry reported two battalions in close support of the 9th in the woods west of Coupru and one battalion in Corps Reserve in the Bois de Fond Jars on the highway.[97] The 23rd was the last regiment to come up to where the rest of the Division infantry was located. With its arrival 13,000 infantry had been placed astride the Paris-Metz road before nightfall between Chateau Thierry and Montreuil-aux-Lions.[98]

The 2nd Engineer Regiment, Colonel [James F.] McIndoe in command, had de-bussed after 20 hours in their camions, at 5:00 am, on 1 June at May-en-Multien. They marched at once on Montreuil, where they arrived

---

90   *War Diary, 4th Brigade, 1 June, Vol. 6. Harbord to 2nd Div., 5:05 pm, 1 June, Vol. 4.*
91   *History of the 6th Machine Gun Battalion.*
92   [According to a very knowledgeable friend, Gilles Lagin of Marigny-en-Orxois, France, the wood was known, incorrectly at that time, as the Bois de Champillon. It was changed on later maps to the Bois St. Martin. The wood opposite the Lucy-Torcy road, facing the Bois de Belleau presently seems to not have a name. GBC].
93   *War Diary, 4th Brigade, 1 June, Vol. 6.*
94   *Catlin to Harbord, 6:50 pm, 1 June, Vol. 6.*
95   *War Diary, 4th Brigade, 1 June, Vol. 6.*
96   *War Diary, 2nd Div., 1 June, Vol. 6*
97   Ibid.
98   Ibid.

at 1:00 pm, less their horse transport, which was proceeding overland. At first the regiment was designated as Division Reserve, but the order was change and it was divided between the infantry brigades, 1/2 to the 3rd Brigade, and the 2/2 to the Marines. Marching forward from Montreuil, 1/2 arrived at Beaurepaire Farm at 7:00 pm, and was set to work strengthening the line of the 9th Infantry. Two/2 proceeded to Lucy-le-Bocage, reporting at 3:00 am, on 2 June, and began the fortification of the Marine positions. Lucy-le-Bocage was placed in a state of defense, and field works were outlined. Thereafter the engineer battalions shared the labors of the brigades to which they attached, the normal distribution being a platoon of engineers to each rifle company. But in the subsequent attacks delivered by the 4th Brigade, the engineers were employed in support and assault as infantry.[99]

At 6:00 pm, 2nd Division Headquarters issued Field Order 6, confirming the details of the deployment. It noted the attack by the enemy in force along the line Chateau Thierry-Bouresches-Monthiers, and the assignment of the 2nd Division to the French XXI Corps, General Degoutte commanding. Degoutte's headquarters was then at Chamigny, a few kilometres southwest of Montreuil, where General Bundy was also established. The French 164th Division, south of the Lizy-sur-Ourcq-Chateau Thierry road, faced the enemy along the line Essomes-Monneaux-La Roche, and the 43rd Division, above his road, prolonged the La Roche line northward. The 2nd Division was allotted the line Bonneil-Le Thiolet-Chateau de Belleau. Here, by the way, was the first mention of the word Belleau in the 2nd Division documents. The occasion is worthy of notice, although no unit of the 2nd ever entered the Chateau de Belleau. To the 3rd Brigade was given the sector south of the Paris-Metz highway, Le Thiolet to Bonneil, the present front of the 9th Infantry, with Brigade headquarters at Ventelet Farm. The 4th Brigade was north of the road, Le Thiolet (exclusive) to Chateau de Belleau, with headquarters at Pyramide, where the 5th Marines were concentrated in reserve. Two/23, near La Longue Farm, and 1/5 southwest of Pyramide constituted the Division reserve. In addition a battalion of engineers, to be assigned, and the 4th Machine Gun Battalion, were stationed at Montreuil. The order further provided for the concentration of the artillery brigade at Cocherel, engineer headquarters at Montreuil, and the employment of the 1st Field Signal Battalion for communications with the French Corps and the elements of the 2nd Division. The ambulance companies, arrived an en route were directed to Vendrest, Dhuisy, and Meaux, and the field hospitals to Bezu, Cocherel, and Meaux. The Divisional mil-

99 *History 2nd Engineers.*

itary police were ordered to establish a barrier on the line Ste. Aulde-Montreuil-Germigny-Gandelu, with an officer post in Meaux.[100]

Of the troops mentioned in Field Order 6, the 4th Machine Gun Battalion was not present—it was then delayed by a broken-down train at Ormoy-Villers. The 2nd Engineers were already assigned to the brigades on the front, and were marching up. The actual deployment of the troops, beginning with the 9th Infantry, had been made on verbal orders given on the ground as the emergency dictated. When the 9th arrived, the threat was from he direction of Hill 204. Later in the day, as the weight of the German thrust swung westward from Chateau Thierry, the line was extended westward to meet it. Information from the divisions of the French Corps fighting out in front continued to be vague and alarming, and the two last-arrived regiments of the 2nd Division, the 5th Marines and the 23rd Infantry, were held in hand to meet developments.

Early in the morning of 1 June, between May-en-Multien and Montreuil and the Ourcq towns, the troops had picked their way forward through the last of the tide of the refugees. But the country where they left the roads and went into position, was drained of life. Around the farmhouses, they found cows and rabbits and fowls, left behind unfed. At Cocherel, Colonel Chamberlaine related, they read a scrawled message on the door of the house in which artillery headquarters were established: "Papa, nous sommes partie a' Rue—, Lizy-sur-Ourcq." The women and children had been obliged to take the road while their man was in his fields.[101] In the area where the Americans deployed they found a few groups of French artillery[102] and scattered details of infantry. "Which way," said a young man in the Marine Machine Gun Battalion, "is this here line?" "Line, hell!" a sergeant told him. "We're going to make one—".[103] As this battalion approached Hill 201, they passed a French battery of 75's, firing from the roadside at some target to the north.[104]

At midnight, 1/2 June, the situation of the 2nd Division was this: from right to left, 2/9 and 1/9 were in line from Bonneil to Le Thiolet, with 3/9 in support, and regimental headquarters at Les Aulnois Bontemps. Two/6 (Marines) and 1/6 were in line from Le Thiolet through Lucy-le-Bocage and the Bois de Champillon to about Hill 142, with 3/6 in support and headquarters at La Voie du Chatel. The 9th Infantry and the 6th Marines were

---

100 Field Order 6, 2nd Division, 6:00 pm, 1 June, Vol. 1.
101 Operations 2nd F.A. Brigade, Chamberlaine, Vol. 9.
102 Brown notes. French XXI CA, had on hand only 6 pieces of artillery, 155mm, with about 10 rounds per gun.
103 Diary J. Bass, 81st Mg. Co, 6th Mg. Bn., file. [Listed in error as "83rd." GBC].
104 Ibid.

deployed on a front of twelve kilometres. The 23rd Infantry and the 5th Marines were in reserve, two battalions of the 23rd west of Coupru and one in the Bois de Fond Jars, and the 5th Marines near Pyramide. Headquarters of the 3rd Brigade were at Ventelet Farm, and Headquarters of the 4th Brigade were at Issonge Farm. The 5th and 6th Machine Gun Battalions were distributed among the deployed battalions and in reserve. The 2nd Engineers were distributed to the 3rd and 4th Brigades. The regimental machine gun companies were en route across country. The artillery was concentrating on Cocherel. The 1st Field Signal Battalion was up and engaged in establishing communications. The motorized Divisional services were up and functioning, as were the hospital and ambulance details. On the right of the XXI Corps was the French XXXVIII Corps, and on the left the VII Corps. Elements of the French XXI Corps, the 164th and 43rd Divisions, were engaged in front of the 2nd Division. The 2nd Division had on its rolls, available for duty, 1064 officers and 25, 614 men, of whom about 13,000 infantry were actually on the ground. The day had been clear and warm, so that the men, moving up, suffered from the heat. No casualties had been reported since only a few German shells had fallen in the area. Small arms ammunition and ration dumps had been established in the rear of the troops, but the field kitchens and regimental supply trains were still absent. They were still marching overland and there was no food except iron rations and what individuals could forage. There were, generally, no maps and no definite information of the enemy and little of friendly troops. But, as the Boche would soon learn, the 2nd Division was between the enemy and the direct road to Paris.[105]

105   *War Diary, 2nd Division*, 1 June, Vol. 6.

Five

Plan of Employment, 31 May–1 June

During the night of 31 May–1 June, following the assignment of the 2nd Division to the French XXI Corps, and on 1 June, while the regiments of the 2nd Division assembled in the Montreuil area, the Division Chief of Staff and the Division Commander, discussed plans for the employment of their troops with the commander of the French Corps. General of Division Degoutte was an old Colonial soldier — like many of the best French leaders and he was presently to be given command of the 6th Army. His Headquarters were, on 1 June, located in Chamigny, a few kilometres southwest of Montreuil-aux-Lions. His plan for the employment of the 2nd Division was to throw the regiments into the fight as they arrived in the battle zone.[106]

Such a plan reflected faithfully the tactics which had governed the French Command since the German break-through five days before. Then the German thrust developed; the line of the Chemin des Dames was, as has been seen, weakly held, and the 11 French divisions in line and in reserve of the 6th Army were quickly overwhelmed. The great French mass of maneuver, the reserves laboriously hoarded since the debacle of the British in March, had been placed by Foch west of Compiegne, and divisions allotted to the 6th Army for the restoration of its front could only arrive in the Marne region at the rate of two a day. Pétain[107] considered that his first task was to weld, by whatever means were found possible, the breach that the Germans had made, and the divisions coming up from the reserve were thrown, any way, into the breach. Presently, said Pétain as the impetus of the German drive dissipated itself, some of those elements would hold some-

---

106 *Notes on Chateau Thierry*, Maj. Gen. P. Brown, 2nd Division File.
107 Pétain report 1918–War College

where; then more of them would hold, and finally the breach would be welded.[108] Then they would see about details. Both of the divisions constituting, on 1 June, the French XXI Corps, had entered the fight in this manner. The 43rd Division had been resting in Compiegne on 27 May: it was rushed up in camions to relieve the shattered 22nd Division, and went into battle from its camions, without organization or supply. The 164th Division had been near Amiens, and was hurried into the fight in the same manner. Both these divisions had suffered heavily, and they, on 1 June, were delivering disorganized and ineffective battle on the north heights of the Clignon, mixed with other fragments of the 6th Army.[109]

Colonel Brown, Chief of Staff, and his Division Commander, would on no account consent to such tactics. The success of the French, in applying them, had not, in the last few days, been conspicuously successful: their broken formations were still reeling back. American prestige was another factor for consideration: American Regulars were about to be engaged, for the first time, on a critical European battlefield. To throw the infantry into the fight, without machine guns or auxiliary weapons, or supplies, unaccompanied by their artillery, armed only with their rifles and 100 rounds of ammunition per man, was not considered justifiable by the 2nd Division command. The infantry Brigades, they insisted, would not fight until their artillery was up. Colonel Brown records that the discussion at the Degoutte headquarters was prolonged, and became acrimonious.[110] Finally, Degoutte gave in. The French were fighting on the Clignon: where would the Americans fight? They studied the map, and the high ground, running southwest through Dhuisy, Montreuil, Coupru, and Domptin, was indicated. The Americans would organize along there. Degoutte, who had seen Chateau Thierry fall that day, wondered if the Americans would stand. Colonel Brown told him that they were American Regulars, and they had never been whipped, and his Frenchmen had been whipped. The Americans would hold.[111]

Such was the understanding reached with French command by daylight on 1 June.

---

108 *Pierrefeu: GKQ 1915-1918.*
109 *Pétain report 1918-War College. Intelligence reports German IV Reserve Corps.*
110 *Notes on Chateau Thierry, Maj. Gen. P. Brown, 2nd Div. File.*
111 *Notes on Chateau Thierry, Maj. Gen. P. Brown, 2nd Div. File.*
    Note: The French disposition to employ their American reinforcement piece-meal is well recognized. The 2nd Division command denied both the necessity and the wisdom of throwing the infantry regiments into the fight, without artillery, machine guns, or supplies, and before the enemy intention had been fully revealed. The outcome of the event justified their judgment.

Chateau Thierry

Chateau Thierry is eighty kilometres northeast of Paris, where the Marne bends sharply southward. The 2nd Division came into a sun-drenched countryside, of rolling wheat-land set with forests that crowned the hills and followed the valleys of the little brooks. Low, sprawling farmhouses and wide barns, with stone walls and roofs of thatch and tile, were set among the fields of grain. There were orchards and some pastureland, but the land grew mostly wheat. The Paris-Metz road marched across it between tall poplars. There were obscure stone villages, presently to be famous nestled in the folds of the hills. Country roads, passable in dry weather, wound between them and fed into the highway. East and south were the milky — turquoise loops of the Marne. To the west was the Ourcq coming down in a curving line to join the flame at Meaux, and a small stream with which the Division was to be concerned, the Clignon Brook, flowed westward to the Ourcq, following a narrow valley that ran east and west a few kilometres above and parallel to the Paris-Metz road. The northern heights of the Clignon slightly overlooked the southern crests, low hills and ridges that ran diagonally towards the Marne. The dominating feature of the terrain was Hill 204, at the bend of the river just west of Chateau Thierry. Monneaux was at its foot: south, it towered over Bonneil and the Marne valley; west, it looked along the Paris-Metz road, which curved around its base, as far as the Coupru-Lucy-le-Bocage road, and north, it commanded Bouresches and the Bois de Belleau.

The country was very beautiful: 1918 was a good year in France for crops and vintages. At the end of May, the wheat was as high as a tall man's knee, and the orchards and the forests were in full leaf. There had been little rain, and the brooks that flowed north to the Clignon were nearly dry. The fields were bright with poppies.

Belleau — Belleau Wood — Physical

All military operations are influenced by terrain. On every battlefield there is some physical feature — wood, or hill, or ridge, or marsh, which dictates the course of the action. This applies to campaigns as well as to the small blood-soaked acres over which battalions fight, So in Lee's invasion of Pennsylvania in 1863, the lone corridor west of the Blue Ridge gave him a covered way for his communications when his army went north, and so at Gettysburg the fight for three days beat upon Culp's Hill and the Round Tops, and Cemetery Ridge that lies between them. In all the long war history of France, invasions have followed the fewest, subscribed channels: the enemy from the east comes through the defiles of the Argonne towards the bottle-neck of the Meuse valley at Verdun, or he comes down across the Belgian plain to the valley of the Marne Northwest of Chateau Thierry, in the same Marne country that has seen invasions since the time of Attila, the 2nd Division, meeting the 4th German Reserve Corps, found the dominating feature of the terrain in the Clignon valley.

The Clignon is a small stream, nowhere very wide or very deep, that rises above Bonnes, flows southwest to Monthiers and Lizy-Clignon and due west from Torcy to the Ourcq. It has a narrow, deep valley, between abruptly rising slopes; hills that have some wooded areas but are mostly under cultivation. The heights to the north of it slightly overlook the south. Leading into it, from either side, are other brooks, flowing north and south, following narrow, wooded valleys, that become ravines a kilometre or so away from the stream. It was the line of the Clignon that the French elements of the 43rd Division were trying to hold on the day which the 2nd Division entered the area, 1 June. Driven from the northern heights, the French tried to hold the southern hills, and the exits from the Clignon line to the south: they stood in the villages of Bouresches, Belleau, Torcy, Bussiares, and Gandelu, all of which lie on the south side. The Germans ejected them from these positions also, generally on June 2, and on that day and the next advanced south of the brook where the ground favored them. The valley in their hands offered a long, sheltered way, parallel to the Paris-Metz road, and only six or seven kilometres north of it, with excellent points of exit to the south when they should decide to drive ahead from that line. Two of these exits may be considered carefully: they were from Bussiares and from Belleau.

Belleau is just east of where the Clignon, coming around the base of Hill 193, above the village, makes its westward turn. The place is very old; it has a church, much ruined now, which dates from the 11th century. Its 40 odd houses are in a deep depression; nothing of it could be seen from the south in 1918. The ground to the south rises abruptly, amounting almost to a bluff, 20 feet high. Under this bluff, at the head of the town, is .a clear cold spring from which the village takes its name — Belleau. Gushing out under the cliff, the water is confined in a sort of tank, of stone and concrete built by the careful villagers; and here, on fine days, the women do their washing. Against the high, overhanging bank, the spring itself has been roofed over with tile, and there is a long stone platform, with the tank in front of it — a platform wide enough for animals to be led along to drink. The natives say that the water never fails; that it is always cold, and clear, and that it is the envy of the countryside. Belleau was in the track of the German invasion in 1914: the inhabitants were caught before they could get away: and they relate that for five days and nights the Germans marched through, during which time women of the village were forced to stand by the spring and hand water to the thirsty soldiers. There is one old woman who declares that when she was fainting with weariness, the Boche kept her at it with a whip. She, by the way, claims also to have been the only citizen who did not leave when the Germans returned in 1918. She is a local character, borne on the records as femme sole, who does washing and odd sewing and has raised 19 children of no stated fathers.

On the platform above the spring, under the bluff, the Germans of the 237th Division set up their field kitchens in June, 1918. Five kitchens they had here, and from this place they sent up food and water to the battalions fighting in the wood just south of Belleau. The spring and its most immediate locality were in dead space: only the most acute of high-angle fire could have reached them and no shells fell here. But west of the spring, across a little cart road that goes steeply up through a cut in the bluff, is the church, and beyond it the Chateau of Belleau. Both of these were much knocked about by shell- fire; the church most of all: it stands gutted and roofless now. The chateau, owned by a wealthy gentleman of Paris, was quite ruined. This gentleman was a sportsman: he kept horses, and their stable, partly underground, running back into the hill west of the spring, was used as a shelter by the Germans: there was room in it for 150 men, and a regimental headquarters functioned there in the first part of June, 1916. The officers slept on beds taken from the chateau. In the chateau, in 1927, workmen found the cadaver of a soldier of the 26th American Division, who had crawled into a corner, died, and was covered by the debris of crumbling wall and ceiling.[112]

The owner of Chateau Belleau kept not only horses; in a thick tangled wood just south of the town, he had a game preserve, maintaining deer, pheasants, and hares, with a small hunting lodge, called the Pavilion, near the northeastern corner of the wood. The natives relate that his hunting parties, held there in the good days before the war, were extremely gay. They mention the baskets of champagne that went out, and the pretty ladies of Paris who came to cheer the sportsmen after their pleasant toils. The wood was called the Bois de Belleau, although the southern two-thirds of it lies in the commune of Bouresches, and was a source of fire-wood and timber to that town. The wood itself began half a kilometre south of Belleau village, and was generally elevated above the surrounding wheat fields. Between it and Belleau ran an improved road, all on high, open ground,

---

112 Captain Charles [sic] Dunbeck, U.S.M.C., retd. Interviews with citizens of Belleau, 1927. [Dunbeck's first name was Charley. His father named him after his favorite horse. GBC].

connecting Bussiares with Bouresches and leading on to the highway at Vaux. From Belleau, you could approach the wood by other roads, unimproved, but good in dry weather. One, coming up from the Chateau, skirted the western edge of the wood and led to Lucy-le-Bocage. The Marines, who became well acquainted with the locality, called it the Double-tree road, because of the low thick trees that were spaced along both sides of it. One road passed east of the spring, climbed the Hill, and went along the east of the wood, shortening an angle of the Bussiares-Vaux road, which it rejoined at Bouresches. South of the wood, another dirt road joined Lucy-le-Bocage and Bouresches, and the wood lay within this triangle: Belleau 500 metres due north, Lucy about 800 metres southwest, and Bouresches just off the southeastern corner. The wood was almost two kilometres long, from north to south, and about a kilometre across at the widest part, and 400 metres at the narrowest. It is shaped, on the map, like a kidney, or like an oyster, very narrow in the middle. In June 1918, as all the wooded areas in the region, its trees were in full leaf, and except for one or two long narrow cuttings in the southern end, and a small clearing in the northern third, it was very much in a state of nature. Tall hardwood trees grow thickly in it, and under the trees it was choked with the heaviest underbrush and second growth. There was a deep ravine in the southern edge, and one narrow, unimproved road in the hunting preserve, and through the rest of it, a few winding footpaths. There was a small stone house called the Pavilion in the hunting preserve. Another deep ravine cuts almost across it, angling northeast and southwest from the western edge, a little below its northern third.

To the east, the ground slopes from the wood down to the main Bussiares-Vaux road, and lifts gently towards Etrépilly, and it opens towards Bouresches. There are scattered trees in the direction of Lucy, and an orchard. To the south, the edge commands a long stretch of open wheat land, but its view of the highway is cut off by a ridge that rises south of Lucy and elopes eastward: it commands all the approaches to Bouresches from Lucy. Westward, the ground towards the Bois de Champillon is all open and lower than the road. In 1918, the surrounding country was in wheat, well grown in June and promising abundant harvest. Within the woods, there is a surprising variety of contour, unguessed from the map. Knolls rise abruptly. Great boulders thrust up from the ground, an outcropping of these crowned the height in the south face of the wood, grey, enormous stones, leprous with moss, and frost-split, offering ideal natural protection from each-fire, and location for machine guns. The high point was in the southwestern corner, Hill 161; but Hill 181 had been, at some time, logged off, and the second growth on it was so impenetrable that it offered no field of fire for any kind of position, or even for an observation post.

Torcy — Bussiares — Tactical

About a kilometre west of Belleau and a little north is Torcy, a town of 40 houses and a church, the same size as Belleau. It is within the Clignon valley, that stream passing just north of it, at Lizy-Clignon. It is a little higher; the slender spire of its church could be seen by the Americans on Hill 142. Like Belleau, it was built against the southern slope of the valley, which was here not so steep as at Belleau. In this hillside was a large cave, used by the Germans, who habitually maintained a battalion in the place. West of it is Hill 126, all wheat land, and two kilometres from it, down the Clignon, is Bussiares, a town slightly larger, also within the valley. But at Bussiares, the land breaks away to the south. Two brooks, that rise near Champillon, enclosing Hill 142, pass here to the Clignon water, and the valley that opens for them, narrow, deep, and wooded, leads as far south as the Marigny depression. To the left, as the Germans faced southward, was the Bois de Bussiares and Hill 142, beyond that the Bois de Champillon. To the right front, you looked as far as Les Mares farm, standing on the skyline over Hill 165; and to the west of Les Mares were the Bois de Veuilly and the Bois de Vaurichart, among valleys and defiles that led down to the Paris-

Capturing Germans in a shell hole

Metz road. The town of Veuilly lay north of Bois de Veuilly. Further west were the villages of Gandelu and Brumetz, with the cover of the forests near at hand to the south of the Clignon. This area was important to any troops along the Clignon line, as was the Bois de Belleau further east.

If you stood along the Clignon, your enemy could approach you by the depressions south of Bussiares, finding cover for his infantry and shelter for his services and battery positions right up to your front. If you intended advancing from the Clignon — and here the Bois de Belleau was important also the Bussiares depression and the wood offered excellent cover of said dead ground for the assembly and formation of assaulting and protected corridors pressing down to the open country beyond. The French gave up this line reluctantly and the Germans holding it, desired also to hold its approaches.

Six

IV Reserve Corps (German): Movements, 27 May–1 June

The IV Reserve Corps was commanded by General of Infantry von Conta, an officer who had made a reputation in the Roumanian campaign. The Corps Headquarters appeared in the 7th Army area on 14 May, one of the three attack groups brought in for the Chemin des Dames drive. Its divisions entered the line immediately before the assault, during the night 26–27 May, and it will be remembered, this Corps in the center of the 7th Army set the pace for the German advance during the next five days.[113]

The IV Reserve Corps attacked on 27 May with three divisions, all shock formations in line. They were, from left to right, the 5th Guards, the 28th, and the 10th. Two divisions, the 36th, an attack formation, and the 231st, a second — or third-rate division followed in Corps reserve. On 26 May, the 36th Division was inserted between the 28th and 10th Divisions. The following day, the 5th Guards was withdrawn to Corps reserve, and the 28th, 38th, and 10th continued the advance, the 231st keeping distance behind, with a new division, the 237th, also a low-rater, added to the reserve. On the 30th, there was no change in the Corps order of battle. On 31 May, the 26th Division, then on the Marne above Chateau Thierry, was withdrawn, the 36th division extending its left to relieve it. The 231st Division came into line on the right of the 36th, investing Chateau Thierry. The 237th was ordered to line on the right of the 231st, but when this movement was partially completed, the 10th Division was shifted in, and the 237th took position on the right of the 10th. The 5th Guards and the 26th rested, and the 197th Division, a sector holding formation, appeared close behind the Corps right, astride the boundary of its right neighbor, the XXV

---

113 *War Diary and Annexes. German Crown Prince Army Group-14-27 Lay-18.*

Reserve Corps.[114] On 1 June, the 197th Division went into line on the right of the 237th. The order of battle was then as the American 2nd Division was to meet it: the Conta Corps, with 5 divisions in line and 2 in reserve, ran north from Chateau Thierry to Etrépilly, thence through Epaux, Bonnes, and Sommelans, in order from the left the 36th, 231st, 10th, 237th, and 197th Divisions. Of these the 36th was immobilized behind the Marne, the 10th was approaching exhaustion, from its losses and exertions in the five days of the drive, the 231st and the 237th were fresh, but not regarded as attack troops, and the 197th, which had been in the front on the Chemin des Dames sector throughout the month of May, had been but five days out of the line. The 5th Guards and the 28th, in reserve, were worn out and much reduced by battle.[115]

The mission of Conta was to form a defensive flank for the thrust to the Ourcq by Winckler's XXV Reserve Corps. With daylight of 1 June, the Conta divisions began a wide wheeling movement to the west and south, the pivot of which was the 231st Division at Chateau Thierry. Beyond the right of the 197th Division, the XXV Reserve Corps attacked straight westward with two strong shock formations, the 33rd Division and the 1st Guards.[116]

At midnight, 31 May–1 June, the Corps line was, roughly, La Charitie, a suburb in the north edge of Chateau Thierry, Etrépilly, St. Gengoulph. The Corps right was in line northeast and southwest through St.Gengoulph to Sommelans. On the right, the 197th Division was ordered to attack between St. Gengoulph and Bonnes, taking Courchamps, Lizy Farm, and Lizy-Clignon. In close liaison on the left, the 237th Division was ordered to attack between Bonnes and Etrépilly, taking Monthiers. The 10th Division would support the 237th with flanking fire, advancing in general conformity. The 231st was to complete the investment of Chateau Thierry and take Hill 204 west of the town.[117]

While, on 1 June, the 2nd American Division was taking up its ground, these orders' were being carried out with thoroughness and precision. With the 33rd Division pushing west into the Ourcq-Clignon corner, the 197th swung southwest, the 237the wheeling on its left, and both divisions made good progress up to noon, the objectives of the 197th being extended, at

---

114 Ibid. *War Diary and Annexes. German 7th Army-14-31 May.* Note: The movements of the German IV Reserve Corps is traced in some detail, since it was with the Conta divisions that the 2nd Division was concerned. JWT. Jr.
115 *War Diary, German 7th Army. 1 June. War Diary and Annexes IV Reserve Corps 1 June. History German Divisions, GHQ, AEF, 1918.*
116 IV Reserve Corps Ia No. 499 operations 1:30 am 1 June 1918.
117 IV Reserve Corps Ia No. 499 operations 1:30 am [1] June 1918.

3:15 pm, to include Hautevesnes. The advance was infiltration, the rolling nature of the terrain, as well as the condition of the French defense, making such tactics most effective. Each division moved well in hand, in columns preceded by skirmishers and mounted points which felt out the foreground.

There was accompanying artillery with each regiment of foot. The points located centers of resistance, and advance forces pushed aside such resistance as could be locally dealt with: but where the French stood with determination and in numbers, word went back to the marching columns, the regiments deployed, the accompanying guns came into action, and the situation was dealt with. The clearing of the area around Monthiers is an example of the actions of this day and the next.[118]

Shortly after midday on 1 June points of the 237th Division came upon French elements, organized at the north edge of Monthiers. Reconnaissance developed a French line, extending south to the Givry-Epaux road, across Hill 193, on the front of the 237th Division. Monthiers marked the divisional boundary, and north of Monthiers, the scouts of the 197th Division located the same French line running from the town towards Sommelans, covering the Petret woods and the approach to Courchamps and Lizy-Clignon. The two advanced regiments of the 237th swung westward to face the southern half of this line, and the 197th, on the right, moved west and then south, enveloping the northern flank of the French. The accompanying artillery opened, from favorable points, on Monthiers and Hill 193, and the infantry went forward. The French line crumbled, the 197th took Courchamps and approached Lizy-Clignon, and the 237th swept through Monthiers and over Hill 193, looking down into the Clignon valley.[119] All over the Corps front, during the day, such desperate actions were fought. At nightfall the 197th Division had Hautevesnes and Lizy-Clignon and Courchamps, the 237th had Bonnes and Monthiers, with its outpost line in the northern edges of Belleau and Torcy, and the 10th Division had taken the Bois des Rochets. The 231st Division had cleared Chateau Thierry of the French and Americans after some street fighting, and seized the crest of Hill 204, to which the weight of the division attack had been directed in the morning.[120] No great effort was put forth by the 231st in Chateau Thierry, because with the hill in German hands, the town was untenable. In the evening, the 231st Division pushed patrols to Vaux. At midnight the German line, from Chateau Thierry, ran through Vaux, the Bois des Rochets, passed some distance south of Etrépilly, then through the north edge of Bel-

---

118 *War Diary, IV Reserve Corps, 1 June: also War Diary, 237th and 197th Divisions 1-2 June.*
119 *War Diary and Annexes, 237th Division, 1 June.*
120 *War Diary and Annexes, IV Reserve Corps, 1-2 June.*

leau, through Lizy-Clignon, through the north edge of Torcy, and northwest of Hautevesnes. From Belleau to Lizy-Clignon they possessed the north heights of the Clignon Brook, and from Torcy to the west they looked down into it. They had taken many prisoners and some machine guns: to date, the Conta Corps alone had captured 333 officers and 11,746 men.[121]

At 11:30 pm, 1 June, von Conta issued orders for the next day's operations.[122]

The day's objective, he noted, had been reached by his Corps: the advance of from 4 to 6 kilometres had, especially on the Corps right, exceeded expectations. The 7th Army would continue the attack until the enemy's resistance broke between Soissons and Villers Cotterets, and the mission of the IV Reserve Corps continued to be the flank protection of the Army on the general line Gandelu-Chateau Thierry. The direction of attack would be the same, generally, as of 1 June. The line to be reached was, for the 197th Division, Gandelu-Marigny, for the 237th Division, Marigny-Bouresches, and for the 10th Division, Bouresches-Vaux. The 231st Division would consolidate its gains on Hill 204 and in the vicinity of Chateau Thierry, and the 36th was preparing to establish a bridgehead up the Marne. Von Conta wanted better cooperation, pre-arranged, between infantry and artillery: the artillery would start the day's work with some preparation on designated points, but by 9:00 am the attack must start.[123]

Two June dawned. No fresh troops replaced the worn French formations along the Clignon, but the word must have gone forward that reinforcements were close behind, for the Germans on 2 June noted the resistance increased every where.[124] The German advance of 2 June is important, because it fixed the terrain which was to be the battlefield of the 2nd Division. Each German division, examining its foreground, set as objectives for the day, places not sheltering, for the most part, headquarters and reserves of the American regiments. The 197th directed its columns on Vinly, Eloup, Veuilly-la-Poterie, and Marigny-en-Orxois. The 237th Division would go as far as Marigny, and seize Champillon, La Voie du Chatel, and Lucy-le-Bocage. The 10th Division would take Bouresches and the Bois de Triangle and Triangle Farm, and the Paris-Metz road west of Vaux. Such an advance, for the Corps, would involve the Paris-Metz road east of Meaux, secure the attractive Clignon line, and neutralize everything between Montreuil and Chateau Thierry, as far as the north bank of the Marne was concerned.[125]

121   *War Diary, IV Reserve Corps, 1 June.*
122   *IV Reserve Corps Ia No. 507 operations 11:40 pm, 1 June.*
123   *IV Reserve Corps Ia No. 507 operations 11:30 pm, 1 June.*
124   *War Diaries and Annexes, 231st, 237th, 10th and 197th Divisions, 1-2 June.*
125   Ibid.

23rd Infantry — 2 June

The German gains of 1 June alarmed the French Army command. From the line of the Clignon brook, now threatened from Belleau to the west, narrow, deep valleys eminently suitable for the screened advance of infantry, led south towards the Paris-Metz Road: even a slight gain in this quarter would be disastrous. About midnight, then — the time that reports of the day's fighting would be received and digested at Corps Headquarters, and the results set forth on the map, the French XXI Corps sent to the 2nd Division for help. A gap of four kilometres now existed in the French line, in the vicinity of Gandelu and the left of the French 43rd Division was in the air.[126]

The 2nd Division detached Colonel Paul B. Malone, with the 23rd Infantry, the 1/5th Marines, the 5th Machine Gun Battalion, less two companies, and Company C of the 2nd Engineers. The three battalions of the 23rd, 2 behind the 9th Infantry position south of the highway, and 1 in the Bois de Fond Jars, on the highway, were roused. and took the road. The First Battalion of the Fifth Marines, in bivouac near the Pyramids, and closest to the line of march, was alerted and sent on as advance guard. The machine gunners and the engineers, with some ambulances and vehicles, followed. The column, about five thousand men, had ten kilometres to go, and it was advisable to get behind the Bois de Veuilly before daylight, which came early.[127] The route laid down was over country roads, by Platriere, Grand Courtmont and Ecoute Pleut, to les Glandons. The gap they were to fill was from the Bois de Veuilly, near which was the left of the 43rd French Division, to Brumetz, where they would endeavor to establish liaison with the French 7th Corps. Battalions filed to the right successively as they came to the rear of their allotted areas, and deployed.[128]

The column moved, and at 6:30 am the battalion of Marines turned off into position along the north edge of the Bois de Vaurichart and west to Premont, its commanding officer reporting liaison with the left regiment of the French division north of Bois de Veuilly at 9:50.[129] At 7:50 am the 3/23 left the column and prolonged the line to the left, from Premont to Moulin du Rhone.[130] At Coulombs the 1/23 filed north, to Brumetz, making patrol contact with the 3/23, and extending westward, to feel for the 7th Corps.[131]

---

126 *French XXI CL to 2nd Division,1:20 am, 2 June, Vol. 4.*
127 *War Diary, 2nd Division 1-2 June, Vol. 6.*
128 *War Diary, 2nd Division, 1-2 June, Vol. 6. Malone to 2nd Division, 6:30 am, 2 June Vol. 4.*
129 *Ibid. [Major Julius S.] Turrill to Malone, 9:50 am, 2 June, Vol. 5.*
130 *Malone to 2nd Division, 7:50 am, 2 June, Vol. 5.*

The remaining battalion, 2/23, went into reserve at Coulombs, with the headquarters of the detachment.[132] The companies of the 5th Machine Gun Battalion were distributed along the line, and the engineers set to work on strong points. The whole force was in position at 1:30 pm, and the Gandelu gap was closed.[133] The movement was observed by the Germans: some of their ground troops reported it; a balloon went up to the north, and the column entering Coulombs came under artillery fire and suffered casualties, as did the 1/23, then going into line around Brumetz. Detachments of French troops, so scattered as to be ineffective, remained in the front of the Americans, passed through the line, or drew off to the 43rd Division on the right.[134]

As for the 2nd Division proper, it found things to do in its own sector. Examination of the country north of Marigny, where the 43rd Division was supposed to be organized, disclosed in the early morning only a few dragoons, and a very weak line of infantry which, in the judgment of the Brigadier of Marines, would not hold very long. He sent word to the 1/5, attached to Colonel Malone, to extend its right across the Bois de Vaurichart, and ordered Colonel Neville, commanding the Fifth Marines, with his regimental headquarters company, and, the 2/5, into line from Hill 142, on the left of the 6th Marines, westward to the Bois de Veuilly, where they connected with the Marines of the 1/5. Unconnected elements of the French were here and there across this front, and the Marines of these battalions and of the Sixth Machine Gun Battalion relate that they found vagrant Frenchmen looting Les Mares Farm, west of Champillon.[135] Also, the Lieutenant Colonel of the 5th Marines, Logan Feland, scouting along the line, found a French regimental commander personally serving a machine gun, while his staff and such men as he could gather were holding back the Boche advance from the Clignon Heights.[136] "Looting," said the French officers "It is very bad at times like these. Everything goes. As soon as we can reorganize, we shoot a few of them, and it stops—." During this forenoon, the Germans were massing near Hautevesnes.[137]

At 11:40 a.m. on 2 June the 4th Machine Gun Battalion detrained at May-en-Multien requesting trucks.

131 *History 23rd Inf.*
132 *Ibid.*
133 *Malone to 3rd Brigade, 1:30 pm, 2 June, Vol. 5.*
134 *Field Messages Malone to 2nd Div., 6:30 am to 1:30 pm, 2 June, Vol. 5.*
    Note: *The Malone detachment was placed under orders of the French 43rd DI-War Diary, 2nd Div., 2 June. War Diary and annexes, 197th DI.*
135 *Harbord to Malone, 10:20 am, 2 June (23 Inf), Vol. 5. History 6th Machine Gun Battalion.*
136 *Brig Gen Logan Feland, Mar. Corps Gazette, 1921.*
137 *Harbord to Malone, 10:20 am, 2 June, (23rd Inf).*

Through the noon hours, machine gunners of the 2nd Division, men of the 5th and 6th Machine Gun Battalions, were in action at long ranges from the high ground cast of Lucy-le-Bocage, on the Germans advancing north and south of Bouresches. The 237th Division was held up by fire from this direction and abandoned their advance because of it.[138]

This day, French 155 batteries behind the 2nd Division ran short of ammunition. A G.H.Q. truck train was commandeered by the Division command and sent 45 miles to the rear for shells. It made the round trip in 13 hours, bringing 32 truckloads of 155 mm. ammunition into the area.[139] As the day went into afternoon, it began to be apparent that the situation on the left of the 2nd Division was not so threatening. The French dismounted cavalry in front of the new line formed by the 23rd Infantry and the 1/5 was holding everywhere, and the Germans were making little progress south of Clignon Brook. Between 3 and 4 o'clock Division ordered the battalion of Marines and 2 machine gun companies detached from the 23rd Infantry and returned to the Division area.[140] Trucks were sent — these same trucks were probably the basis of the German balloon report that the French near Gandelu were receiving reinforcements.[141] About midnight the Marines and the machine gunners were relieved by the 2/23, em-bussed, and transported back by the Grande Courmont-Platerie Road, the Marines to their former station near the Pyramides [*farm*] and the machine gunners to Ventelet Farm, the movement being accomplished with slight loss; 1 killed and ten wounded.[142] The German guns were busy with Bouresches and Veuilly, and the terrain south of the Highway. The 23rd Infantry line now extended to the right, connecting with the Marines of the 2/5, west of Les Mares Farm.

During the forenoon of this day, it was found that the line of the 2/5, with the regimental headquarters company, was stretched very thin, from Hill 142 to the Bois de Vaurichart.[143] Accordingly, two companies of the 3/5 hitherto in reserve, were dispatched to strengthen it. In the 6th Marines and in the 9th Infantry, minor adjustments were made. At noon the 2nd Division covered the widest front it was to hold, in the sector. From Bonneil, southwest of Hill 204, to Le Thiolet, to Lucy, to Hill 142, to Brumetz, beyond Gandelu, was more than twelve kilometres on an air line, and about 20 kilometres as the front ran. Except for a battalion of the 9th Infantry, a battalion of the 6th Marines, and two companies of the 5th Marines, the

---

138 *History of the 6th Machine Gun Battalion. War Diary, 237th DI, 2 June, Vol. 5.*
139 *War Diary, 2nd Div., 2 June, Vol. 6.*
140 *Brown to Malone 3:55 pm, 2 June, (23rd Inf), Vol. 6.*
141 *War Diary, 237th DI, 2 June-see IV Reserve Corps WD.*
142 *Turrill to CO, 5th Marines, 9:30 am, 3 June, Vol. 5.*
143 *War Diary, 4th Brigade, Vol. 6.*

entire Division was in line. Nowhere, however, was it engaged, except in long-range machine gun activity. The French, now from a kilometre to two kilometres ahead of it, held their ground with resolution. Their thin and fragmentary lines had not been reinforced, but the knowledge that fresh troops were behind them strengthened their morale, and they met the thrusting Boche with confidence. They lost, however, Bouresches, Belleau, Torcy and Bussiares, and during the night of the 2nd and on the 3rd of June they retired from the Bois de Belleau, since the fall of Bouresches at the southeast corner of the wood threatened the rear of the troops holding its northern part. It remained for them to extricate their forces from enemy contact, and to reassemble behind the 2nd Division. Elements of them began to pass to the rear through the lines of the 2nd Division.[144]

In general, little of importance occurred during 2 June in the Division area. Telephone communications were improved. The field messages, from battalions to regiments to brigade, were full of rumors, meaning little.[145]

Colonel Malone warned the 23rd Infantry that a Boche division was attacking from the north: the word was passed from the French Division Commander that the French were counter-attacking, and that the Americans would hold their support lines at any cost. The Marine Brigadier anticipated movements against Triangle Farm and possibly Clerembauts Wood, but nothing came of it. The 9th Infantry, a singularly uncommunicative regiment, in no way prone to excitement, reported that its Colonel had relieved a major for inability to read a map, and, a Captain for a reason unspecified, and replaced them; it also asked for ambulances to move 26 wounded men, its lines lying in an area now under shell fire, as the German 10th Division tried to push south. The 6th Marines strengthened their works between Le Thiolet and Lucy through the day, and watched the Germans attack towards Bouresches, 1200 to 2000 yards off. In the afternoon a report, originating with the French, that the 2/6 was withdrawing in the region of Triangle Farm, annoyed General Harbord, and he admonished the regimental commander that they were supposed to hold.[146] The 2/6 reported that it was holding, that nothing had happened, and that since they had received plenty of ammunition, nothing was going to happen, 4th Brigade Headquarters later received the apologies of the French.[147] Meantime, the 1/6, now in the

---

144 *War Diary, 2nd Division-2 June. War Diary, 237th Div., 10th Div., 197th Div., 2 June.*

145 *War Diary, 2nd Division-2 June. War Diary, 3rd Brigade-2 June. War Diary, 4th Brigade-2 June.*

146 *Harbord to Catlin, 2:40 pm, also to Holcomb, 2:45 pm, 2 June, Vol. 5.*

147 *Holcomb to Evans, 2:45 pm, 2 June, Vol. 5. Harbord to Catlin, 3:50 pm, 2 June, Vol. 5.*

French soldiers

Bois de Champillon, and stretching westward to Hill 142, was having its troubles as to liaison with the left battalion of the 5th Marines: most of the day 1/6 and 2/5 fumbled for each other's flank in the woods finally welding it at Hill 142. This situation was complicated by the French troops of the 43rd Division, some of which were in the line of Marines, some ahead of it, and some behind it.[148]

Almost everybody moved somewhere during the day: men, already worn out from camions, forced marches, and organizing positions, had no rest and very little food. Certain units stripped wire fences and erected obstacles on their fronts. Little engineer material was up as yet, and a few trench lines, mostly around Triangle Farm and Lucy, and in the Bois de Champillon, were cited. Elsewhere the weary men dug foxholes by individuals, shallow or deep as the distribution of Boche shelling inspired them. There was much lost motion and some confusion. But the front was stabi-

148 *War Diary, 4th Brig, 2 June, Vol. 6.*

lizing. The lines upon which the action was to take place began to come later in shape. Division Headquarters were established in Montreuil-aux-Lions, where also were the Headquarters of the 2nd Field Artillery Brigade, its guns still en-route, and in the vicinity of which town the trains and auxiliary services began to group themselves.[149] Montreuil was on the Paris-Metz Road, ten kilometres in the rear of Le Thiolet. Five kilometres southward was Charmigny, headquarters of the French Twenty-first Corps.

Headquarters of the Third Infantry Brigade set up at Ventelet Farm, just south of the highway. The 9th Infantry Headquarters were at Les Alnois Bontemps; those of the 23rd Infantry, for the time being, at Coulombs, in the area of the 43rd French Division.[150] The Fourth Brigade of Marines set up at Issonge Farm at 4:45 p.m. 1 June, having held forth from the Brigadier's automobile during the day. The Colonel of the 5th Marines was in Carrieres, 300 meters Northwest of Marigny, and the 6th Marines were at Voie du Chatel. All these establishments, were, by the evening of 2 June, linked up by telephone, and lines run out to most of the battalions.[151]

In the Third Brigade, all battalions except the 3/9 were in line. The 3/5, less two companies, was stationed at La Loge Farm as Corps Reserve, and the 3/6, in Marigny, was designated as Fourth Brigade Reserve. The 1/5 was also allotted as a reserve, but up to midnight, 2 June, it was still waiting relief in the 23rd Infantry position.[152]

---

149 *War Diary, 2nd Division, 2 June, Vol. 6.*
150 *War Diary, 3rd Brigade, 2 June. Hist. 9th Infantry. Hist. 23rd Infantry.*
151 *War Diary, 4th Brigade.*
152 Ibid.

SEVEN

IV Reserve Corps (German): 2 June

As soon as it was light on 2 June, the German guns opened on selected points in the terrain, shelling all the towns and farm houses in sight south of the Clignon, and searching out roads and troop movements. At 9:00 o'clock the infantry of the three divisions went forward. The 197th cleared the Clignon stream and mounted the crests on its south side, meeting determined French resistance in Bussiares and west of that village. The 237th took Torcy and Belleau, turning French rear guards out of both places. The 10th Division moved generally westward, pivoting on its left flank, took La Gonetrie Farm by 9:45 am, Hill 201, southeast of Bouresches, at 11:40 am, and pushed its elements to the narrow gauge railroad east of Bouresches. Up to about noon, the advance was orderly and controlled. Then things began to go wrong.

The 197th Division, pushing south from Bussiares and the high ground between Bussiares and Torcy, was held up by machine gun fire from Hill 165, and on Hill 126. The 237th and the 10th, swinging southward on Bouresches and the Bois de Belleau, were assailed by fierce small-arms fire coming from the north end of the Bois de Belleau and the Belleau-Bouresches road east of the wood, and from the valley opening southward towards Lucy-le-Bocage.[153] In Bouresches also the French resisted vigorously, and liaison between the two divisions, on the line running northeast of Bouresches, withered under the machine guns. Contact was lost, and both the left of the 237th and the right of the 10th slowed up and lost headway.

The 10th Division was attacking in two groups; the 47th Infantry Reg-

---

153 *The records of the 6th Machine Gun Battalion, and reports of the Adjutant 6th Marines, show that the 6th Machine Gun Battalion had some of its guns in action between Lucy and Triangle, opposing this attack.*

iment on the left and the 398th Infantry Regiment[154] on the right, with elements of the 6th Grenadiers supporting each.[155] The left group, the 47th Regiment and attached details of the 6th Grenadiers, made good progress, driving from the Bois des Rochets through Bascon le Bas and the Bois de la Roche and crossing the Paris-Metz highway, south of Vaux, before noon. The troops which passed the highway, however, came under such heavy artillery fire that they were ordered back to about the Vaux-Bouresches narrow-gauge railway, where a line was organized, contact with the 231st Division in Vaux having been firmly established. The right attack group, the 398th Regiment and attached elements, suffered with the flank of the 237th Division from the fire that struck them east of the Bois de Belleau.[156] At noon they were definitely stopped, and the 237th Division on their right, was also checked as it emerged from the Clignon valley south of Belleau and Torcy and came over the exposed crest of Hill 126. Both attacks lapsed through the afternoon, fumbling for each other's flank, and, struggling to gain ground towards the woods and the village Bouresches. After some hours; the 10th Division reported driving the French across the Belleau-Bouresches road, but the machine guns in the east face of the wood still held out, and the 237th was repeatedly repulsed from the north end.

 The afternoon was a period of confusion in the ranks of the 10th Division. About 2:00 pm the General Staff Officer of the Division, passing along the line of the attacking troops, noted that casualties wore heavy, and that the men gave an impression of nervousness and exhaustion. There were reports from the front that elements of the 10th Division had occupied Triangle Farm; Bouresches was reported taken at 11:00 am, and the report denied at 2:45 pm. About 3:00 pm, also, forward details of the 398th Regiment reported, the enemy was massing his strength at Triangle Farm and asked for artillery upon them; the Division Artillery Commander refused to fire on the place because he had information that it was in German hands, and he ordered mounted officers forward to reconnoiter. At 4:00 pm it was again reported that Triangle Farm was taken. In the meantime, the Division orders had been extended to include Triangle Farm as part of the objective, and the 398th Regiment, the right attack group, was specifically directed to occupy it. These orders were reiterated during the afternoon, while the 398th was still struggling to get into Bouresches.[157]

 154 *War Diary, 237th Division, 2 June.*
 155 *War Diary, 10th Division, 2 June.*
 156 *War Diary and annexes, 10th Division, 2 June. War Diary and annexes, 237th Division, 2 June.*
 157 *War Diary and annexes, 237th Division, 2 June. War Diary and annexes, 10th Division, 2 June.*

Late in the afternoon, the 398th turned westward into the sector of the 237th Division, and forced its way to the railroad east of the Bois de Belleau, contact was strengthened with the left attack group, south of Bouresches. At 7:00 pm, by a last effort, the 2/398th carried Bouresches with a rush, ejecting the French defenders. About the same time, a battalion of the left flank regiment of the 237th Division, the 461st Infantry, forced its way into the northern end of the Bois de Belleau, and west of the wood, the 462nd Regiment of the 237th Division established itself on the southward slope of Hill 126, in liaison with left of the 197th Division, which had gained a little ground south of Bussiares, and taken Vinly and Eloup.[158]

With nightfall on 2 June, the German effort ceased. The IV Reserve Corps was everywhere short of its objectives. It had cleared the line of the Clignon Brook, but it had not approached near enough to the Marigny-La Voie du Chatel-Lucy le Bocage-Triangle Line to involve the Americans in those places, except for long-range machine gun fire, near Triangle, and some sniping at extreme ranges in the vicinity of Les Mares Farm.[159] The losses of the Germans were unexpectedly heavy. The 10th Division immediately issued orders for its regiments to prepare their positions for a protracted defense, and the 197th and 237th examined their dispositions with a view to local improvements only. The night was spent in reorganization, with careful reconnaissance and patrolling to the front. All German divisions had seen and reported new troops moving upon their front, and deduced from the stiffened. resistance of the French that they had been materially reinforced.

At midnight, the Corps line lay along the Clignon from Eloup to Bussiares. It included Hill 126 and Torcy, and the Bussiares-Belleau Road; Belleau, with a foot-hold in the north edge of the Bois de Belleau; the Belleau-Bouresches road, and Bouresches; and it passed along the Bouresches-Vaux road to the fork 500 metres north of Hill 192, curved out to the west edge of Bois de la Cote 192, and thence to the highway at the south corner of the Bois de la Roche, and into Vaux. From Vaux southward, the 231st Division was on Hill 204, and had cleared Chateau Thierry of the last of the defenders.[160]

Corps orders for 3 June noted the mission of the Corps: flank protection of the Army attack towards the Ourcq, which was progressing slowly. To this end, some further advance on the part of the 237th and 197th Divisions was necessary: the 10th could mark time until they were up. The

---

158 *War Diary and Annexes, 197th Division, 2 June.*
159 *War Diary, 237th Division, 2 June.*
160 *War Diary, IV Reserve Corps, 2 June and War Diary, 231st Division, 2 June.*

French soldiers charging a machine gun nest

depressions leading south of the Clignon line were to be cleared and occupied; the Germans still wanted Marigny, La Voie du Chatel, and Lucy-le-Bocage, as well as Triangle. Then they would see about Hill 201 on the Paris-Metz road. In the meantime, all ranks were enjoined to retain the spirit of the offensive: if, for a few days, they slackened their attacks, it was in conformation with the general strategic plan and not because the enemy had brought their victorious advance to a halt. Also, the Corps Commander took occasion to make severe remarks about discipline: discipline must be tightened everywhere, and any tendencies to looting and horse-play in the rank — the General had seen German soldiers wearing plug-hats and women's draperies, and skylarking in ranks as they marched — would be discouraged.[161]

The losses of the IV Reserve Corps on 1 June and 2 June were 45 officers and 917 men killed, wounded and, missing. A few men began to go sick, with influenza.

Three June was quieter on the Corps front than the preceding day. The 237th Division reported that its 461st Regiment had pushed straight through the Bois de Belleau from north to south, meeting little opposition: as a matter of fact, the French in the wood were effectively turned when Bouresches was taken the evening of 2 June, and they largely withdrew from the wood during the night. But the 197th Division, moving south from Bussiares on Hill 165, and further west, on Veuilly-la-Poterie, made little progress. It came in view of Les Mares farm on Hill 165, but encountered artillery and small-arms fire from the wooded strips north of Lucy and between Bussiares and Champillon. The French, during the day, delivered several ineffective counter-attacks in this region, and while the Germans lost no ground to them, they appear to have proceeded with more caution, influenced by the bare fact that the retreating enemy had enough vitality left for counter-strokes. The day's loss was 43 officers and 793 men killed, wounded, and missing. There were a few more sick.[162]

Up river from Chateau Thierry, the 36th Division had gotten a few men across at Jaulgonne to form a bridgehead, and the French began to attack them.

---

161 *War Diary and Annexes, IV Reserve Corps, 1-2-3 June.*
162 *War Diary and Annexes, IV Reserve Corps, 3 June.*

Eight

2nd Division and French XXI Corps d'Armée 3–5 June

3 June

The French XXI Corps, at 1:35 am, 3 June, announced the loss of Bussiares, Torcy, and the woods of Belleau.[163] It had been intended that the 2nd Division would take over command of the sector where its troops were now deployed, but a counterattack, to recover the lost fore-ground, was decided upon by the 43rd French Division. Accordingly, plans for the passing of command to General Bundy were delayed until the counterattack could be carried out.[164]

In the small hours of this morning, the regimental machine gun companies of the 2nd Division's infantry regiments passed through Montreuil, pressing eastward to join their commands, having. marched overland from the area Chaumont-Gisors. The machine gun company of the 23rd Infantry was turned off to the left to report to Colonel Malone at Coulombs; the others proceeded by the highway to their commands. The trains of the 3rd and 4th Brigades and of the 2nd Engineers were sent to Cocherel.[165]

At 4:00 am, a lieutenant of the 6th Marines, scouting north from Lucy-le-Bocage, reported the Germans a kilometre north of that town.[166]

163 *Compte-rendu XXI C A, 3 June.*
164 *XXI C A to HQ 2nd Div,. 3 June & War Diary, 2nd Div., 3 June.*
165 *War Diary, 2nd Div., 3 June & G-3 2nd Div. to CG 2nd Div., 2:50 am, 3 June, Vol. 4.*
166 *Gulliver-memo 6th Marines, 4:00 am, 3 June, Vol. 5.* [Lt. C.C. Gulliver was not a Marine officer, he was U.S. Army and served on the 2nd Division, General Staff, as a secretary. GBC].

2nd Division and French XXI Corps d'Armée: 3–5 June

Early on 3 June, such elements of the 43rd as could be gotten together delivered a series of ineffective counter thrusts in front of the 4th Brigade of Marines, around Hill 142 and Hill 165, mainly against the German 197th Division. They were easily stopped, and regained no ground: it was nothing more than a gallant gesture. But it had the result of slowing up the German advance: the 197th could not understand why the exhausted French attempted anything in the nature of a counter-stroke, and they proceeded during the rest of the day with elaborate caution.[167]

The Divisional Artillery, detraining on 1 June north of May-en-Multien, had been marching steadily, 38 to 40 kilometres, on its assembly point at Cocherel. It had out marched its ammunition trains, which had proceeded overland, and was obliged to wait for them.[168] The 2nd Field Artillery Brigade, with HQ at Montreuil, was assigned the general line Domptin-Coupru-Marigny en Orxois, and had now under its command 3 groupments of the French 37th and 2 of the 232nd Regiments of field artillery, and[169] groupment of the French 236th Regiment —155mm. On June 3, in the afternoon, the American regiments were added to these. The 15th Field Artillery was assigned to the 3rd Brigade, took up positions south of the Paris-Metz highway, with HQ at Domptin, its batteries moving in after dark. The 12th Field Artillery went to the Marine Brigade, emplacing its guns north the highway, with HQ at La Loge Farm. The 17th Field Artillery, the 155's, was distributed, a battalion behind each brigade, the third battalion south of the highway, assigned to counter-battery work. Some of the French artillery was withdrawn upon its entry, but they were replaced by other units under American command.[170]

The German observers saw and reported these batteries as they moved in, and noted the formation of battery nests north and south of the highway, but allowed them to take up their ground without loss or incident.[171]

French avions reported Germans in the Bois de Belleau who fired with machine guns on their planes;[172] the 10th Division, on the left front of the Americans, pushed forward somewhat, improving positions south of the metro gauge railway which faced the 6th Marines.[173] The 197th Division, pushing ahead south of Bussiares and Veuilly, met energetic French resistance and made no substantial gains.[174]

167 War Diary, 197th Div., 3 June.
168 War Diary, 2nd Div., 3 June & History 2nd FA Brigade, Vol. 9.
169 History 2nd FA Brigade, 2 June, Vol. 9.
170 Ibid.
171 War Diary, 237th Division, 3 and 4 June & History 2nd FA Brigade, Vol. 9.
172 War Diary, 237th Div., 3 June & Air report to 2nd Div. HQ, 3 June, Vol. 4.
173 War Diary, 10th Div., 3 June.
174 War Diary, 197th Div., 3 June.

American Infantry and Marines, lying in their lines, noted movements of the enemy on their front; they saw him on the Clignon crests, from one to three kilometres away. A few bursts of machine gun fire were gotten off at him, where the target was tempting[175] and in front of Les Mares Farm men tried long-range rifle shots.[176] More shells came upon the American positions and it was evident that the German guns were getting up.[177] There was a readjustment of formations, all over the Division areas. The guns of the 5th and 6th Machine Gun Battalions were redistributed as the regimental companies took their places in line. The work of organization and fortifying went on. Hill 201, just west of Le Thiolet, was placed in a condition of defense; two companies of the reserve battalion the 9th Infantry, with the aid and counsel of the Engineers, went up in the dark from the wood west of Les Aulnois Bontemps and turned this point on the highway into a redoubt.[178] German air service was very active, both planes and active, both planes and balloons.[179] The French artillery in the area — 5 groupments of 75mm and 1 of 155mm, sent representations to Division HQ about Americans showing themselves on the road near important points.[180] Such exposures, they pointed out, were always followed by shelling. It became necessary, in the first days of June, to post sentries around Headquarters and artillery position, for the purpose of driving away casual passers-by who might be inclined to loiter in sight of the German sausages on the skyline.[181]

A matter of pressing importance to the troops was that on 3 June the rolling kitchens arrived, having marched overland.[182] They were sent as far forward as was compatible with safety. It was possible for some battalions, in the back areas, to have their kitchens with them. The others, hidden among trees, tucked into ravines, or against the sides of farm houses, were enjoined to lay low and use only dry wood: smoke brought prompt shelling.[183] Since leaving the area Chaumont-en-Vixen, on 31 May, the men had been issued no hot food.[184] They had eaten their reserve rations or gone without. A few companies had been lucky enough to fall in with cattle and hogs, left behind by the French inhabitant, and with fowls and rabbits.

175   *History of the 6th MG Bn.*, 3 June.
176   Diary, Major J.[ohn] D. Murray, 3-5 June (2/5 Marines).
177   *War Diary, 2nd Div.*, 3 June.
178   *Ibid* and *Field Messages, 2nd Div.*, 3 June, Vol. 4.
179   *War Diary, 2nd Div.*, 3-4 June.
180   *Field Messages, HQ 2nd Div.*, 3 June Vol. 4.
181   *War Diary, 4th Brigade* 3-4 June.
182   *War Diary, 2nd Div.*, 3-4 June.
183   *War Diary, 4th Brigade*, 3-4 June.
184   *Ibid.*

These went promptly into the pot. But most of the infantry went hungry until the trains came in.[185]

On 3 June occurred an incident around which many stories have grown. The French on the front of the 2/5 Marines, in line west of Hill 142, covering Les Mares Farm, fell back during the afternoon. Passing through the Marines, a French Major ordered Captain [*William O.*] Corbin of 2/5 to fall back with them. This order was passed quickly to Captain Lloyd R. Williams, the 51st Company, and the senior officer present. He sent the following message to Lieutenant Colonel Wise, commanding 2/5:

"3:10 pm

"To: Battalion Commander —
    Second Battalion —

"The French Major gave Capt. Corbin written orders to fall back — I have countermanded the order — kindly see that the French do not shorten their artillery range — 82nd and 84th Companies are on their way to fill gap on the right of this company' —

Lloyd W. Williams,
Captain, U.S.M.C."[186]

On this foundation, the "Retreat Hell! We just got here —" myth grew up.[187]

On 4 June command of the Division sector passed from the French to Major General Bundy, the 2nd Division taking over as of 8 o'clock am. During the night the withdrawal of the French 43rd Division had begun; attended by some confusion due to the disorganized condition of the French elements.[188]

Up to this time, most dispositions within the division had been made under French command, and with a view to bolstering the advanced French lines. Now the 2nd Division was free to effect organization according to its own ideas and requirements. Comparative inactivity on the part of the Germans aided these measures: this day there was fighting with the French around Hautevesnes and southward, but it did not involve the Americans.[189]

---

185 Ibid.
186 Capt. Williams to Battalion Commander, 2nd Battalion, 5th Regt. 3:10 pm, 3 June-Vol. 5. [See also Clark, G.B. "Retreat Hell! We Just Got Here." Brass Hat, Pike, 1992. GBC].
187 Brigadier General Logan Feland, Marine Corps Gazette, 1921.
188 2nd Div. War Diary, 4 June.
189 Ibid & 4th Brigade War Diary, 4 June.

Chapter Eight

The sector of the 2nd Division stretched from Monneaux at the base of Hill 204 to Le Thiolet, to Lucy-le-Bocage, to Hill 142, to Les Mares Farm; and the 23rd Infantry extended westward from that point. The line ran generally northwest, with Lucy at the point of a reentrant angle. At present, the portion north of the highway was in the hands of the Marine Brigade: the 3rd Brigade, south of the highway, lacked one of its regiments, and its further organization was not practicable. But the 4th Brigade made new dispositions.

Fourth Brigade Headquarters was shifted from Issonge Farm to La Loge, a kilometre to the south and less exposed to German observation.[190] The 3/5, which had been serving as Corps Reserve near La Loge, returned to the Brigade and was sent to a point 1½ kilometres southwest of Marigny, in the woods, as Brigade reserve. This brought it nearer the left of the line, where the German activity seemed the greatest. The front of the 5th Regiment continued to be held by 2/5, with certain reinforcements from the disengaged 1/5 and 3/5 and the Headquarters Company: during the 4th this regiment was heavily shelled and reported some loss. The 6th Marines remained in its original position.[191]

On 4 June the Germans were organizing the Bois de Belleau for defense: the 461st Regiment of the 237th Division, now in liaison with the 10th Division at the southeast corner of the wood, near Bouresches, established positions along the south face of the wood to the base of Hill 181, and thence northwest, and north along the wood's western edge. Hill 181 and the long narrow strip of woods thrust towards Lucy were included in tho outpost zone but not organized. Patrols of this regiment penetrated the Bois de Champillon, and some of them, operating southward towards Lucy-le-Bocage, picked up the corpse of a 6th Marine which they carried back to regimental headquarters for the intelligence officers. It was the first American they had seen. The regiment suspected that a relief was being carried out on their front[192] and the IV Reserve Corps recorded the identification in its reports.

The records of the Conta Divisions all note, on 4 June, an increase in the hostile shell fire, and mounting loss, especially in their rear areas and along lines of supply. Their main line of resistance, from the Bois de Belleau, ran westward along the high ground south of the Clignon Brook, to the flank of the 197th Division. The 197th's left was advanced to Hill 142, its line run westward to Veuilly, and north towards Hautevesnes.[193]

---

190 *War Diary, 4th Brigade, 4 June, Vol. 6.*
191 Ibid.
192 *War Diary, 237th Division and annexes, 4 June.*
193 Ibid & *War Diary, 197th Division, 4 June.*

5 June

The principal event of 4 June was the return of the 23rd Infantry and attached units to the 2nd Division. Colonel Malone had been on the extreme left for 4 days, and although not engaged, his men had suffered losses from shelling and had effected a great deal in the way of organization and patrolling. They were relieved by the French 167th Division during the night 4–5 June, and were extricated from the front without incident. The 1/23 and 2/23 moved at once to the 3rd Brigade, relieving Marines of the 6th Regiment in the line from Le Thiolet to Triangle Farm. The 2/23 went to La Langue Farm as Division Reserve.[194]

On this day, 5 June, there occurred a contact with the enemy. The 2/5 Marines, in line on the ridge of Les Mares Farm, noted activity on their front during the afternoon. The wheat was high here, and Marines saw the grain shake, as though men crawled through it. Gunnery Sergeant [David L.] Buford and eight Marines of the 55th Company went out and came upon a German patrol of twelve men, with a light machine gun. Shooting ensued; ten Germans were killed, and two wounded, together with the light Maxim were captured. They were identified as Saxons of the 26th Jager Battalion of the 7th Regiment, a formation of the 197th Division.[195] They were the first prisoners taken by the 2nd Division in the area northwest of Chateau Thierry.

Neither on 4 June or 5 June, after the area had been taken over from French command, is there record of any systematic patrolling or reconnaissance by the 2nd Division of the terrain in front of it. During the night of 5 June, a small patrol was sent out from the 6th Marines. It went along the Lucy-Belleau road, west of Belleau Wood and returned. It reported hearing a man cough in the direction of Torcy, and it heard a wagon coming down through the Bois de Belleau. It discovered no abnormal activity on the part of the Germans. It discovered nothing of consequence.[196] The wood itself, the ravine leading toward it from Lucy, and the ravines enclosing Hill 142, do not seem to have been approached. The Germans, however, reconnoitered the American lines in the Bois de Champillon, and filtered up the ravines towards Champillon, and towards Lucy.[197]

---

194 War Diary 2d Division, History 23rd Infantry, 5 June, Compte Rendu XXI AC, 5 June.
  195   Ibid & Diary, Major John D. Murray, USMC, 2/5 Marines, 5 June.
  Following the last statement was Capt. Mathews hand-written comment that the first prisoners were "captured by me. I still have the watch of one of them." GBC].
  196 Patrol Report, 6th Marines, 5 June, Vol. 8, 2nd Division Records. [The patrol was led by 1stLt William A. Eddy, the regimental intelligence officer. GBC].
  197   War Diary, 237th Division and annexes, 461st Regiment, 5 June.

Officer issuing orders

2nd Division — Midnight 5–6 June

At midnight, 5–6 June, the 2nd Division formed the right of the French XXI Corps d'Armee. On its right was the French XXXVIII Corps, the 10th Colonial Division, with the 30th U.S. Infantry attached. On its left was the French 167th Division, of the XXI Corps. The four regiments in line from right to left, the 9th, the 23rd, the 6th Marines, and the 5th Marines. The 1/9, at La Langue Farm, was the Division reserve, the 1/6 Marines, near La Loge, Corps reserve. The 2/23 and the 2/5 were, respectively, 3rd and 4th Brigade reserve. With the entry of the 23rd Infantry, the 3rd Brigade was assigned a sector from the southeast corner of the Bois de La Marette to Triangle Farm; the 4th Brigade a sector from Triangle Farm to a point 800 metres north of Champillon on the Champillon-Bussiares road, where the French 167th Division took over. This arrangement on the left was subject to the relief of elements of the 1/5 and 2/5 Marines still to the westward, as far as Les Mares, whose relief by French Infantry was ordered but not completed by midnight.[198]

Each regiment had two battalions in line and one in reserve. The artillery was emplaced and firing. The Engineers were distributed, as were the machine guns, only the 4th Machine Gun Battalion being held in reserve. The divisional services were all up and functioning. The only element absent was the 2nd Trench Mortar Battery, which had just received its guns and was engaged in target practice.[199]

Attached to the Division were five groupments of French artillery, the dismounted cavalry in the Bois de La Marette, and the 27th Escadrille of the French Air Service; Balloon 21 of that service made ascensions on the Courboin Blesmes road. The Field Hospitals, 1, 15, 16, and 23, were distributed between Bezu-le-Guitry, Chateau La Rue, and Meaux, Ambulance companies were in Sablonniere, Coupru, and Bezu-le-Guitry; one, the 16th, was detailed to the artillery. The railhead was at Meaux; the axis of liaison and supply was the Paris-Metz Road.[200]

---

198 *War Diary, 2nd Division, 5 June; War Diary, 4th Brigade, 5 June; Field Order 8, 2nd Division, Vol. 1.*
199 *History 2nd Trench Mortar Battery, 6 June.*
200 *War Diary, 2nd Division, 5 June & Field Order 82nd Division, Vol. 1.*

Nine

IV Reserve Corps (German)

4 June

For 4 June, Corps, as far as the 237th and 197th Divisions were concerned, repeated its attack orders of the 3rd. The 237th, with little difficulty, cleared out and organized the Bois de Belleau, and pushed its right flank elements as far south as Hill 142. Hill 142 is enclosed between two brooks, at this season dry, one of which rises at Champillon and flows north along the west side of the hill. The other rises in the Bois de Champillon and passes along the east side, approaching this western brook several hundred metres to the north of the hill, and both pass around the base of Hill 126 to the Clignon. There was a confusion between the 197th and the 237th Divisions as to which of these brooks was designated as the division boundary. The 237th, on the 4th, advanced its left generally along the brook east of the Hill. The 197th Division, during the night 3–4 June, seized Veuilly la Poterie, pushed advanced elements down the Bussiares depression, and mounted Hill 165, casting for Les Mares Farm. They established a line from the north western edge of Hill 142, across Hill 142, considering the brook on the west side of the hill as their sector limit. During the day, they attempted to get forward to Les Mares Farm, but abandoned the effort in the face of artillery fire, and of rifle fire from the 2/5th Marines, in line across the wheat fields to left and right of Les Mares. A gap, between Bussiares and Hill 142, was not occupied by either division, and the 237th complains, through its liaison officer, that the 273rd Regiment on the left flank of the 197th Division was not as far forward as it reported itself.[201]

    201   *War Diary, IV Reserve Corps, 4 June & War Diary and annexes, 197th and 237th Divisions, 3-4 June.*

This regiment, about noon, also reported that it had taken Les Mares Farm, which it never entered at all. During the closing hours of the day, the situation on Hill 142 was adjusted, and the flank elements of both divisions took positions on the northern end of that height, the flank of each overlapping, a little, the eastern and western brooks. The day ended with the German line inclosing the whole of the Bois de Belleau, following the trace of the Bussiares-Bouresches road across the high ground south of Torcy, and inclining southwestward to cross Hill 142, the northern end of the Bois des Mares, Hill 165, the Bois de Baron, and Veuilly. From Veuilly the flank of the 197th Division was refused to the Clignon immediately north. The casualties of the Corps on this day were light: 10 officers and men killed, wounded, and missing. The Corps reported the capture of 30 machine guns, 12 trench mortars, one cannon, and prisoners. The corpse of a Marine of the 6th Regiment had been found and brought in from the front of the 237th Division, the presence of the Americans deduced there from. All divisions made careful reconnaissance to their fronts, and reported trace of the American lines with accuracy. The Germans noted the increase in enemy artillery, and their air service, reported guns moving in, and foot and vehicular traffic behind the enemy front.[202]

Those elements of the 36th Division on the left flank of the Corps, thrown across the Marne at Jaulgonne, were cut off and captured.[203]

5 June;
Condition of 10th Division

On 5 June Corps ordered definitely that all offensive operations be suspended, and, that the divisions organize their lines for defense. Division staffs were ordered, however, to prepare and have in readiness plans for further attacks, on 48 hours notice towards the Paris-Metz road. The immediate relief of the exhausted 10th Division, by an extension of the lines of the 231st and 237th Divisions, was announced. The 36th Division was also to be relieved, the Army placing the 10th Landwehr Division at the disposal of the IV Reserve Corps for that purpose. The 10th was to be withdrawn between 5 June and 8 June, the 36th between 9 June and 12 June, and it will be noted that the 10th was not to be replaced, Corps considering that the line could be held with 4 divisions, none of them of the attack order.[204]

202 *Ibid.*
203 *Ibid.*
204 *Ibid.*

The 10th Division was, on 5 June, the only first-class formation in line with the IV Reserve Corps on the 2nd American Division front. Reports are available on its condition.[205]

Immediately before the Chemin-des-Dames offensive, the 10th Division was reported satisfactory as to combat strength and training. At that time the German authorized rifle strength was 850 men per battalion, 2550 to the regiment, and 7650 for the infantry brigade of 3 regiments, which, with attached machine gun and artillery details and special troops, made up an infantry division. The 10th Division had a shortage of 950 men evenly distributed through the 3 regiments, in the infantry brigade, giving it a strength of 6700. The division attacked on 27 May and remained in the front line through 5 June and for some days thereafter. During the period 3–4 June,[206] all regimental commanders forwarded reports on the strength and condition of their commands. In the 47th Regiment, there were five rifle companies without a single officer. The 2/47 had one officer present, and the remnants of the battalion had been formed as one company under his command. Two machine gun companies attached to the regiment were without officers. This report bears the notation that the relief of the 47th was contemplated on 5 June, but was not carried out because of hostile attacks. There is a return of this regiment on 2 June which gives its loss, since 27 May, as 27 officers and 684 men. The 398th Infantry Regiment reported, on 4 June, that its troops were not fit for front line service. Its companies averaged 40 men, not enough to man the light machine guns of the organization, and not enough to get the heavy machine guns into action. Its rifle shortage was 1200 men. The 6th Grenadier Regiment, on 4 June, reported as exhausted and incapable of further effort. Elsewhere, its shortage is given as 1155 rifles, with proportional loss in the attached machine gunners. The 17th Machine Gun Sharpshooter Detachment, on 4 June, reported a similar situation all respects. The Divisional Artillery Commander reported his command reduced and worn out. The Divisional Commander, Sydow, later forwarded these reports with the most urgent representations as to the need of the Division for rest and replacements: his rifle shortage in the 3 regiments he gave as from 2700 to 3000.[207]

The Chemin des Dames offensive was the second drive in which the 10th Division had been employed in 1918, and it was destined to attack again on 14 July in the Champagne.[208] But on 5 June, it was at the lowest

---

205 *Annexes and War Diary, 10th Division: Open documents "C," 1 May 18-18 June, 18-91789/4413 & Report of 22 May.*
206 Ibid.
207 Ibid

The Leathernecks

ebb, and cases of influenza, aside from battle casualties, were beginning to multiply.

    208   *Ibid. Each regiment had, on 27 May, an approximate shortage of 300 rifles. This would make the casualties of the 6th Grenadiers about 855 men, and of the 398th about 900 men, calculation from the last report before 27 May, dated 22 May. To check with the Division Commanders report above, it must be assumed that several hundred replacements were received between 22 May and 27 May.*

Of the other divisions on the front between Vaux and Eloup, the 231st, the 237th and the 197th, were fairly fresh: they had entered the line 31 May to 1 June, and had encountered no heavy fighting. But they were not attack divisions: they were sector-holding troops. In Corps Winckler, (CO) the XXV Reserve, on the right, the 1st Guards and the 33rd Divisions were excellent troops, and there can be no doubt that the French XXI Corps regarded their presence in the line as significant and dangerous. But it was evident that Corps Conta, the IV Reserve, from its order of battle, intended nothing serious. Two excellent divisions, the 5th Guards and the 28th, were known to be in reserve behind it, but they were also known to be exhausted.

On 5 June, to the north of the 7th Army, the Germans began the battle of Noyon, which the French call the Noyon-Montdidier Defensive. It raged from 5 June to 9 June, and was broken off when it was seen that it promised no decisive results. Its object was to drive in a salient towards Montdidier, and pinch out the Soissons corner where the French still held.

The movement of the right wing of the 7th Army towards the Ourcq was subsidiary to the Noyon battle, and after it broke down the Ourcq line was not immediately important.[209]

209 *War Diary, German 7th Army, 1-6 June 18.*

Ten

4th Brigade Field Order #1—Hill 142

French XXI C.A. 81/P.C.

At 15[00] hours on June 5, which is three o'clock, French time, and an hour later by the clocks of the German headquarters across the Clignon Brook, the Twenty-first Corps issued Order 81/P.C., directed to the 167th French Division and the 2nd American. This order reviewed briefly the situation on the front of the Corps, in much the same strain, though from the opposite side—as the order of the German Fourth Reserve Corps, received by the German divisions this same day. The line of resistance established at the end of the fighting, said Twenty-first Corps, on the front Veuilly la Poterie-Bouresches, had inconvenient features. Close in the front of it, and on the line marked by the Clignon Brook, and on the low ground between Lucy-Clignon and Bussiares, the terrain offered the enemy every facility for concealment and assembly. In these woods and depressions, hidden from observers, his infantry could form for attack, while his artillery immobilized our line of resistance. It is of the first importance, then, before the enemy can reinforce his artillery—that is to say, as soon as possible—to carry our line forward to the commanding heights south of the Clignon, from Veuilly la Poterie to Bouresches. In consequence, proceeded Corps, on the morning of 6 June, the General commanding the 187th Division would take measures to recover these heights, from Veuilly la Poterie to the Champillon brook on his right.

East of the Champillon brook, the left of the 2nd American Division would go forward in conformity with the French advance, clearing the long ridge of Hill 142, the rest of the 2nd Division taking steps to assure liaison from the east with the new line so established. The General commanding the 2nd American Division will give orders to the troops charged with the reduction of Hill 142. He is charged also with the task of maintaining contact with the progress of the French on his left: let the officer commanding his attack see to it. The Colonel commanding Corps artillery would consult with the Division commanders and arrange artillery preparations on the terrain to be conquered.[210]

Under the same condition, added Corps, and as soon as possible after the execution of this operation, a similar advance would be carried out by the 2nd American Division, to occupy the Bois de Belleau and the length of the ridge running southeast and northwest, immediately dominating Torcy and Belleau.

Following the receipt of the XXI CA order at 2nd Division Headquarters, the Chief of Staff, Colonel Preston Brown, informed the Commanding General of the 4th Brigade of Corps' intentions, and discussed them with him. He gave him the objective, and the instructions for the artillery. The infantry, he directed, would advance by infiltration rather than by waves. There should be close liaison between artillery and infantry, and the advance of the Marines was to guide on the advance of the 167th Division, the guide being left.[211]

A little later in the day, the hour for the attack was communicated to the 2nd Division Headquarters. It was 3:45 am., 6 June.[212]

Division passed the order along to the 4th Brigade of Marines, holding the left sector of the Division front. 4th Brigade issued at 10:25 pm., Field Order 1. The Brigade would attack, in conjunction with the French, its objective being a line between the Little Square Wood 400 metres southeast of the Calvarie and the brook Crossing 174.0 & 263.4 — this is the language of the order. The attack would be made by the 1st Battalion, 5th Marines, supported by the 8th (regimental) Machine Gun Company and the 77th Machine Gun Company. The 3rd Battalion, 5th Marines, in line east of Hill 142, would advance its left along the brook on that side of the

---

210 *XXI C.A. #81/P.C.-5 June.*
211 *Colonel Preston Brown, Chief of Staff, to General Harbord, CG, 4th Brigade, 3:00 P.M., 5 June, Vol. 4.*
212 *CG, 2nd Division to CG, 4th Brigade, 4:53 p.m., 5 June, Vol. 1. Note: That the phrase "as soon as possible" occurs twice in this French Corps Order. [This was a problem that JWT was hinting at that was deadly to the men of the 1st Bn, 5th Marines. The orders were delayed by brigade until after midnight of 6 June and the half-battalion was forced to travel several miles to positions it had not had a chance to reconnoiter and to be ready to jump-off at 0345. They barely made it after being forced to move, in darkness, rapidly over ground no man of 1/5 had ever been on before. GBC].*

Hill, to conform with the progress of the attack. Artillery to be provided by the 2nd Field Artillery Brigade. Aviation as ordered by the 167th French Division. The objective, when attained, would be seized and held against counter attacks. Thus, in substance, Field Order 1.[213]

Officers concerned examined their maps— it was too early in the action for the elaborate plenty of maps afterward realized: the map referred to was the old French hachured [*indicating terrain features like height etc.*] map Meaux —1:50000, made by the Depot de la Guerre in 1832, corrected in 1912. On it the roads were accurate in their trace, and the hills, for such things do not greatly change in Europe; but more trees had grown since that time.[214] Over the terrain concerned, the wooded areas were generally more extensive than indicated by the map, and this was important. Also, when the 2nd Division moved into position, French troops were in action on its front, and reconnaissance were not made in any effective way; the French troops, much disorganized, drew off through the Americans, and there is no record of any careful scouting done between the relief of the French, and the attacks of the 6th of June. It does not appear that the German forward elements were exactly located, although the German divisions had careful and accurate reports on the lines of the Americans in front of them.

There were not many maps. Battalion commanders had them, and Company commanders. Platoon commanders and some sergeants were allowed to look at them, and the zealous made sketches in their notebooks. The others were told. Examining the map now, the officers found the Little Square Patch of Woods; it lay more east than south of the symbol on the Champillon-Bussiares Road, which stands for a wayside cross, and it stood just north of an unimproved road which branched east from the Bussiares road to provide the farmers of Champillon with a short cut towards Lucy and Belleau. Some 600 metres eastward, the line of the designated brook crossed the unimproved road at the point established by the coordinates given in the order. Thus the unimproved road was the line of the objective. At this time the 3/6 was in line across Hill 142, north of Champillon. From its foxholes to the objective was a little more than a kilometre, and the two brooks, east and west of the Hill, bounded the area to be seized into a fair rectangle.[215]

The line of the 3/6 was within the edge of some heavy timber, looking out on an open stretch of wheat. About 300 metres to the north was another belt of woods, running almost across the hill from the right, low

---

213   Field Order #1, 4th Brigade-5 June, 10:25 p.m., Vol. 2.
214   Map Atlas, 2nd Div.-Meaux-1:50000.
215   About 1150 metres-Map Chateau Thierry 1/20000.

and thick and heavy with underbrush. Beyond was more wheat, on land sloping gently northward to the nose of the Hill, enclosed right and left by the steep wooded lines of the brooks; and more than half-way out, a triangular clump of trees, very dense, thrust up from the Champillon brook on the west, into the wheat. At the very end of the ridge, where the slope went abruptly down into the valley, was a line of tall pines and hardwood. The northern face of the hill was steep and covered with bushes, as was its eastern edge, and from the end of the hill you looked, on the right, to the northern top of the Bois de Belleau, which stood a kilometre and a half eastward. Out in front, there was a long, curving valley of wheat, with trees along the stream lines that angled across the low ground, then a gentle bare slope of wheat, treeless except for five tall poplars in a row half a kilometre north, then the open crest of the ridge called Hill 126, across which you could see the spire of the Torcy church. Bussiares lay behind the ridge, but the Bussiares-Champillon road was visible, climbing it to the left. Looking west, across the ground over which the French must attack, you saw Hill 165, the Bois les Mares to the south, the Bois Triangulare to the north, and the tops of the Bois de Veuilly on the skyline. The objectives of the 167th Division lay west as far as Eloup.[216]

Attack on Hill 142, 6 June

In the afternoon of 5 June the 2nd Division ordered fire of interdiction around the zone to be attacked, and the guns of the French 167th Division were engaged on the same mission. A steady, harassing cannonade fell upon the towns in the Clignon valley, on towns to the north of the brook, and on all the paths and woods used by the enemy. German artillery replied, and there was counter-battery work and harassing fire on the front lines and, the rear areas.[217] Through the night the sky was alight with gun flashes, and the German troops under that fire record losses and confusion, as their units moved into positions of increased combat readiness: for the commanders of the 197th and 237th Divisions considered, from the growing artillery activity, and the reports of their front line observers, that an attack was coming.[218] In the 2nd Division area, battalions moving to carry out the ordered readjustments suffered casualties from the German reaction.[219]

216   XXI C.A. #81/ P.C.
217   *War Diary, 2nd Div, 5-6 June, Vol. 6. & War Diary, 4th Brigade, 5-6 June, Vol. 6.*
218   *War Diaries, 237th and 197th German Divisions, 5-6 June.*
219   *War Diary, 2nd Div., 5-6 June, Vol. 6. & War Diary, 4th Brigade, 5-6 June, Vol. 6.*

The 1/5, designated for the assault, was at daylight on the 6th partly in and partly out of the line west of Champillon. The 67th and 49th Companies had returned to the 4th Brigade sector, and were in hand near Champillon, but the 17th and 66th Companies, with the 8th (regimental) Machine Gun Company, deployed with 2/5 near Les Mares Farm in the area of the incoming French 167th Division, still awaited relief by the French 116th Regiment. The French infantry had been expected at 9:00 pm, and guides were duly posted to bring them in, but they did not arrive until about 3:00 am on 6 June. By 3:00 o'clock, less than an hour before the battalion was to attack, the 49th and 67th Companies had proceeded to the line on Hill 142, relieving the companies of the 3/6, which withdrew to the woods north of la Maison Blanche.[220]

Shortly before zero hour Major [*Julius S.*] Turrill, commanding the 1/5, moved his command post forward from Champillon to the jump-off line. He found his 49th and 67th Companies deploying in the open, just north of the woods— the line ran 100 metres north of the figure 142 on the map.[221] But his other companies were not up, nor had the engineers and machine-gunners reported to him. The 15th Machine Gun Company (6th Machine Gun Battalion) was in position north of Champillon ready to deliver a machine gun barrage. The Marines of the 49th Company, Captain [*George W.*] Hamilton, on the right, and, the 67th, 1st Lieutenant [*Orlando C.*] Crowther, on the left, formed platoons in four waves as taught by the French: it was 3:45 am, and the sun was rising: the officers blew their whistles and the Marines went forward.[222]

The American guns had been firing on the zone of the objective since 3:15 am, and although the exact trace of the German front was not known, their fire was effective on the approaches to the line, and the woods and villages used by the Germans as assembly points:[223] shortly after daylight

---

220   Major J.S. Turrill [CO 3/5] to Col [Wendell C.] Neville, CO, 5th Marines, 7:00 p.m. 6 June, Vol. 5.

JWT added a note here "(F.O.I.): "The so-called brooks, running east and west of Hill 142, were, at this time dry ravines. In this text they are referred to as ravines, except in quoting orders which used the word 'brook.' Hill 142 was really a ridge, running two kilometres north of Champillon: but the text follows the records in calling it a hill."

[*The two companies, 17th and 66th, both of which had been on detached service with 2/5, to the west, arrived well after the assault began. Upon arrival they immediately took their place and provided necessary support to the remnants of the 49th and 67th Companies. This was an example of poor planning and implementation from the leadership of the brigade. JWT's commentary looks like a cover-up, possibly brought about by the 2nd Division history project leadership. GBC*].

221   Chateau Thierry 1/20,000.

222   Major J.C. Turrill to Col Neville, 5th Marines, 7:00 p.m., 6 June, Vol. 5.

223   War Diaries, German 237th DI and 197th DI, 6 June.

84   Chapter Ten

a German aviator, on patrol above the front, reported shells on every path and road.[224] The covering fire delivered by the 15th Company's machine guns fell with effect on the waiting German infantry: the 10th and 11th Companies of the 460th Regiment had many men hit before they were engaged.[225]

The sun was up, and the short night of northern France over, but the Marines, formed across Hill 142 from west to east, could not see what lay in front of them. About 300 yards from the jump-off line, across an open Wheatfield, was a belt of woods extending westward, from the ravine east of the ridge. In this was the 9th Company of the 460th Regiment. Past this belt of woods, jutting up from the Champillon ravine west of the ridge, was a low, thick coppice, which sheltered a heavy machine gun detachment from the 273rd Regiment: the 2/273rd, which had the regimental left and the flank of the 197th Division, lay in the Bois des Mares and across the Champillon-Bussiares road at the north end of the ridge. Among tall pines and underbrush immediately to their left was the 10th Company of the 462nd Regiment, attached to the 3/460, the right regiment of the 237th Division.[226]

The 10th and 11th Companies of the 460th were in the square patch of woods just east of the ravine, a wood not shown on the map, lying on X — line 263, and the 12th Company was in reserve north of them.[227] Hill 142 was, it will be remembered, the junction point between the German 127th and 237th Divisions, and the exact boundary line seems to have been in dispute between the flank elements. From Corps orders, it appears that the ravine east of the hill was the designated limit, but liaison on the ground was imperfect, and on 2 June and 5 June the 237th Division complained that its right neighbor was nowhere near as far forward or as far to the left as it was ordered to be, and as it reported itself.[228] Within the 197th Division there was also some uneasiness regarding dispositions on the Hill; and on 5 June the General Staff Officer of the Division advised either the abandonment of the advanced positions, or a thrust towards Champillon and Marigny to improve them. When the attack came, the 3/460, reinforced by a company of the 462nd Regiment, lay generally along the east side of the Hill, the 2/273 of the 197th Division lay on the west side, extending towards Les Mares Farm. The ridge running north from 142 was, in effect, a joint in the German harness, and when attack shattered it, divided local authority in defense contributed to the American's success.

    224   Annexes to War Diary, 197th DI, 6 June.
    225   Annexes to War Diary, 237th DI, 6 June: report 460th RI.
    226   Annexes to War Diary, 237th DI, 6 June: report 460th RI.
    227   War Diary and annexes, 237th DI, 6 June: see report 10th and 11th Companies, 460th RI, 6 June.
    228   War Diary, 237th DI 2-3 June: also War Diary, 197th DI.

The line of Marines, advancing at a foot-pace through the open wheat, and guiding center with great care, came first under fire of the 9th Company of the 460th Regiment, and overran it in spite of sharp resistance. At once the 9th Company sent up a red rocket, the barrage call, and the signal was repeated by the 10th and 11th Companies to the east. The 67th Company, on the left, overlapped and swept past the position of [*the 9th Company*] 9/460, and then came under the fire of the heavy machine gun in the coppice thrust up from the Champillon ravine west of the Hill, losing heavily in officers and men. It penetrated the cover, bayoneted the machine gunners and such infantry as stood, and forced the 2/273rd violently aside. The 49th Company emerged from the woods it had pierced, and the fight streamed, confused — down the north end of the Hill, Marines and Germans mixed together. The [*10th Company*] 10/462nd was next encountered and, broken up, and 49th Company, passing down the eastern side, took enfilading fire at close range from the 10th and 11th Companies in the wood across the ravine. There was further disorganized combat on the brushy north end of the hill; here Gunnery Sergeant [*Charles F.*] Hoffman of the 49th Company bayoneted the crew of a heavy Maxim [*machine gun*] had the Congressional Medal of Honor for it. The Germans in the woods to the east record that very little was taken of them, the Marines, whom they believed, to be English soldiers, passing straight through their fire and pressing north after the fugitives, so that the 10th and 11th Companies were presently isolated. They lay in cover, holding the edge of the wood, and attempting no movement.[229]

The Marines reached the objective, without recognizing it, for most of their officers were down. They climbed the slope of Hill 126, towards Torcy, and some of them followed the Germans into the town. A Corporal sent back word by a wounded man that he had taken the place and wanted reinforcements and ammunition.[230] He, and the man with him, never came out. Just south of the first house in Torcy, by the Bussiares road, there was a deep, dry hole from which rock had been taken.[231] In 1927 the French farmer who owned the land cleared away a tangle of weeds and brush that had grown up around the hole, and found in the bottom of it the weathered corpses of 2 Marines of its 5th Regiment and 2 German soldiers, their arms and equipment lying undisturbed upon them. Since on this occasion only the Marines approached Torcy, they must have fallen in the close and savage fighting of the 6th of June.

229 *War Diary and annexes, 237th DI-report 460 RI-6 June.*
230 *Major Turrill to Col Neville, 7:00 pm, 6 June, Vol. 5.*
231 *Capt C. Dunbeck. Belleau Wood memorial.*

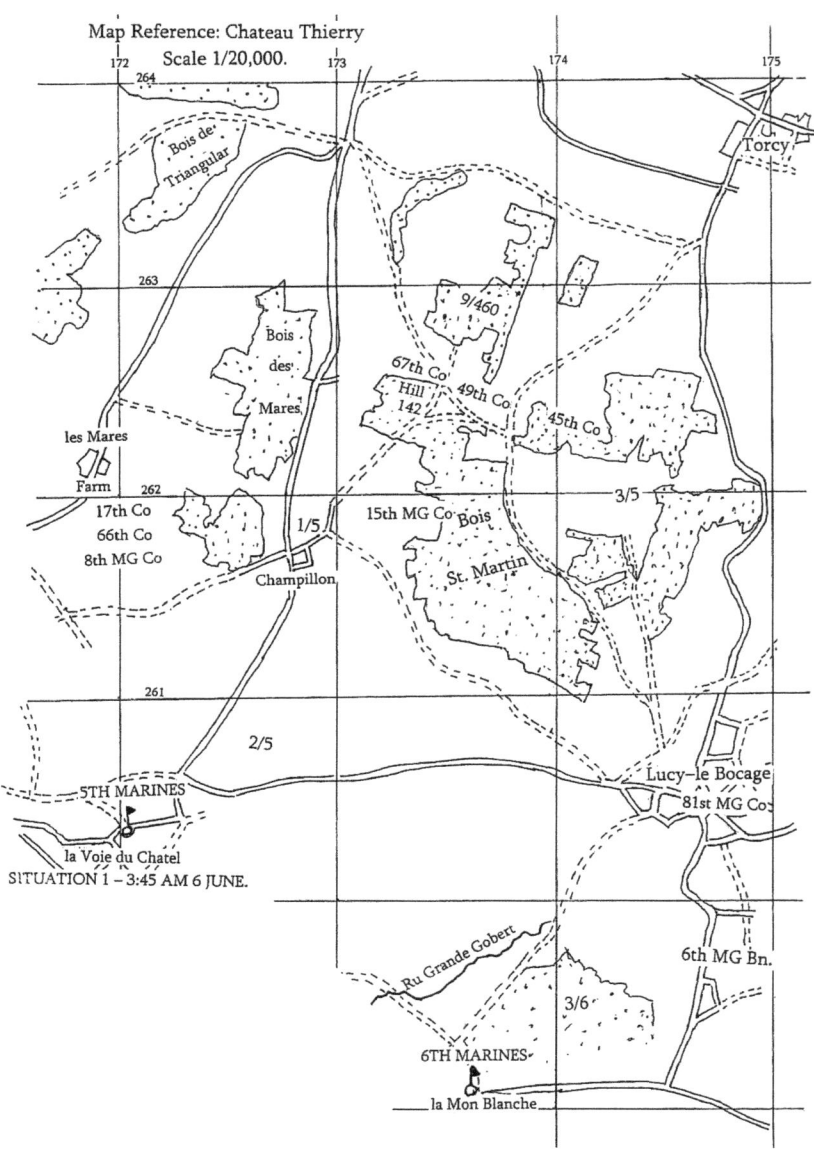

Map 3

After the attack passed Hill 142, the German 12th Company of the 460th Regiment, local reserve, delivered a counter attack from the northeast, and the elements of the 460th further east laid heavy fire on the slopes of Hill 126. A Jager battalion in support of 2/273 came into position from the direction of Bussiares, and many of the Marines were killed, and a few captured, who rejoined, in Germany after the Armistice. But the commanding officer of 12/460 was shot and the Germans did not press the advantage gained.[232] The surviving Marines of the 49th and 67th Companies fell back across the valley to the north end of Hill 142, and clung there, the 49th grouped to the right and the 67th to the left. The 49th had lost 5 officers out of 6, and the 67th 4 officers out of 5, including the company commander. Captain Hamilton was the senior officer present, and under his direction a semblance of a line was formed and, organization of the position begun.[233] His message at this stage are not timed, but from the German reports, the attack phase of the action was over by 6:00 am.[234]

In the meantime, Brigade and Regimental Headquarters of the Marines were without definite information. The Battalion commander, who had expected to attack with 4 rifle companies and 2 machine gun companies, had gone forward with 2 infantry companies only, supported by the 15th Machine Gun Company, delivering fire of position. Perhaps 15 minutes later, a platoon of his 66th Company arrived at 4:30 am, 45 minutes after he started, the remainder of the 66th arrived, and Major Turrill put it in line[235] across the Hill, on the north edge of the first belt of woods, The 8th Machine Gun Company, Captain John Fay, followed the 66th, and was sent forward to the fight. At 5:37 the 17th Company, Captain [Roswell] Winans, reported, and was passed to the front by the bordering ravine on the right: he moved up without incident, and deployed on the right of the 49th Company, which, by the time it arrived, had fallen back to the north end of the Hill and was organizing. These three companies were not wholly relieved from the Les Mares Farm vicinity by the French until after daylight, and their last orders were to remain until the French were satisfied and had taken over. Once out, they had hurried around to Champillon and thence to Hill 142.[236]

At 5:37, as the 17th Company was entering the line, the adjutant of the 1/5 reported to Col Neville that all seemed to be going well, although the expected engineers had not yet reported.[237] D Company of the 2/2 came up

232   *War Diary and annexes, 237th DI: report on 460 RI, 6 June.*
233   *Hamilton to CO 1/5: 9:50 am: also No. 2, 6 June.*
234   *Major Turrill to Col Neville, 7:00 pm, 6 June, Vol. 5.*
235   *Ibid.*
236   *Ibid. and conversation between Harbord and [Preston] Brown, 2nd Div., 3:00 pm, 5 June, Vol. 4.*
237   *[Capt Keller E.] Rockey [1/5 Adjutant] to Col Neville 5th Marines, 5:37 am, 6 June, Vol. 5. [Rockey had been, until very recently, skipper of the 67th Co. For some reason Capt Francis Kieren had been designated his successor but wasn't there at this time. Hence Crowther was acting in that capacity until KiA. GBC].*

a little later, and was passed to the front, acting thereafter as infantry during the German counterattacks and furnishing details for carrying parties and entrenching during quiet intervals.[238] Walking wounded carried incoherent and fantastic rumors to the rear as the attack progressed: the Brigade Commander saw the wounded, and records that their bearing was cocky, and that they were in fine spirits.[239] At 6:30 the adjutant of the 4th Brigade sent word from the front that all was going well.[240] At 7:10 he reported to Division Headquarters that all objectives were taken and the position being organized.[241] Headquarter's, 5th Regiment, thought there might be 65 prisoners;[242] the French Liaison officers of the 167th Division sent word, at 10:45, that the Americans had taken 300 Germans.[243] Eventually, 1 officer and 15 men were accounted for.[244]

Lieutenant Colonel Feland, 2nd in command of the 5th Marines had gone forward to command all troops on the ground. At 6:00 he called on Colonel Neville for a company to cover the left of the 1/5, for the French advance had not kept pace with the Marines, and that flank was uncovered: Colonel Neville sent up the 51st Company, Captain Williams, of 2/5, which was Brigade reserve near La Voie du Chatel, and the 51st Company went immediately to Champillon and thence forward by the Champillon ravine, connecting with the left of 1/5 and forming a line west of the Hill, facing at right angles to the advance.[245] The messages of Major Turrill, during the forenoon, indicate anxiety over his flanks, for his advance had formed a salient, more than a kilometre long and less than a kilometre wide, and for some hours both his flanks were in the air.[246]

Attack orders had contemplated the advance of 3/5, Major [*Benjamin S.*] Berry, on the right of 1/5, in conformity to progress made, and it was expected that the advance would be made by the flank elements of 3/5 along the bordering ravine east of Hill 142.[247] But there appears to have been no liaison between the two battalions at the time of the attack or for hours after it. The flank company of 3/5 was the 45th, Captain [*Peter*] Conachy, and when it advanced, its effort was directed, not along the ravine, but

---

238 Hist. 2nd Eng. pg. 27.
239 War Diary, 4th Brigade, 6 June, Vol. 6. [*The first portion sounds plausible, the latter doesn't.*]
240 Adjutant [*Major Harry R. Lay*] 4th Brigade 6:30 am, 6 June, Vol. 4.
241 Ibid: 7:10 am.
242 Harbord to 2nd Div., 10:19 am, 6 June, Vol. 4.
243 Ibid.
244 War Diary, 4th Brigade, 6 June, Vol. 6.
245 Feland to CO 5th Marines, 6:00 am, 6 June, Vol. 5.
246 See all Turrill messages to Neville, 6 June, Vol. 5.
247 F.O. 1, 4th Brigade, 5 June, Vol. 2.

across the open, well to the right of the ravine, and against the Germans in the woods on X—line 263.00, 10/460 and 11/460. Captain Conachy threw forward two platoons, supported by two machine guns firing from the edge of the Bois de Champillon. The left platoon, nearest the ravine, was unable to make any progress, German fire pinning it to its line of departure. The right platoon, [First] Lieutenant [Edward B.] Hope, advanced some 200 metres, as far as an unimproved road which angled across the company front, and dug in, 200 metres short of the objective, at 6:05.[248] Reporting this action at 7:20, the Battalion Commander informed, Colonel Neville that he would advance along the ravine as soon as Major Turrill was on his objective. At 9:00 am a report from Major Turrill noted that Berry was fighting in the woods on his right, but there was, as late as 1:10 pm, no contact between 3/5 and 1/5.[249]

The 23rd Machine Gun Company, designated as support in the attack order, took no part in the movement,[250] but at 12:30 pm 6 guns of the 81st Machine Gun Company, stationed at Lucy in reserve, were ordered to 1/5 and reinforced the positions on the Hill.[251] As the morning advanced, some reorganization was effected in the 49th and 67th Companies, and with the reinforcement received from the 17th Company and the 8th Machine Gun Company, and later, the 51st of 2/5, several German counter attacks were repulsed. There were a great many wounded, both German and American, on the hill and in front of it, and German snipers and machine gunners harassed the Marines steadily, until they were located and disposed of. Little could be done for those wounded in the open, on both sides, for German and Marine alike fired at everything that moved. The Regimental Band of the 5th Marines were utilized to move the wounded, and many of them were shot while so engaged.[252] Ambulances could only be gotten forward as far as Champillon.[253]

At 1:10 Major Turrill reported the French in sight on his left, and with that flank secured, the most apprehensive period was past, although the right of 1/5 remained open. Fortunately, the two companies of Germans who lay behind it were not aggressive.[254]

The attack was carefully reported by the Germans. The 197th Division had on its left flank the 273rd Regiment, from Hill 142 to Veuilly, with 2 battalions in line and 1 in support. The French appear to have struck Veuilly

---

248 Capt Conachy to BMC, also Berry to Neville, 7:20 am, 6 June, Vol. 5.
249 Turrill to Neville, 2:00 pm, 6 June, Vol. 5.
250 F.O. #1, 4th Brigade, 5 June, Vol. 2.
251 Hist. 6th MG Bn, 6 June.
252 Regt. Hist. 5th Marines.
253 See all Turrill messages to Neville, 6 June, Vol. 5.
254 Turrill to Neville,1:10 pm, 6 June, Vol. 5.

about the same time that the Marines went forward on Hill 142, for at 4:50 am — German time was an hour ahead of French — the 273rd Regiment reported both flanks attacked and giving ground, while its center held. The regiment asked for a barrage, and its Brigade reserve, the 25th Jager Battalion of the 7th Saxon Regiment, was to help, counter- attacking effectively towards Veuilly. The 273rd thought, at first, that it could contain the situation on its left: then confused messages came in from the 2/273 and from[255] neighboring elements of the 237th Division; and at 6:10 the 273rd called for artillery fire on its old line, and German shells began to rake Hill 142. At 7:15 the 273rd reported the attack in more detail, saying that it had been assailed by a Brigade of American troops. At 8:10, the Infantry Brigade of the 197th Division advised the 237th Division that Americans, French, and English were attacking. Immediately afterward, the 197th Division notes that it threw in its last reserve to maintain its left. The 26th Jager Battalion went forward to fill the gap left by the 2/273, when it was forced away from the Hill. The 273rd Regiment was also ordered to retake at any cost the lost ground; but none of it was ever regained, although efforts were made repeatedly during the forenoon. The command post of the 273rd, which had been in Bussiares, retired across the Clignon to the Petret Woods. At 9:10 the IV Reserve Corps was called on for additional troops and denied them. Later, however, Corps was alarmed for the safety of the Clignon line, and ordered up 2 battalions of the 3rd Regiment of Foot Guards Division, from Corps reserve. They moved, to position behind the left flank of the 197th. At the same time, the left neighbor, the 237th Division, was advised that the 197th must be supported and its lines maintained, and the 2/460 was sent hurriedly to Hill 126. By the end of the day the 273rd Regiment was so badly mauled that its front was reduced, and the 237th Division extended its right to include the front from Torcy to Bussiares, while Corps ordered preparations for the immediate relief of the 197th by the 5th Guards Division. [256]

The 197th Division had been in line since 1 June. The Corps War Diary states that it suffered about 2000 casualties on 4, 5, and 6 June, 6 June being the only day on which it was heavily engaged. The 273rd Regiment records a loss, on 6 June, of 13 officers and 405 men, of whom 8 officers and 273 men were missing. The regiment also reports the capture, on 6 June, of 120 prisoners, Colonials and Frenchmen, and a few Americans. Through its papers persists the idea that it had British on its front.[257]

    255   *War Diary and annexes, 197th RI, June 6.*
    256   *War Diary and annexes, IV Reserve Corps and the 197th DI, 6 June (see reports 273rd Regiment and 210th Infantry Brig., 6 June).*
    257   *Ibid. [The uniform coloration and the Kelly helmet were similar, as was the language, even though the dialect was decidedly different. GBC.]*

By noon on the 6th the action of 1/5 was definitely over; there were enough troops up to hold its gains against any effort the Germans might make. The 1/5 suffered a loss of 8 officers and 325 men, killed, wounded, and missing, most of the casualties occurring in the 49th and 67th Companies. The 8th Machine Gun Company lost 10 men, the 51st Company, 1 officer and 45 men, and the 45th Company, 2 officers and 71 men.[258] As finally organized, the line was short of the designated objective, but was tactically upon it: the Little Square Woods 400 metres southeast of the Bussiare Calvarie [*wayside cross*] was not occupied, but it was untenable to anybody, and the unimproved road running east to the brook-crossing 174.0-263.5 was under the rifles of the Marines. On the left, the French were abreast, and on the right, the line was refused along the ravine east of the Hill to the Bois de Champillon, with the two German companies lying low in the woods on X-line 263:

45th Company — 7 June

On the left of the Marine Brigade, 6 June closed with the small square woods east of Hill 142 on X-line 263 still in the hands of the 10th and 11th companies of the German 460th Regiment. Captain Conachy faced them from his old line, with one platoon of the 45th Company, and the line of the Turrill battalion passed along the ravine a hundred metres to the west. Captain Conachy, returning to his company from Hill 142, where he had been summoned to receive orders for the projected 2nd phase of the evening battle, found himself with 50 odd Marines where he should have had more than 200. While the attack against Belleau Woods went forward, 2 platoons of engineers passed in rear of the 45th company area, and were promptly impressed. Later, 30 men of the 16th company, drifting back from the repulse of 3/5, joined him, and scattered survivors of other commands. With these in hand, he stood by until dark, prepared to advance at Lieutenant Colonel Feland's orders, but the 2nd phase was not undertaken. During the night 6–7 June, some reorganization was effected in 3/5.[259]

---

258 *Casualties from the Adjutant and Inspector, U.S.M.C. Those of the 45th Company include losses during the attack in the afternoon on Bois de Belleau. Casualties while attached to 1/5 were probably light, but exact figures are not available.*

259 *Captain P. Conachy, USMC, to Battle Monuments Commission and to 2nd Division Historical Section. Note: The advance of the 45th on 7 June was made by passing one platoon ([2nd] Lt. [Willis T.] Conway) along the ravine east of the hill to a point adjacent to the wood, and then rushing across the narrow open interval, the other platoons covering. Compare with the attempt of 6 June, made over 500 metres of fire-swept ground.*

During the night, also, the German 10th and 11th companies retired quietly from the little wood, taking their wounded and material with them, and rejoined their regiment in Torcy. Their reports say that they cut their way through the enemy; 'but they did not: the north was open to them, and they got out unmolested.[260] The Marines, however, did not know that they were gone. On the 7th, Captain Conachy was directed to take possession of the woods, by way of cleaning up the Hill 142 vicinity. He advanced, with his company, at 5:00 pm, and occupied the woods without incident, establishing contact with the 17th company of 1/5 on his left. At 8:00 pm, 2/5 took over the 3/5 position, and the 45th company was replaced by the 55th of the Wise battalion.[261]

---

260 *War Diary and annexes, 237th DI, 6-7 June:* reports 10/460 and 11/460.
261 *War Diary, 4th Brigade, 6-7 June.*

Eleven

First Attack on the Bois de Belleau

pm 6 June

The reports received by the French XXI Corps during the morning were encouraging. By noon, the French 167th Division had made good progress towards Veuilly, across Hill 165, and towards Bussiares, and the left of the Marine Brigade had advanced 1100 metres, throwing the enemy off of Hill 142. The Bussiares depression leading to the Clignon line, which was the objective for the combined attack, was now denied to the Germans, and the 167th Division would push on to the stream. Corps saw no reason to delay the next step. About noon, General Degoutte ordered the 2nd Division to proceed with the second part of its operation, the reduction of the Bois de Belleau, and the seizure of the dominating ridge above Torcy, to the west of the Wood.[262]

At 2:05 pm, Headquarters, 4th Brigade, issued Field Order 2, the general plan of which had already been communicated verbally to the regimental commanders concerned. Field Order 2 announced that this Brigade attacks on the general line Bouresches-Torcy. The attack would be in two phases: first, to take the Bois de Belleau; and second, to take the railroad station of Bouresches, the town of Bouresches, the brook crossing 173.9–264.1, Hill 126, and Hill 133. The final designated objectives would place the line of the Marine Brigade on the south heights of the Clignon,

---

262 XXI C.A. 87/PC, 6 June.

from a point 900 metres east of Bussiares, through the edge of Torcy, around and including Hill 133 at the northwest corner of the Bois de Belleau, thence around and including the entire Bois de Belleau, to the railroad station a hundred metres east of Bouresches village. The brook-crossing was 600 metres north of the point reached by 1/5 during the morning.[263]

For the first phase, to take the Bois de Belleau, the 3/5, MajorBenjamin S. Berry, less one company attached to 1/5 on Hill 142, and the 3/6, Major Burton W. Sibley, were designated. Colonel Albertus W. Catlin 6th Marines, would command the first phase. The 77th Machine Gun Company was placed under his orders to support the operations against the Bois de Belleau and Bouresches. The 2/6, Major Thomas Holcomb, would advance its left to conform to the progress of the attack.[264]

For the 2nd phase, the movement was more elaborate. The 3/6, and the 3/5 on its left, having cleared Belleau Wood, would constitute the right and center. The 1/5, from Hill 142, plus the attached companies' of 3/5 and 2/5 would constitute the left. The machine guns with the 1/5, the 8th Company and 6 guns of the 81st Company, with the 15th Company also available — would support the second phase. Lieutenant Colonel Logan Feland, 5th Marines, would command the movements on the left, Colonel Catlin remaining in command of the right and center. The Bois de Belleau being in the possession of 3/5 and 3/6, 1/5 would sweep northeastward from Hill 142, to Hill 126 and the high ground between Bussiares and Torcy, as far east as Hill 133. Three/5 in the woods, would carry the advance from Hill 133 around the northeastern perimeter of the woods 3/6, partly in the woods and partly south of them, would take Bouresches and the line of the metre-guage railroad to the east. All positions when attained would be held, against counter attack. Artillery as ordered by the 2nd F.A. Brigade. Aviation as ordered by the French XXI Corps. Two/5, less the 51st Company with 1/5, was Brigade reserve in the Woods northwest of Lucy. Brigade and Regimental PCs to remain in place.

The first phase would begin at 5:00 pm. The second phase would begin as soon as the objectives for the first phase were reached.[265]

Written copies of this order did not reach the battalion commanders until after the attack.[266]

---

263 *Field Order # 2, 4th Brigade, 2:05 pm, 6 June, Vol. 2.*
264 *Ibid.*
265 *Field Order # 2, 4th Brigade, 2:05 pm, 6 June, Vol. 2.*
266 *History 3/6, also letter Holcomb to McClellan, Historical Section, U.S.M.C.*

First Attack on the Bois de Belleau

No details as to artillery arrangements, or liaison organization, exist in the Division records.[267]

Of the troops designated, 3/6 had been relieved south of Hill 142 by 1/5 at daylight, and had withdrawn to the woods north of Mon Blanche Farm, on the Paris-Metz road. Three/5 was in line from Lucy-le-Bocage, along the ridge running north, west of and parallel to the Bois de Belleau, around the northern edge of the Bois de Champillon, to the ravine east of Hill 142. The right companies of 3/5 faced east, the 2 left companies northeast and north, the 4th Company was in reserve. Three/6 would have to move 2 kilometres to get into position for attack, and 3/5 would have to readjust its lines and move its left companies through the Bois de Champillon.[268]

One/5 lay in the lines it had taken from the enemy that morning, two of its companies short of officers and much shattered. Two/5, relieved the night before by the French in the Les Mares-Veuilly line had 3 companies close behind the line of 3/5; the other company had been in action all day with the Turrill Battalion. Two/6 had, since 1 June, been in line from Le Thiolet to Lucy, and after midnight, 5–6 June, it had been relieved from Le Thiolet to Triangle Farm by 2 battalions of the 23rd Infantry, taking out 1 company and moving another to the left of its front. The machine gun companies had been in position through the Brigade area, and in action, during the preceding days. The 8th and part of the 71st Companies [*I'm sure he meant the 81st Company*] had participated in the morning operation of 1/5. Only one battalion of the Marine Brigade was not involved; 1/6, Major Hughes, lay in Corps Reserve.

In effect, the order called for a thrust, pivoting on 2/6 in the Triangle-Lucy line, by the whole Marine Brigade, less 1 battalion. The average advance demanded was about 2 kilometres.

The Brigade Commander has stated that the French informed him that the Bois de Belleau was not occupied except by a few Germans in its northern end, and that he considered a surprise attack, without extensive artillery preparation practicable.[269] No reconnaissance was effected by the Brigade between 4 June, when they took over the front from the French, and 6 June, when the Brigade attacked, to correct this impression.

---

267 From study of field messages and Brigade instructions, the infantry [Marines] was, at this time, expected to keep in touch with the artillery in addition to its other duties. There is no mention of artillery liaison officers with infantry battalions. [JWT's personal attitude comes out very clearly in this note. This was no doubt part of the reason the material was never published as produced. GBC].

268 See positions 3/5: Berry to Neville,1:45 pm, 6 June, Vol. 5.

269 Gen. James G. Harbord to U.S. Naval Institute, Nov. 1928, comment on Battles for the Possession of the Woods of Belleau. [Lieutenant] Colonel [Ernst] Otto, Reichsarchiv, U.S. Naval Institute, Nov. 1928.

96   Chapter Eleven

As for the German dispositions, most of the objective assigned lay within the area of the 237th Division, which had entered the Bois de Belleau between 2 June and 4 June, and lost no time in organizing the entire wood. The German 460th Regiment, with attached details of the 462nd, held Hill 126 and Torcy, and by the evening of 6 June, this regiment had extended its line to Bussiares, relieving broken elements of the 197th Division. The 461st Regiment,[270] Major Bischoff, held the Bois de Belleau, with 2 battalions in line from the northwest corner of the wood, down its western face, including Hill 169, to Hill 181, and from Hill 181 to the to the southeastern corner of the wood. Hill 181 and the thickly-wooded area stretching westward towards Lucy-le-Bocage had been left out of the line, although included in the outpost zone, since the growth was so thick and the ground so broken that no field of fire was possible. The regimental reserves were in the northern end of the wood. The local commander was Major von Hartlieb. Major Bischoff was an old West African soldier, who had learned the art of bush-fighting in the German colonies. His infantry positions were everywhere stiffened by machine guns and minenwerfers [*mortars*], and his dispositions took full advantage of the great natural defensive strength of the woods.[271]

From the southeast corner of the Bois de Belleau the German main line of resistance angled east to the line of the metre-guage railroad and ran south towards Vaux, the zone of outposts including Bouresches village, and the Bouresches-Vaux road. This was in the area of the 10th Division, and one company of the 2/398th Regiment held Bouresches, the village being fully commanded by the high ground beyond it.[272] For both the 237th and the 10th Divisions there had been two days to perfect their organization, for there was no fighting of importance on 4 June or on 5 June. The German positions were nowhere exposed to observation, and were chosen with skill and experience. Their exact trace was unknown to the Americans, and the targets of the American gunners were of necessity indefinite. The rear areas were heavily shelled on 5 June and during the forenoon of 6 June, and while the lines of communication suffered, the front line troops were for the most part untouched prior to the attack.[273]

Shortly after noon, Colonel Catlin conferred at Regimental Headquarters with his battalion commanders, and there was a final conference about 4:30 pm in the orchard east of Montgivrault-le-Grande, following which

270   *War Diary and annexes, 237th DI, 4-6 June.*
271   Ibid.
272   *War Diary and annexes, 10th DI, 4-6 June.*
273   *War Diary and annexes, 237th DI, 4-6 June.*

First Attack on the Bois de Belleau

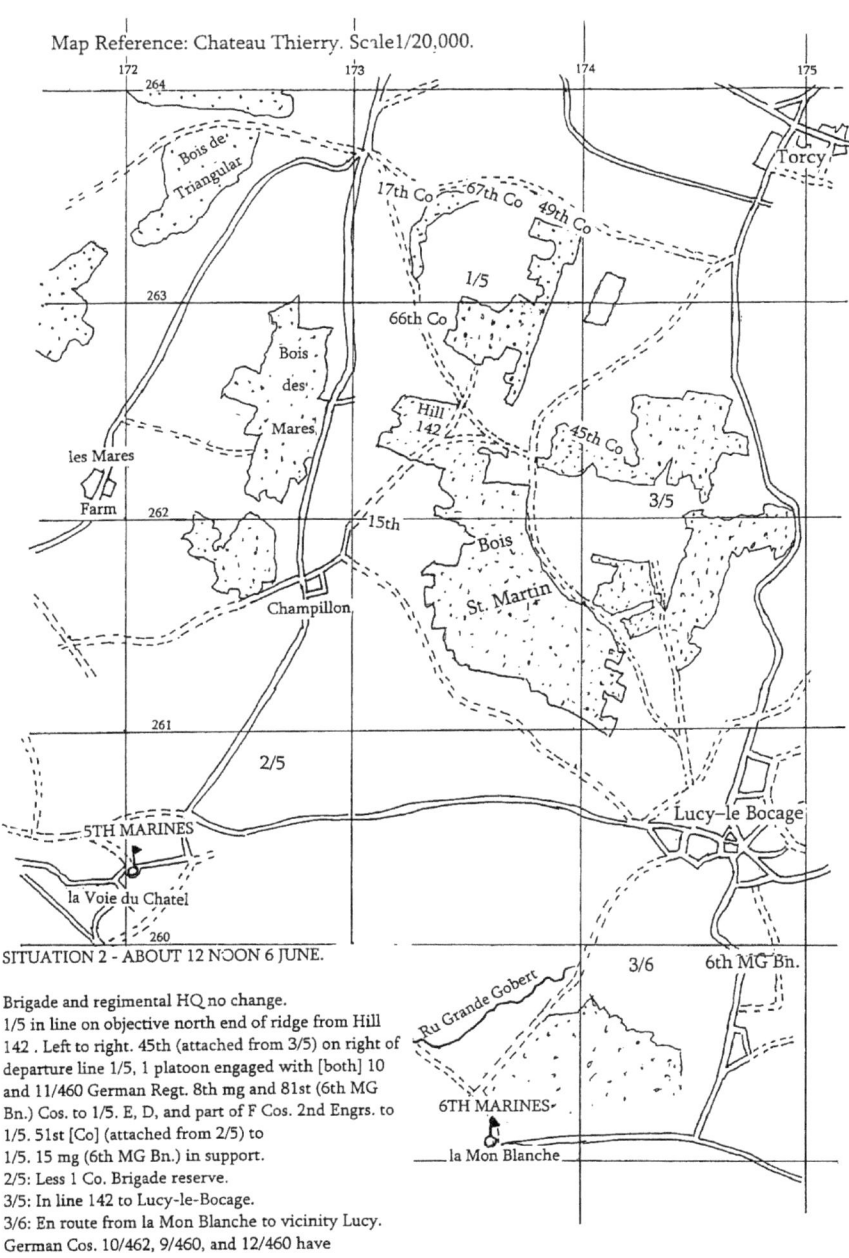

SITUATION 2 - ABOUT 12 NOON 6 JUNE.

Brigade and regimental HQ no change.
1/5 in line on objective north end of ridge from Hill 142 . Left to right. 45th (attached from 3/5) on right of departure line 1/5, 1 platoon engaged with [both] 10 and 11/460 German Regt. 8th mg and 81st (6th MG Bn.) Cos. to 1/5. E, D, and part of F Cos. 2nd Engrs. to 1/5. 51st [Co] (attached from 2/5) to 1/5. 15 mg (6th MG Bn.) in support.
2/5: Less 1 Co. Brigade reserve.
3/5: In line 142 to Lucy-le-Bocage.
3/6: En route from la Mon Blanche to vicinity Lucy. German Cos. 10/462, 9/460, and 12/460 have disappeared. 10/460 and 11/460 surrounded.

Map 4

Colonel Catlin moved forward to Lucy.[274] The 3/6, which had the longest way to go, started from its cover above La Mon Blanche at 3:00 o'clock, and filtered into the front line by small detachments, using such dead space as was available.[275] Its movements were seen and reported, as it concentrated around Lucy, by the German observers of the 237th Division, but no fire was laid upon it.[276] Major Berry regrouped 3/5 behind the ridge running north from Lucy, facing the Bois de Belleau. Captain Conachy, whose 45th Company was attached to Major Turrill, was sent for by Colonel Feland in the middle of the afternoon, to receive instructions regarding the 2nd phase of the attack. Returning, just before 5 o'clock, he found that 3 platoons of his company had been taken away by the battalion adjutant, among them the Hope platoon, withdrawn from the advance position it had attained in the morning. The lieutenant commanding his 4th Platoon, [Second] Lieutenant [Edward E.] Conroy [USA], had refused to leave the place to which Captain Conachy had assigned him. This platoon appears to have been the only force left on the north edge of the Bois de Champillon during the attack.[277] The battalion was formed, roughly, between X-lines 261 and 262, facing east, just west of the Lucy-Torcy road. Major Sibley's 3/6 took up position facing northeast, on the outskirts of Lucy and astride the ravine that ran from Lucy along the south face of Belleau Woods. Major Holcomb, at 4:30, was ordered verbally by Colonel Catlin to detach one company to operate on the right flank of 3/6, covering the area south of Bouresches. The part performed. by 3/6 will be considered. later, since this company never made contact with Sibley's companies.[278] Three/5 and 3/6, much hurried, were in position by 5:00 o'clock.[279]

During the afternoon, the 2nd Engineers moved a train of entrenching material to 4th Brigade Headquarters, and 3rd Brigade was directed to have 2 companies of engineers ready to help the Marines in consolidation at dusk.[280] Lieutenant Colonel Feland at the Turrill PC perfected his arrangements for the 2nd phase. The artillery assigned to the 4th Brigade laid raking fire, as ordered by General Harbord on the Bois de Belleau, Bouresches village, and the approaches to the assigned area, without effect as far as the German front line was concerned. At 5:00 pm, the officers' whistles shrilled, and the two battalions of Marines went forward. The sun was low behind,

274 Holcomb to McClellan. Historical Section, U.S.M.C.
275 History 3/6, 6 June.
276 War Diary and annexes, 237th DI, 6 June.
277 Captain Conachy to BMC and to 2nd Div, Hist. Sec. file.
278 Holcomb to McClellan.
279 Regt. Hist. 5th Marines. War Diary, 4th Brig. 6 June, Vol. 6.
280 Col. Brown, Chief of Staff [2nd Div.] to 4th Brigade, 6 June, Vol. 4.

them, their lines were carefully dressed in the 4-wave platoon formation taught by the French, and their shadows lay long and level on the wheat in front of them. They were at once assailed by a furious machine gun fire from the edges of the Bois de Belleau, and high explosive and shrapnel from the 237th and 10th Divisional artillery to the east and north.[281]

Major Berry's battalion had before it the western face of the Wood, here curving like the inner line of a crescent. Hill 169 flanked the battalion from the left, and the woods in front commanded all the right and center. There was no cover anywhere. The battalion had, in order from the right, the 47th, 20th, and 45th Companies, with the 16th in support.[282] Of these, the 47th Company, on the right, was favored somewhat by the unoccupied tongue of woods lying west of Hill 161; the company pulled to the right, kept contact with the left of 3/6, and entered the southern part of the woods with Sibley.[283] But the rest of 3/5 was quickly shot to pieces. Small, desperate groups rushed more than half-way across the open wheat between the Woods and, the Lucy-Torcy road: their bodies were salvaged weeks afterwards. The battalion commander went forward, was shot, and evacuated. The remnants of the companies drifted back to the line of departure, except for elements of the 47th Company, which remained with 3/6. At 6:10 pm the Battalion Adjutant, Captain [*Henry L.*] Larsen, reported to 4th Brigade from the old battalion PC: "What is left of battalion is in woods close by — " In little more than an hour, 3/5 was decisively repulsed. It had in no place penetrated, or even closely approached, the German line.[284] Its losses on 6 June were 4 officers and 268 men killed and wounded. These figures include the losses of the 45th Company in its action with 1/5 earlier in the day (total for 45th Company, 6 June: 2 officers and 71 men) and, one of the officer casualties was the Battalion Commander.[285]

The 3/6 advanced over ground slightly more favorable. Orchards on the outskirts of Lucy covered it as it formed, and small scattered trees stood north of the ravine, between Lucy and the southwest corner of the Wood, which was half a kilometre distant. A road paralleled the ravine, from Lucy to Bouresches, and the ground south of this road was open, rising further south

---

281   *War Diary, 4th Brigade: 6 June, Vol. 6: also Histories, 5th and 6th Regiments.*
282   *Berry to Neville, 1:45 pm, 6 June, Vol. 5.*
283   *History 3/6, 6 June.*
284   *War Diary and annexes, 237th DI, 6 June.*
285   *Adjutant and Inspector U.S. Marine Corps.* Note: The records of the 10th and 237th Divisions mention the capture, on 6 June, of between 40 and 50 Americans: 7 from the 23rd Inf. and the remainder from the 5th and 6th Marines. The Adjutant and Inspector, USMC, lists no captured Marines, nor are authoritative figures available from the War Department for the Army units of the Division. [Major Berry lost part of his left hand but would remain a Marine for many years afterward. GBC].

to the Bois de Bocage, immediately east of Lucy, and the Bois de Triangle, a scattered wood further east. As the battalion went forward, it was deployed on a two-company front of about 900 metres, the 82nd and 84th Companies left to right leading, and the 83rd and 97th in support. Battalion Headquarters followed in the ravine, which was in the center of the battalion, and approximated the axis of advance. The battalion scouts flushed German outposts in the ravine, at the very edge of Lucy, and although fire was opened at once from the woods, the companies on the left advanced swiftly and with little loss through the southwestern end of the Bois de Belleau, overran the unoccupied Hill 181, and recoiled from the German main line of resistance beyond the Hill. The two right companies were altogether in the open, and as soon as Hill 181 no longer covered them, they came under severe machine gun and artillery fire and began to lose men. Checked on the left, the battalion pivoted and extended along the south face of the wood elements of the right companies halting in the open, and other elements of the companies taking cover in the ravine and driving up from the ravine into the face of the Woods. It was seen at once that the German position was immensely strong.[286]

Within the south face of Belleau Wood the ground rises abruptly by some 30 metres above the banks of the ravine; and east of Hill 181, the upper slopes are open, commanding all the country to the south. There are outcroppings of grey, gigantic rocks, frost split, and overgrown with low bushes. In those rocks, so securely emplaced that direct hits from heavy artillery would have been necessary to dislodge it, was the main line of the 461st Regiment, held by machine guns, with supporting infantry.[287] The 3/6 silenced two machine guns just east of Hill 181, and then attempted to mount the rocky ledges east which the Germans with fire and showers of potato-masher grenades. The Marines had only their rifles—lacking themselves grenades and auxiliary weapons and they were unable to reach the crest. Extending always to the east, they cut off and captured a detachment of Germans in the clump of trees at the extreme southeastern corner, towards Bouresches, and formed a line in close contact with the enemy, from that point to Hill 181. The combat continued without a lull from about 5:30 to 8:45 pm.[288]

Observers from Headquarters, 4th Brigade, were on the front and saw the attack start. They reported that it had gotten away well, with the formations dressed and everything in order. Success was anticipated. But subsequent reports were incoherent and confused.[289]

At 5:37 pm, Colonel Catlin, in a shallow trench in front of Lucy, was

---

286 *History 3/6*, 6 June.
287 *War Diary and annexes, 237th DI*, 6 June.
288 *War Diary, 4th Brigade*, 5-6 pm, 6 June, Vol. 4.
289 *History 3/6*, 6 June.

First Attack on the Bois de Belleau

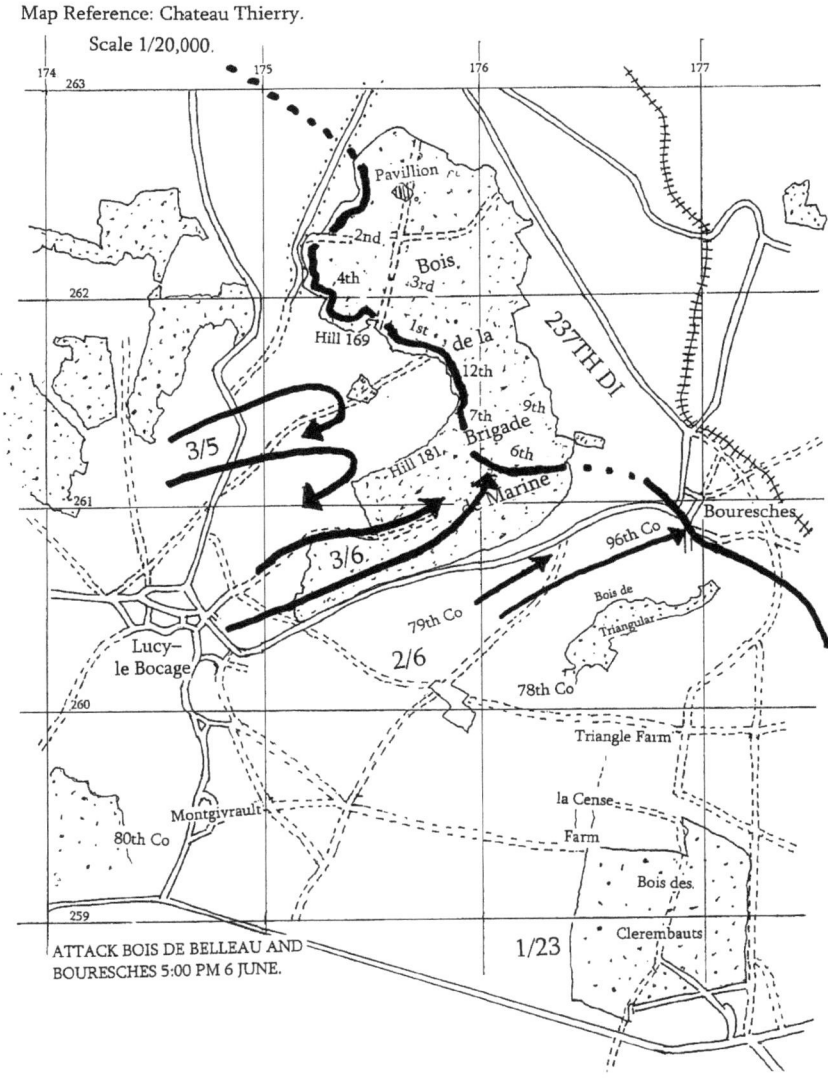

Map 5

shot through the shoulder by a machine gun bullet and evacuated.[290] Report of this reached Brigade Headquarters at 5:50 pm, in a message from Captain [*Thibot*] Laspierre, the French Liaison Officer attached to the 6th Regimental Headquarters.[291] It was confirmed by a second report, through

290   War Diary, 4th Brigade, 5-6 pm, 6 June, Vol. 6.

Colonel Neville, at 5:54.[292] At 6:00 pm, General Harbord sent orders to Lieutenant Colonel [*Harry*] Lee of the 6th Marines, directing him to assume command "if Colonel Catlin was too badly wounded to continue."[293] For some hours afterward, no reports were received by Brigade from Lieutenant Colonel Lee.[294] Brigade had various reports on German movements in the vicinity of Bouresches, sent in by observers near Lucy, and from French avions: one of the latter reported, at 6:22 pm,[295] that Americans were on the Belleau-Bouresches road — in the light of events, incorrect. A little earlier, at 6:13,[296] General Harbord noted that French batteries were moving forward on the left, which would indicate that the French 167th Division was making progress towards the Clignon line. At 7:22 the first report came to Brigade from the attacking forces: Major Berry, 3/5, reported that the German positions in the western edge of the Bois de Belleau were taken; and at 7:55 he asked instructions as to the disposition of his Battalion reserve, the 16th Company. His losses, he thought, had been heavy, and he anticipated counter-attacks. These messages were received long after they were sent, and nothing further was heard of Major Berry, until, at 9:50 pm, his adjutant, Captain Larsen, sent word that Major Berry had gone forward with 4 runners to find his front line and had not been seen again. Meantime, at 7:35, a report had come in to the effect that the 83rd Company of 3/6 had taken the railroad station of Bouresches — a report wholly incorrect and misleading. At 7:51 Brigade heard from Captain Larsen regarding the 45th Company: "3 platoons went over. Only a few returned." At 7:55 Lieutenant Colonel Feland requested 5 minutes artillery fire on his front: he would then attack in the 2nd phase. But this was followed in 2 minutes by another message from Feland: the French on the left appeared to he withdrawing instead of advancing, and an advance by 1/5 would have to be made with the left flank in the air. Lieutenant Colonel Feland awaited further instructions as to progress of the first phase, since the wounding of Catlin.[297]

With this information in hand, amplified by the usual rumors that follow an attack, General Harbord reported at 8:07 to Division Headquarters. First, it appeared that the French on the left had not come forward and showed no disposition to advance further against the German resistance they

291 Captain Laspierre to 4th Brigade 5:37 pm, 6 June, Vol. 4. [Laspierre, physically a little man, helped drag Catlin, a huge man, back out of further danger. GBC].
292 War Diary, 4th Brigade, 5-6 pm, 6 June, Vol. 6.
293 Ibid.
294 Ibid.
295 Ibid.
296 Ibid.
297 Field messages at times indicated in text, 6 June, 4th Brigade, Vol. 4.

First Attack on the Bois de Belleau 103

had developed in front of and to the west of Bussiares. Regarding the 4th Brigade General Harbord believed that he had the Bouresches station, and the east edge of the Bois de Belleau. Touching upon the 2nd phase, he thought that, in an hour he could get his Brigade reserve into line on the left of 1/5 and go ahead, taking Hill 126 and connecting up with the north edge of the Bois de Belleau. Would Division assist him if he needed help? Colonel Brown replied that Division would.[298]

At 8:15 the first direct word was received concerning 3/6: Major [Frank E.] Evans, Adjutant, 6th Marines, advised Brigade that Major Sibley was held up by machine guns on the rocky plateau to the left of the Lucy-Bouresches road, and had asked for a Stokes mortar, which was being sent him. Major Sibley reported that his right had not advanced as far as his left, and was then at the edge of the woods, not having taken all the machine guns.[299]

At 8:55, no report having been received. from Lieutenant Colonel Lee, the Brigade Commander addressed a message to him, enjoining the necessity for prompt and. systematic communication. The message repeated the general instructions for the attack, and ordered that it be pushed vigorously. The left half of Holcomb's battalion, 2/6, was placed at his disposal if it was needed to support Major Sibley.[300]

It is evident, from this message to Lieutenant Colonel Lee, that Brigade had been without reports from 2/6, since long before 8:55 pm, the left half of the Holcomb battalion — the 96th and 79th Companies — was in Bouresches, and as events turned out, Sibley sent half his battalion to support them.

Major Cole, commanding the 6th Machine Gun Battalion, had gone forward, as was his custom, to observe the progress of the attack. At 9:45 he reported on the Bois de Belleau. He found the whole outfit — 3/6 — held up by a machine gun nest on the north edge of the Wood. He had seen Major Sibley, who was attempting to encircle it. He thought that, with mortars and hand grenades the nest could be reduced, and that, if they had been furnished, 3/6 would already have reduced it. He had seen Colonel Lee,

---

298 Harbord to 2nd Div. 8:07, 6 June, 4th Brigade, Vol. 4. Note: Harbord to Brown, (2nd Div) 8:07 pm, 6 June, Vol. 4, refers to wood SE of Bouresches. This can only mean Bussiares-Bouresches was on the right, not the left. Hill 106 certainly refers to Hill 126. There is no Hill 106. It appears from this report that Harbord believed the Bois de Belleau penetrated and held, by 8:07 pm, 6 June. See War Diary 5pm-9pm, 6 June, 4th Brigade, Vol. 6.

299 Evans to 4th Brigade 8:15 pm, 6 June, Vol. 4.

300 Harbord to Lee, 4th Brigade, 8:55 pm, 6 June, Vol. 4. [In his first message to Lee, Harbord was not cordial, in fact he was quite insulting; he was obviously concerned with Lee's abilities. GBC].

who was at the north edge of Belleau Wood, and, who had had difficulty in finding Colonel Catlin after that officer was wounded, and was not yet in touch with some of the attacking elements. Major Cole had given Major Sibley 2 guns, and had 12 more in place to cover his flank. There were 15 or 16 prisoners. Major Cole had, also, [*heard*] the rumor that Bouresches was taken.[301]

This was the most comprehensive message that Brigade had yet received from the action. Yet, it was misleading in essential points. The machine guns were holding Major Sibley to the south edge of the Wood: not the north edge. Colonel Lee was on the north edge of the wooded strip thrust out from the southwest corner of the wood, west of Hill 181—for in a message, written about the time of the Cole report, Lieutenant Colonel Lee located himself by coordinates.[302]

The mistakes in these reports were not immediately apparent, and they were communicated to Division Headquarters as they came in. At 9:40, the situation as summed up for Division by Colonel [*Lorenzo D. ?*] Gasser, placed the Marines in the Bouresches railroad station, and around the north and east edges of the Bois de Belleau with General Harbord strengthening his left from his reserve to proceed with the 2nd phase. There were also French reports that Americans were in Torcy, and Division forwarded to the XXI Corps a report that Marines were in Chateau Belleau also. It was further reported that Sibley and Berry were in liaison, Berry's left resting near Hill 133.[303]

The foregoing messages sum up the impression in force at Brigade and Division Headquarters at the close of the day. These impressions were slowly rectified.

At 9:45 pm, the first news came in from 2/6. Major Holcomb, through the old Catlin PC near Lucy, advised that 2½ platoons of his 96th Company held Bouresches. He had no information of the 3/6, and asked for orders.[304]

At 9:50 Colonel Neville reported the repulse of 3/5, 3 companies of which were accounted for at about their starting points. Captain Larsen was trying to find the 47th Company, which, as has been seen, was then with Sibley. Further news of 3/5 cane in the first message from Lieutenant Colonel Lee, at 10:10 pm, who located, himself near the southwest corner of

---

301   Cole to 4th Brigade, 9:45 pm, 6 June, Vol. 4. [*For some reason JWT had numbered the machine gun battalion "4th" instead of 6th, which I changed. GBC*].

302   Lee to 4th Brigade, 9:15 pm, 6 June, Vol. 4. (*Received at 10:10 pm*)

303   Gasser to 2nd Div., 9:40 pm, 6 June, Vol. 4. [*Cannot locate a first name for this officer in division records. Found a listing in that name in a 1902 USA roster and assumed that there would not be many other persons with the same last name. GBC*].

304   Holcomb to 4th Brigade, 9:45 pm, 6 June, Vol. 4.

First Attack on the Bois de Belleau

the Bois de Belleau. He had the 47th Company with him, and was in touch with the left of Sibley Battalion. Later reports from him detailed the reorganization of 3/5. He forwarded a report from Sibley, who, at 8:45 pm, had found further advance impossible, and now clung to a line under the muzzles of the German guns. Lee also thought the hostile position too strong, and waited instructions.[305]

Immediately upon hearing from Lieutenant Colonel Lee, at 10:10, Brigade advised him that 2 companies of engineers, with tools, were arriving in Lucy and would report to him. He was ordered to organize and hold what he had taken, and to attempt no further advance.[306]

Lieutenant Colonel Feland had been ready to start the 2nd phase since 5 o'clock. The inaction of the French on the left had caused some uncertainty, and Brigade had entertained the idea of adding its reserve, 3 companies of 2/5, to Feland's left and going ahead regardless. Some special artillery preparation had been given him. The situation with him seems to have hung in the air during the closing hours of the day, for at 10:25 General Harbord, in touch with him through [*First*] Lieutenant [*Fielding S.*] Robinson, ADC, informed him that no barrage could be given him because of ignorance of his whereabouts. (Apparently Feland had asked for a barrage) He was ordered — if by the receipt of this message he had already advanced — to consolidate where he was, and be prepared to hold his ground on the next day. He would use the Wise battalion — 2/5 was now at Feland's orders— to connect up his right with the left of the Berry Battalion, believed to be near Hill 133 and the north end of the Bois de Belleau.

This message disposed of the 2nd phase, which, except in preparation, was never undertaken.[307]

This text has confined itself to dealing with the execution of the 1st phase of the attack, as ordered, in 4th Brigade Field Order 2. One of the developments of the 1st phase, not as contemplated in the orders, was the seizure of Bouresches by 2/6, the Holcomb battalion.

It will be remembered that 2/6 was in line from Le Thiolet on the Highway to Lucy-le-Bocage, from 1 June to the night 5–6 June, when the 23rd Infantry returned to the 2nd Division area from the Veuilly-Premont-Coulombs area. With the 23rd Infantry again in hand, a 3rd Brigade sector was formed, from the right boundary of the Division to Triangle Farm, the 9th Infantry on the right, and the 23rd on the left. Two battalions of

---

305   *Lee to 4th Brigade, 9:15 pm, 6 June, Vol. 4. (Received at 10:10 pm)*
306   *Harbord to Lt Col. Lee, 10:10 pm, 6 June, Vol. 4.*
307   *Harbord to Lt Col. Feland, 10:25 pm, 6 June, Vol. 4. (See Neville's report to Brigade re'd 9:50 pm, 6 June, Vol. 4.)*

the 23rd took over from the 2/6, Major Holcomb, that portion of the line between Le Thiolet and Triangle Farm. The movement released two companies, the 96th and 79th. Major Holcomb had held his position with three companies of his battalion, and one, immediately to the right of Lucy, from the 3/6. His 79th Company being relieved by the 23rd Infantry, he passed this company around his rear, and replaced with it the company of 3/6, which was returned to Major Sibley. The 96th Company was not relieved before daylight on the 6th, however, and after coming out of the line, it lay up in the northwestern corner of the Bois des Clerembauts during the day. In the afternoon of the 6th, the 2/6 had, in line, between Triangle Farm and, Lucy, the 78th and 79th Companies, with the 80th Company in reserve and the 96th disengaged in the rear of the 23rd Infantry.

Major Holcomb was present at the conferences held by Colonel Catlin in the afternoon, following the receipt of attack orders from Brigade. At the final conference, in the Montgivrault-le-Grand orchard, about 4:30 pm, Colonel Catlin received the written Brigade order, and reading it, he directed Major Holcomb to put one company into line on the right of 3/6, to take that part of the objective south of Bouresches.[308] In accordance with these instructions, Major Holcomb despatched a pencilled order to Captain [Donald F.] Duncan of the 96th Company. Captain Duncan was to place the 96th Company in line on the right of 3/6, his objective the enemy line being south of Bouresches. He was to regulate his advance on 3/6. He was to get into position in time to attack at 5:00 pm.[309]

Captain Duncan received this order at about 4:45 pm. He at once assembled his company, and started on a trot for the left of his battalion which was 1000 metres north of the Clerembauts Wood. La Cense ravine skirted the northwest corner of the Wood and angled toward Bouresches, and the 96th Company followed the ravine to the edge of the Bois de Triangle, near which it passed. Emerging from the ravine, the company entered the woods just as the first gusts of enemy machine gun fire began to tear through them. Three platoons of the company went into line near the eastern face of the woods, to the left of the ravine. The 4th Platoon, [First] Lieutenant [Clifton B.] Cates, was sent further to the left, with instructions to find the flank of the Sibley battalion, now already attacking. Four/96 was not far enough past the ridge on which the Bois de Triangle stands to see into the low ground beyond, where 3/6 was advancing, but the platoon entered the area of the 79th Company, Captain [Randolph T.] Zane, in line

---

308   Holcomb to McClellan, Hist. Sec., and 2nd Div. file.
309   Ibid.
310   Capt. Clifton B. Cates to BMC.

at the edge of the wood. Captain Zane did not want it there, and the platoon moved to the east again, near the tip of the woods towards Bouresches, and saw the rest of the 96th Company, some distance to its right. Straight down the hill from them, about 600 metres distant, was Bouresches.

The German artillery fire now fell with great violence on the line of the 79th Company,[310] searching, also to the right and rear. Captain Duncan, on the eastern tip of the Bois de Triangle, was wounded; stretcher bearers picked him up and a shell killed him, the stretcher bearers, his first sergeant [*Joseph A. Sissler*], and, Lieutenant (jg) Weeden E. Osborne of the Navy Dental Corps. Command of the 96th Company devolved on First Lieutenant James F. Robertson. Lieutenant Robertson moved to the front, waved his pistol, and called, "Let's go!" Bouresches was in plain sight, and the 3rd and 4th Platoons of the 96th ran down the hill to the village.[311] Heavy fire was at once opened up on them, from the town, and from the Bois de Belleau squarely on the left hand. The 2nd Platoon followed the 3rd and 4th at a little distance, and the German machine guns raked them all. The 3rd Platoon, and then the 2nd, sideslipped into La Cense ravine on their right. The 4th Platoon, with a few men of the 3rd, went into the town. Lieutenant Cates was stunned by a bullet 200 yards from the first houses, and when he regained consciousness, he went forward, with several men of the 3rd Platoon who attached themselves to him, and entered the town from the southwest, establishing a chaut-chaut post to command the main street. Meantime, Lieutenant Robertson had ejected the company of the German 398th Regiment which held the place, and now Lieutenant Cates saw him, with his men, retiring from the village. He attracted Robertson's attention, who returned, handed over the Marines following him, and then went towards the rear to bring up ammunition and, reinforcements. Lieutenant Cates and his detachment were at once caught in a burst of machine gun fire, and several Marines were killed or wounded. The others took cover, and methodically cleaned out the village, killing or driving out the Germans who persisted among the houses, and capturing one German and one light machine gun. The prisoner was made to take the light machine gun to the rear, which, it is related, the prisoner resented. Having then 21 Marines, Lieutenant Cates set about organizing the town for defense. The 96th Company had reached the Bois de Triangle a little after 5:00 pm, had lost a few minutes in looking for the flank of 3/6, and some of its men had taken Bouresches by 5:45 pm. The 2nd and 3rd Platoons, much thinned by casualties, came into town by La Cense ravine soon afterward. At about 6 o'clock the 79th Company advance from the Bois de Triangle, over the same

311   Ibid.

ground as the left of the 96th, and Captain Zane took over the defense. Close behind the 79th, the 1st Platoon of the 96th came in. The platoons were posted on the east, north, and northwest edges of the village, as the houses and ground favored. They had no liaison with 3/6 along the south face of Bois de Belleau, and during the remaining daylight hours, Marines on the northwest side[312] of the town were exchanging shots with the eastern edge of the Bois de Belleau. About dark — between 9 and 10 o'clock, the 78th Company, Captain [*Robert E.*] Messersmith, shifted its line along La Cense ravine from Triangle Farm, establishing a flank 200 metres to the southwest, and maintaining contact with the town by patrols. The Germans placed heavy artillery fire on Bouresches, and raked it with machine guns, but they threw forward no infantry to counter-attack. Their records indicate that they attached little importance to Bouresches, and did not, on June 6, consider efforts to regain it.

The Marines in Bouresches were most apprehensive as to their left, for they had no contact with 3/6, which, by dark, had established a flank at the southeast corner of the wood, 500 metres from the town. It was 10:45 before Major Sibley, whose PC was in the ravine in the south edge of Belleau Wood, was advised by Major Holcomb that some of 2/6 were in Bouresches, needing support. Major Sibley had heard of Catlin's wound at 10:15, and he seems to have had no orders or information from anybody before that hour. On receiving Holcomb's message, he at once detached the right half of his battalion, the 84th and 97th Companies, and sent them into Bouresches to report to Captain Zane. They went along the Lucy-Bouresches road, arriving at 11:40 pm, and bringing the Bouresches force up about 600 men — remnants of 4 companies. Later food ammunition were rushed into Bouresches by truck, in spite of the heavy harassing fire maintained on the approaches by the Germans. Bouresches was firmly held, and the Germans never retook it.

At midnight, 6–7 June, 4 of the 6 battalions of the 4th Brigade had been in action. One/5 with attached details of 2/5 and 3/5 and machine gunners had advanced the line 1100 metres on Hill 142. Three/5 was back on its old lines, after an attack that left its dead scattered along the west front of the Bois de Belleau. Three/6 had a foothold in the south face of the Wood. Two/6 had gotten a company into Bouresches, and extended its lines to include the village. The morning attack had been successful; the evening attack, except for the taking of the town in the German outpost zone, unsuccessful.

The 3/6 lost, in killed, wounded, and gassed, 5 officers and 194 men.

312   *Cates to BMC.*

The losses of 2/6 were, from all causes, 6 officers and 126 men. Losses in the machine gun companies which participated in the attacks of the day were light. The total casualties for the day in the Marine Brigade were 31 officers and 1056 men, of which number 6 officers and 222 men were killed or died of wounds.[313]

The German casualties for the day were excessive only in the 197th Division, which, alone of the IV Reserve Corps, lost any important ground. The 237th Division reported a loss of 5 officers and 48 men killed, 7 officers and 348 men wounded, and 1 officer and. 72 men missing. The weight of these losses fell upon the 460th Regiment, the 3rd battalion of which was torn to pieces by 1/5 on Hill 142.[314]

The 10th Division reported a loss of 24 killed, 101 wounded, and 26 missing.[315]

7 June

During the night of 6–7 June the combat in the south end of the Bois de Belleau continued.[316] Officers of the 6th Regiment, surveying the situation in the early hours of the 7th, decided that things looked better than they had the night before.[317] Fourth Brigade, studying its front lines, decided to straighten the angle immediately to the east of Hill 142, where the 1/5 now lay with its right flank sharply refused; and to this end a new attack was ordered on the Square patch of woods at 174.2 — 264.0, where the Germans still held out.[318] In the south end of the Bois de Belleau, the 3/6, Major Sibley, made some readjustments, and prepared to renew its efforts against the German machine guns which had halted it the night before.[319]

There had been heavy fire on the Wood all night, from both American and German guns, and the 3/6 records the distress it suffered from the fumes of high explosive, which hung thickly in the dense underbrush.[320] The Germans, especially their ration details and rear echelons, were harassed by

---

313 Adjutant and Inspector, U.S. Marine Corps.
314 War Diary and annexes, 237th DI, 6 June. (Report of 9 June)
315 War Diary and annexes 10th DI, 6 June. Note: The Corps map and records, and the divisional maps and War Diary, 10th Division, locate and refer to Bouresches as being in the outpost zone. The War Diary of the 10th Division on 6 June, however, states that the right flank of the 398th Regiment was forced out of Bouresches, and shifted its main battle position to the railroad embankment east of the village.
316 War Diary, 2nd Division, 7 June.
317 Lee to 4th Brigade, 6:50 am, 7 June, 6th Regt.
318 War Diary, 4th Brigade, 7 June.
319 History 3/6, 7 June pg's 21-22. War Diary, 2nd Division, 7 June.
320 History 3/6, 7 June, pg's 21-22. War Diary, 4th Brigade, 7 June.

artillery directed upon the center and north of the wood, and the approaches to it.[321]

The 80th Company, Captain [*Bailey M.*] Coffenberg, now the only company of 2/6 not yet engaged, had taken position after midnight in support of 3/6 astride the Lucy-Bouresches road, having been ordered by Major Holcomb at 1:30 am to connect up between Bouresches and Major Sibley's 3/6. Major Sibley moved it from the Lucy-Bouresches road to the southeast corner of the wood on Hill 181.[322]

The Battalion Adjutant of the 3/6 was sent back to 4th Brigade Headquarters to explain the situation in the woods. The Battalion Quartermaster, [*First*] Lieutenant [*Hugh*] McFarland, with three of his men, in an effort to get food up to the 3/6, were caught by shellfire on the Lucy-Bouresches road and wounded. Two companies of the 2nd Engineers, Major [*Milo P.*] Fox, reported to Major Sibley and took position on the right rear of the Battalion. The 82nd and 83rd Companies, disposed in close contact with the enemy along the ledges from Hill 181 to the southeastern corner of the wood, dug in and improved their arrangements. These companies were much exhausted and generally without rations, although Ford trucks had made, before daylight, a run into Bouresches by the Lucy road, and delivered food and ammunition to the companies there.[323]

In the afternoon, Major Sibley was notified that he would attack again early on 8 June, and was ordered to Brigade Headquarters for detailed Instructions.[324]

---

321   *War Diary, 237th DI, 7 June. War Diary, 4th Brigade, 7 June.*
322   *CO 2/6 [Holcomb] to 4th Brig., 1:30 am, 7 June-4th Brig., Vol. 4.*
323   *History 3/6, pg's 20-21.*
324   *CO 2/6 to 4th Brig. 1:30 am, 7 June-4th Brig., Vol. 4.*

Twelve

3rd Brigade — 6 June

23rd Infantry

With the return of the 23rd Infantry to the 2nd Division, on 5 June, the organization of Brigade sectors as set forth in Field Order 8, 2nd Division was carried into effect.[325]

Under Field Order 12, 3rd Brigade, 7:30 pm, 6 June, the details of the Infantry organization were confirmed. The 9th Infantry was left in the sector which it had originally occupied, from Le Thiolet on the Paris-Metz road to the right boundary of the Division, its line covering the Bois de la Marette and running to a point on the highway 200 metres northeast of Bourbetin.* The 23rd Infantry covered the Bois des Clerembauts north of the highway, its line in the eastern face of the woods, and extending to the flank of the 4th Brigade at Triangle Farm. The 15th Field Artillery lay behind the 3rd Brigade, with designated elements of the 17th Field Artillery Regiment. The 1/2 Engineers was detailed to the Brigade. Each infantry regiment had its regimental machine gun company, and Company D, 5th Machine Gun Battalion was assigned to the 9th Infantry: Company C, to the 23rd. One infantry battalion was allotted to Division reserve, and Brigade reserve consisted of an infantry battalion, with two companies of the 5th Machine Gun Battalion (A and B) and the engineers of 1/2 not engaged in construction work on the front. Brigade reserve was stationed

---

325 F.O. 8, 2nd Division, 10:00 am, 5 June, Vol. 1.
*Spelled Bourbelin on French hachured maps used by division before Plan Directeur 1/20000 was issued. Spelled Bouretin in F.O. 12, 3rd Brigade and in most official communications.

112   Chapter Twelve

at Coupru, with 2 infantry companies forward in the redoubt at Hill 201. The order provided for the relief of the French dismounted cavalry which had been holding the forward edge of the Bois de la Marette. Each infantry regiment occupied its line with two battalions, organized in depth. The 9th had in line the 1/9 and 2/9:[326] 3/9, under Lieutenant Colonel [*Alfred C.*] Arnold, constituted Brigade reserve. The 23rd placed in position, from left to right, 1/23 and 3/23, 2/23 going to Division reserve at La Longue Farm.[327]

On 6 June, all the dispositions enjoined in F.O. 12 were already in force, except the relief of the French dismounted cavalry, which was ordered for the night of June 6–7.[328] The 23rd Infantry had marched directly from the French area on the left, and took over the Le Thiolet-Triangle line from the 2/6 Marines during the night of June 5–6.[329]

The 23rd had come in after midnight. Some of its officers had looked over the position during the afternoon of 5 June, but there had been no opportunity for reconnaissance or examination of the foreground. Each battalion placed two companies in line and two in support and reserve. Three/23, Major [*Charles B.*] Elliott, held its front with Companies K and M; I Company was near the southwest corner of the Bois de Clerembauts, and L Company was south of the highway, a kilometre to the rear. The Battalion PC, with the dressing station and attached special troops, was located just off the highway at the southwest corner of the Wood. An outpost was stationed in the Bois de Bourbetin, 400 metres east of the battalion front. The arrangements of 1/23, Major [*Edmund C.*] Waddill, were similar, and the battalion was in liaison with the flank company of 2/6, the 78th, Captain Messersmith, which prolonged the line from Triangle Farm. In addition to C Company of the 5th Machine Gun Battalion, 4 guns of the 6th Machine Gun Battalion had been left near Triangle by the Marines.[330]

On the front of the 23rd Infantry, extending from Bouresches to the Bois de la Roche, were the 398th and 47th Regiments of the German 10th Division. The 231st Division joined at Vaux. The 10th Division lay in the lines which it had established on 2 June and 3 June, its outpost zone following the Bouresches-Vaux road to the road-fork 400 metres north of Hill 192, including the Bois de la Cote 192, and angling back to la Roche. The main battle position was based on the metre-gauge railway which paralleled the Vaux-Bouresches road. It was held in strength, and powerfully commanded by the high ground beyond it. Patrol reports of the German

326 *F.O. 12, 3rd Brigade, 7:30 pm, 6 June, Vol. 2.*
327 Ibid.
328 Ibid.
329 *War Diary, 23rd Infantry, 6 June. (Also regiment history)*
330 Ibid. *War Diary, 2nd Division, 5-6 June, Vol. 6. History, 6th M.G. Bn.*

regiments indicate that they were thoroughly familiar with the ground between the lines, as far as the west edge of the Bois de Bourbetin.[331]

The 3rd Brigade received, on 6 June, no information of the movements of the 4th Brigade, until the early afternoon, when arrangements were being made for the attack on the Bois de Belleau. Brigade was then directed to send a staff officer to Division Headquarters for orders and Major [*Charles P.*] Hall, Brigade Adjutant, was despatched. He returned with information outlining the plans of the 4th Brigade, and the intention of Division concerning the Infantry Brigade, which were expressed by [*Brigadier*] General [*Edward M.*] Lewis in 3rd Brigade Field Order 13, issued at 3:15 pm, 6 June.[332] This order is quoted verbatim:

> "1. The 4th Brigade attacks at 5:00 pm today in the direction of Bouresches.
>
> 2. The 23rd Infantry will maintain close tactical liaison during the attack, advancing the left battalion where necessary to prevent a reentrant angle in the line near Triangle Farm.
>
> 3. The Brigade Reserve, 3rd Brigade, will be kept well in hand during the attack for use at any time if called upon.
>
> " /s/ E.M. Lewis,
> Brigadier General, N.A.
> Commanding."

It will be noted that this order was timed 1 hour and 10 minutes later than Field Order 2 of the 4th Brigade, and 1 hour and 45 minutes before zero hour for the Marine attack. Headquarters of the 3rd Brigade were at Ventelet Farm, 3 kilometres by road from Headquarters of the 23rd Infantry at Coupru, and Coupru was about 4 kilometres by road from the nearest line battalion of the regiment — 3/23, in the Bois des Clerembauts.[333]

Major Hall was sent by motor with F.O. 13 to Headquarters of the 23rd Infantry, Colonel Malone at once proceeded, by motor, Major Hall accompanying him, to the PC of his 3rd Battalion, Major Elliott, and personally communicated the orders.[334]

From this point, all subsequent orders were given verbally. The map used by Colonel Malone, on which he indicated to Major Elliott the advance the 3/23 was to make, is available for reference.[335]

---

331 *War Diary and annexes, 10th DI, 6 June.*
332 *Report of operation 6 June, CG 3rd Brig., 7 June, to 2nd Div., 3rd Brigade, Vol. 6. Major General E.M. Lewis to 2nd Division Historical Section, 15 February 1929.*
333 *See map Chateau Thierry 1/20000.*
334 *Report of the operations, 23rd Infantry, 6 June, dated 11 June, Vol. 7.*
335 *Section of hachured map, Chateau Thierry-1/20000, 2nd Div. file.*

The line of the 23rd Infantry ran almost north and south from Le Thiolet to Triangle Farm. From Triangle Farm, the line of the Marine Brigade ran west and little north towards Lucy (about west-northwest) If the Marine right went forward to Bouresches, a slight reentrant angle might have been formed between the village and the left flank of the 23rd.

A few hundred metres south of Bouresches on the Bouresches-Vaux road, an unimproved road branches off and goes directly south to the northeast corner of the Bois de Clerembauts where it intersects an unimproved road running from Triangle Farm to Hill 192. Colonel Malone indicated, on his map, a line, angling forward from Triangle Farm, and traced about 100 metres in advance of these roads and parallel to them, as far as the northern tip of the Bois de Bourbetin, stopping west of Hill 192. He ordered Major Elliott to advance the left of his battalion to the line indicated, cautioning him that his right would hold its present position.[336] *–** Colonel

---

336 Letter, Maj-Gen. Paul B. Malone to 2nd Division Historical Section, 12 Dec. 1928. This letter follows in all essential respects Malone's Operation Report, 23rd Infantry, 6 June, 1918, dated 11 June, 1918, Vol. 7. The time element is authenticated by all available data in Division records. Col. Malone reached Elliott at or about 4:15 pm, proceeded immediately to Waddill, who was perhaps 1400 metres north; and finished communicating the instructions at or about 4:55 pm. One detail is confusing: the only Marines advancing within his probable range of vision were those of the 96th Company, which at 4:45 pm was moving from the Bois des Clerembauts toward the Bois de Triangle, by La Cense ravine. The Bois de Triangle and the Bois de Bocage cut off view to the north, where 3/6 was then attacking. Some elements of the 78th (right flank) Company of 2/6 may have been readjusting themselves, but this company did not advance until about dark, and then not in attack.

* Major Elliott, commanding 3/23, is not in agreement with the foregoing statement of orders as received by him. In a statement to the Historical Section, 2nd Division, on 15 November, 1928, he says that, at 4:15 pm, on 6 June, Col. Malone came to his PC and said to him, "you attack at 5:00 pm," and indicated Hill 192 as his objective. Major Elliott understood these orders to be peremptory, although he represented to Col. Malone the time given-45 minutes-was insufficient for preparation, that the objective was useless and untenable. He says that he received no instructions regarding cooperation with 1/23, other than that it would advance also. He did not understand the movement to depend in any way upon the action of the Marines. He had never had opportunity to reconnoiter the ground over which he advanced.

** Study of the 3rd Brigade Field Order 13, shows that the 23rd Infantry was charged with one definite mission: it was to "maintain close tactical liaison during the attack." At 5:00 pm, this liaison existed at Triangle Farm, and the Marines on Station there never moved, so it continued to exist. F.O. 13 enjoined a conditional mission: "advancing the left battalion where necessary to prevent a reentrant angle in the line near Triangle Farm." It appears, then, that the actual and collective mission of the 23rd Infantry was merely to observe the movement of the flank of the 4th Brigade with action to be taken only in case of an anticipated development. The anticipated development did not take place. This movement resolves itself into a study of the different interpretations placed on Colonel Malone's orders by the Battalion Commanders who received them, and on a consideration of Colonel Malone's orders as set down by him in his report, and the objective line marked on his map.

Malone reached the Elliott PC at 4:15 pm, and as soon as he had given his orders, he went hastily to Major Waddill, reaching him at 4:30 pm, near Triangle Farm, and gave him similar instructions regarding 1/23, except that Major Waddill was told that he would advance with the Marines on his left. Colonel Malone finished his instructions to the Waddill battalion at 4:55 pm. He saw the Marine advance, north of Triangle Farm, begin at 5:00 o'clock. Observing that the support company of 1/23 was stationary, he sent a runner to inquire why it was not moving forward, and received word by runner that the Marines on Waddill's left were standing fast. Colonel Malone then sent an order, verbally, by the same runner, directing Major Waddill not to advance unless the Marines, with whom he was in contact, went forward. After watching the Marines for some minutes, Colonel Malone, with the Brigade Adjutant, left the field and proceeded to Brigade Headquarters, where he was summoned for conference.[337] *–**

The actions of Major Elliott and Major Waddill, in execution of the orders given by Colonel Malone, differed widely. Major Elliott understood his attack orders to be unconditional, and believed his objective to be Hill 192 immediately notified his company commanders of the mission of the battalion, ordered his reserve company, L, south of the Highway, to come forward, and his support company, I, to advance to the front line. His battalion dressing station was ordered to move up with the advance. His line companies K and M, were quickly formed for attack and, by extraordinary efforts he got K and M in motion by 5 o'clock, Captain [Frank C.] Valentine, on the left, and M, Captain [James O., Jr.] Green on the right. K Company was charged with the additional duty of maintaining contact with 1/23, which, Major Elliott expected, would advance at 5:00 also.[338]

Three/23 burst into the open from the Bois des Clerembauts and went forward, rapidly, coming under very heavy machine gun fire from the start, and receiving the attention of the German artillery immediately afterwards, for the Germans had perfect observation of every stage of the movement. Then the advance passed the Bois de Bourbetin, and came upon Hill 192, the whole German line from Bouresches to Vaux blazed upon it, and the German infantry laid down such a heavy fire that they expended, by nightfall, all their small-arms ammunition, and the 6th Grenadiers, resting in the rear, had to be formed for carrying parties to supply the rifles and machine guns of the 47th and 398th Regiments The fact that the infantry expended their entire stock of cartridges is noted in the records of the 10th Division as unusual.[339]

337   Ibid.
338   Major Elliott to 2nd Div. Historical Section.
339   War Diary and annexes, 10th DI, 6 June 1918.

116   Chapter Twelve

At 6:00 pm, Major Elliott was able to locate the German machine guns firing from the metre-gauge railway, and he sent for his battalion one-pounders and trench mortars.[340] As these auxiliaries hurried up to his battalion PC, now established in the edge of the Bois de Bourbetin the area was heavily shelled, and [First] Lieutenant [Gordon] Kaemmerling, commanding the special weapons, was killed. The Battalion Medical Officer Captain [William G.] Hearington [sic Herrington], was also killed, the French Officer attached to the Battalion was wounded, and numerous casualties occurred in the Battalion Headquarters group.[341] At 6:40, Major Elliott, having moved back to a less exposed point near the Bois des Clerembauts, reported to Colonel Malone that he was heavily engaged but holding his ground.[342] At 7:30, his line was facing the Bois de la Cote 192, south of the metre-gauge railway, with both flanks in the air: he had his rear and left elements seeking contact with 1/23.[343] At 7:40 his advance was able to locate, from Hill 192, German machine guns along the line of the railroad, and he asked, through Colonel Malone, for artillery fire upon the enemy positions. The enemy line, he reported, ran from Hill 192 towards la Roche.[344] Five minutes later he ordered his support company, I, into line on his left, now deeply refused in an endeavor to guard that flank and make contact with 1/23. At 8:15, he asked regimental headquarters for support.[345] At 8:55, I company, part of which had emerged from the Bois des Clerembauts and worked northward reported contact with the Waddill battalion. At 9:10 he ordered Captain Smith of the regimental machine gun company to support I company on the battalion left.[346]

All messages from Major Elliott went back by runner, and reached him through the same medium since there was not enough wire for the field telephone to extend from his old PC to the front.[347] About 9:15 or 9:30, 3/23 appears to have established parts of M and K Companies on Hill 192, the advance reaching and crossing the road which passed through the western end of the woods that stand just east of the Hill. Germans of the 47th Regiment were encountered in these woods: an officer was captured, and one machine gun was taken and sent back by M Company. The battalion right was wide open. The left was refused sharply and had liaison with 1/23 east

---

340 Elliott to Kaemmerling, 6:00 pm, 6 June, Vol. 5.
341 Major Elliott to 2nd Div. Historical Section.
342 Elliott to Malone, 6:40 pm, 6 June, Vol. 5.
343 Elliott to Malone, 7:30 pm, 6 June, Vol. 5.
344 Elliott to Malone, 7:40 pm, 6 June, Vol. 5.
345 Legg to Elliott, 8:55 pm, 6 June, Vol. 5.
346 Elliott to Smith, 9:20 pm, 6 June, Vol. 5.
347 Elliott to Malone, 6:40 pm, 6 June, Vol. 5.

of the Bois des Haies, near the small ravine leading down towards the Bouresches-Vaux Road. Heavy casualties had occurred, particularly in M Company.[348]

Major Waddill, on the left of 3/23, understood his attack orders to be conditional upon the advance of the Marines on his left. He ordered his B and D Companies, supported by attached engineers to advance with the Marines, and held them in readiness until 6:30, when he received word from the Marines that no advance would be undertaken by them. Later, he saw, from the high ground near the Triangle, troops on the ridge north of Hill 192, and he decided to connect up with them, leaving his left flank exposed. The men he saw were Elliott's, probably K Company. He ordered his battalion to advance at 7:00 o'clock, and worked forward until 9:30, when be dug in, on a line from the ridge north of 192 to a point east of Triangle Farm,[349] under machine gun fire from the Bois de Bouresches. D, B, and finally A Companies were fed into the line. About dark, the enemy fire was so heavy that he refused his left flank towards Triangle Farm and the position of the Marines.[350] One/23 did not at any point come to close contact with the Germans.[351]

Colonel Malone, after giving his orders to his front line battalions between 4:15 and 5:00 pm, proceeded in obedience to orders, to a conference at Brigade headquarters. In the course of the conference, he mentioned the movement which he had ordered, and which was then in progress. He was informed by the Brigade Commander that no such advance by the 23rd was contemplated, unless it became necessary to straighten out a reentrant angle incident to the 4th Brigade attack. Colonel Malone at once transmitted orders, by telephone, to stop the advance where it then was.[352] But, by that time, Major Elliott and Major Waddill were out of reach of the telephone, both their battalions were engaged, and communications had to be relayed forward by runner, through the inevitable confusion in the rear of an action.

At 9:35 an order from Colonel Malone directed Major Elliott to hold his present position, and report his location, for the information of the supporting artillery.[353] At 9:41, Colonel Malone ordered Major Waddill to maintain close liaison with the Marine flank, and to report his location to the

---

348 Malone to CG 3rd Brigade, 6:15 am, 7 June, Vol. 5.
349 Line of 23rd Inf. at farthest advance is given in War Diary, 3rd Brigade, 6 June, as 177.7-260.2 to 178.4-258.8, Chateau Thierry 1/20000.
350 CO, 1/23 to Malone, rec'd 1:45, 7 June, Vol. 5.
351 Operation report, 1/23 to CO 23, 7 June, Vol. 5.
352 Operation report, CG 3rd Brig. to CO 2nd Div., 7 June, Vol. 6.
353 Malone to Elliott, 9:35 pm, 6 June, Vol. 5.

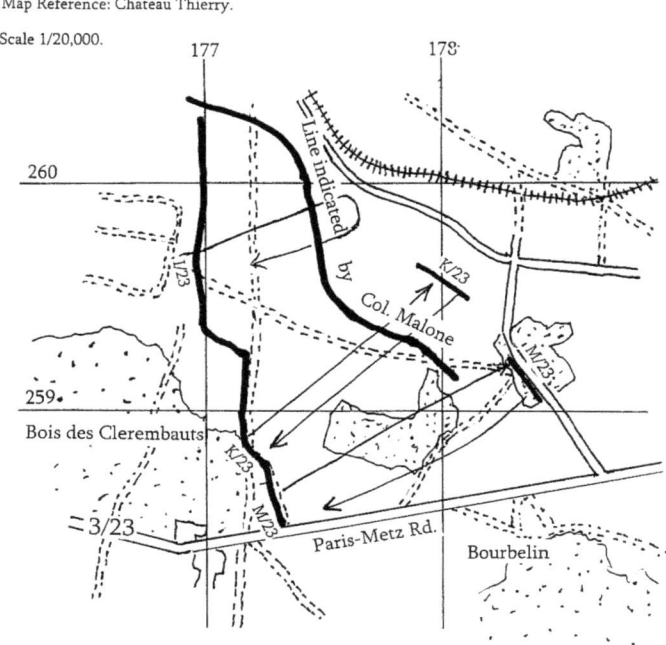

23rd Infantry, 5 PM 6 June — 3:45 AM 7 June.

Map 6

artillery.[354] These messages, sent forward from Coupru by motorcycle, had to be forwarded to the advanced PCs of the officers concerned. At 10:55,[355] Major Elliott was ordered by his Colonel to "use utmost endeavor to restore the situation and get your battalion back to its original position by dawn." It is quite possible that this message, started from Coupru, did not reach Major Elliott before midnight.*

At about the time it was issued, 1/23 and the left of 3/23 were readjusting their lines in less advanced positions, and digging in under fire, some distance east of Triangle Farm. At 11:30 pm, 2 companies of the Brigade Reserve were sent forward under Major [Alfred C.] Arnold.[356]

The final phases of the action are obscure. Both battalions were fighting on ground that they had never seen before, and their locations are con-

354 Malone to Waddill, 9:41 pm, 6 June, Vol. 5.
355 Malone to Elliott, 10:55 pm, 6 June, Vol. 5.
* Note: These messages are timed on leaving Coupru: not on receipt. From Coupru to Elliott's advanced PC was between 7 and 8 kilometres (nearly five miles) and the last kilometre had to be covered on foot. 1 hour for delivery is a safe estimate.
356 War Diary, 3rd Brigade, June 6, June 7, Vol. 6.

sequently indefinite. It is evident, however, from the German records, that 3/23 was able to occupy the western part of the Bois de la Cote 192, on the front of the 47th Regiment, and at 1:00 am, (2:03 am, German time) the 47th Regiment counterattacked from the north and forced the Americans out of the woods and back upon the Hill, capturing 4 soldiers of the 23rd Infantry. Following this attack, it was reported that the line of the 23rd Infantry was broken; but the Germans did not press the attack beyond the recovery of their own positions, and moved 2 battalions of the 6th Grenadiers up as reinforcement south of Bouresches.[357]

Three/23 maintained itself with the forces in hand, not finding it necessary to call on the reserves. Major Elliott disengaged his companies and fell back on the Bois des Clerembauts, and Colonel Malone reported to Brigade that the PCs of both 1/23 and 3/23 were reestablished in their old positions at 3:15 am.[358] The first reports of casualties from 3/23 were alarming: M and K Companies were rumored to be almost destroyed.[359] By daylight, however, more men turned up, and Major Elliott reorganized his battalion sector without assistance, the two reserve companies being returned to Brigade. I Company had been lightly engaged, and L Company not engaged at all, and they occupied the battalion front M and K were stationed in support.[360] Major Waddill took up his former lines without incident. His battalion had at no time been heavily engaged and his losses were 1 killed, 1 missing, and 11 wounded. The losses of 3/23 brought the regimental casualty list up to 27 killed and 225 wounded or missing, officers and men.[361] The weight of the losses fell in M Company of the Elliott battalion, which reached the Bois de la Cote 192. Unburied dead from its fight were found in front of the woods when 3/23, on 1 July, attacked across the same ground in the Vaux operation.[362]

At dawn, 7 June, the 23rd Infantry held the lines occupied at 5:00 pm, the day before.

---

357   *War Diary and annexes, 10th DI, 6 June, 7 June.*
358   *Malone to 3rd Brigade, 3:15 am, 7 June, Vol. 5.*
359   *Operations report CO 23rd to 3rd Brigade for 6 June, dated 11 June, Vol. 7.*
360   *War Diary, 3rd Brigade, June, June 7, Vol. 6.*
361   *Col. Malone to Brigade CC, 11 June (on report 23rd, 6 June, Vol. 7). Brigade Commanders estimate on 6 June was 15 officers and 288 men.*
362   *Major Elliott to 2nd Div. Historical Section. There has been some controversy as to the responsibility for movement of the 23rd Infantry. Major Hall, in the 3rd Brigade History, ascribes it to a general misunderstanding of orders, and charges the losses to "lack of experience, lack of time for preparation and, lack of information as to what the 4th Brigade was doing." General Ely, in his report on 3rd Brigade Operations, 1 June-15 July, states that a copy of 4th Brigade F.O. 2 of 6 June was not received by 3rd Brigade until 2:00 am, 7 June. Study of 4th Brigade intentions, and, of the map, leads to the conclusion that the possibility of a reentrant angle being formed was exceedingly remote.*

Chapter Twelve

9th Infantry

The 6th of June held yet another event for the 2nd Division: in the afternoon, Division Headquarters was informed that the French XXXVIII Corps, on the right, was to advance on the north bank of the Marne. On the adjoining flank of the XXXVIII Corps, in liaison with the flank of the 9th Infantry, was the 10th Colonial Division, General Marchand, attached to which was the 30th U.S. Infantry of the American 3rd Division. At 4:20 pm, Division Headquarters received details of the projected movement from XXI Corps. The 10th Colonials, in the sector Saulchery north of the Marne, would attack Hill 204, advancing their left flank past Monneaux. The right of the 2nd Division would maintain liaison with this advance, establishing a new flank halfway between Monneaux and Vaux, its line following the ravine that leads east from Bourbetin to the Vaux-Monneaux road.[363]

Brigadier General Lewis was advised of the movement at 4:30 pm, the execution of the part assigned to the 2nd Division fell upon the 9th Infantry. Colonel Upton at once made his preparation, getting in personal touch with the Colonel of the neighboring French 53rd Colonial Regiment.[364] Zero hour was 9:30 pm. The French started to climb the lower slopes of Hill 204, and the 9th Infantry pivoted forward on Bourbetin, moving out of the Bois de la Marette and the old line of the French dismounted cavalry, this night relieved. Generally, the movement was unopposed except for routine harassing artillery fire at 12:12 am, 7 June, 3rd Brigade reported to Division that the right battalion of the 9th was on its objective and digging in. Some difficulty followed in the establishment of liaison. Contact was not maintained during the advance[365] and when the objective was reached, the flank of the 10th Colonials could not be found. Elements of the 30th Infantry had been expected on that side, and an officer sent by Colonel Upton to look for them learned that while the 30th had been alerted, it had taken no part in the advance and had gone back to its billets.[366] The 9th proceeded, however, to organize the new line, which ran at almost right angles to the old one, from a point on the Vaux-Monneaux road half-way between those villages, to the Paris-Metz road 40 metres east of Le Thiolet, covering the Bois de la Marette and Bourbetin, and based on the Bourbetin ravine. About 3 o'clock in the morning of 7 June, contact was firmly established with the

---

363 *War Diary, 2nd Division, 6 June, Vol. 6. XXI Corps PC/84, 6 June. Operations report 3rd Brigade to 2nd Div., 7 June, Vol. 6.*
364 *Col. Upton to 3rd Brigade, 8:05 pm, 6 June, Vol. 5.*
365 *War Diary, 2nd Division, 6 June, Vol. 6.*
366 *3rd Brigade to 2nd Div., 12:12 am, 7 June, Vol. 4.*

Others lay on the ground

10th Colonials.[367] The 9th Infantry had 76 casualties, largely from artillery fire, during the advance.[368] Vaux, at this time was not included in the German main line of resistance, nor does the German 231st Division appear to have carried out much organization on Hill 204.[369]

---

367 *General Lewis to 2nd Div., 1:40 am, 7 June, Vol. 4.*
368 *War Diary, 2nd Div., 6-7 June: also War Diary, 9th Inf. and War Diary, 3rd Brigade.*
369 *War Diary and annexes, 231st DI, 1-15 June.*
Note: 'Then the 201st Division relieved the 231st in the Vaux-Hill 204 positions, they complained that nothing in the way of sector organization had been done, and that they were obliged to construct a new front.

Thirteen
Relief of 10th and 197th Divisions, 7–9 June

During the period 7–9 June, the German IV Reserve Corps relieved two of its divisions on the front of the 2nd Division. The 197th Division, in line from Torcy westward, had been hard hit on the 6th June by the 5th Marines and by the French 167th Division, and that portion of the Clignon Line which it held was seriously threatened. The 5th Guards Division was in Corps Reserve, resting after its toils in the Chemin des Dames drive. As early as the afternoon of the 6th, some of its battalions were brought up to the rear of the 197th, and about 7–8 June, it replaced the 197th in the line, the 237th Division having already extended its right to include Torcy when the 197th was hard-pressed on the 6th.[370]

The German 10th Division, in line from the Bois de Belleau south, lost Bouresches. It had been in line since May 27, and was exhausted. The 28th Division, a Baden regular formation of high reputation, but also much exhausted from the late offensive, relieved it during 7–9 June, taking over the sector the forenoon of 9 June.[371]

In the progress of these relief's, a readjustment of the Corps line was effected. The 231st Division, in line from Chateau Thierry and Hill 204 to Vaux, extended its left, taking over with its 444th Regiment a portion of the 10th Division front. The 28th in turn extended its left beyond the former limits of the 10th Division, relieving those elements of the 237th Division in line across the southern portion of the Bois de Belleau, which shortened the front of the left regiment of the 237th by the width of a battalion — in this case, some five hundred yards.[372]

370 *War Diary, 197th DI, 6 June, also [on] 5th, 28th DI.*
371 *War Diary, 10th DI, 7-9 June, also 28th DI.*
372 *War Diary, 197th DI, 6 June, also [on] 5th, 28th DI.*

The regiment of the 237th thus relieved was the 461st, Major Bischoff, which had held the wood against the attacks of the 3/6 and 3/5 on 6 June, and the second attack by the 3/6 on 8 June. Liaison with the 398th Regiment of the 10th Division had been near the southeastern corner of the wood. In the organization of the 461st, six infantry companies, backed up by six heavy machine guns, with reserve closely echeloned with in the wood, had been disposed in the positions which the 28th Division now assumed. These arrangements were thoroughly tested by the assaults of the Marines and they were adequate. But the 28th Division changed them.[373]

The 40th Fusilier Regiment of the 28th Division went into line from about the Bouresches Railroad Station to the western face of the Bois de Belleau, joining the 461st Regiment just north of Hill 181. In front of Bouresches it placed its third battalion and within the wood, the 2/40. Here, where the 461st had employed six companies, it employed two, the 8/40 and 7/40 The other two were located well to the rear, the 5/40 on the east edge of the wood, and the 6/40 on the metre-gauge railroad further to the east. Two heavy machine guns and 3 minenwerfers were stationed in the wood, and two more heavy machine guns east of the Bouresches-Belleau road. The 461st Regiment left behind, for 24 hours, six of its heavy machine guns.[374]

These dispositions wore vigorously protested by Major Bischoff, who carried his complaint far as his Division Commander. Two companies, he insisted, were not enough to hold that line; and the battalion reserves of the 2/40 were too far to the rear to be of any value in counter attack. He pointed out that the dense woods necessitated a strongly-held line, with reserves in close support. His protests were disregarded by the 28th Division, and he was advised that Corps had approved the plans for the new organization, and that it would remain in effect with the forces at his disposal. He set about the organization of a switch line, running east and west across the wood, to cover his left flank and rear.[375] His front extended along the western face of the Bois de Belleau, making contact with the 462nd Regiment in the high ground east of Torcy. His regimental reserve he placed in Belleau and in the northern end of the wood.[376]

These relief's were effected by the Germans during the nights of 7, 8, and 9 June, in good order as far as the front lines were concerned; but they

---

373 *Annexes to War Diary, 237th DI, reports 461 RI, 1-15 June.*
374 *Situation map, 28th DI, 9 June (annexes to War Diary).*
375 *Colonel Otto, Reichsarchiv, 2nd Div. file.*
376 *Annexes to War Diary, 237th DI reports, 461 RI, 15 June.*

A sprinkling of old-time Marines

note heavy losses from harassing artillery fire, through their rear areas and along all approaches to the front, both outgoing and incoming troops suffering casualties beyond expectation.[377]

   377   *War Diary, 10th DI, 5th Guards DI, 237th DI, 28th DI, 97th DI, 7-9 June.*

Fourteen

Bouresches and Bois de Belleau

2nd Attack on Bois de Belleau by 3/6 on 8 June

At 12:30 am 8 June the Bouresches defense reported an attack on that village, and heavy fire was laid upon its approaches by the machine guns assigned to its support, and by the divisional artillery, and by the Marines of the 6th Regiment in the town. The Germans effected no contact with the place.[378]

During the night of 7–8 June, Major Sibley completed within the south face of the Bois de Belleau his arrangements for renewing the attack on the German positions in front of him. Elements of the 83rd Company, which had passed the southeastern corner of the wood during the fighting of the 6th, were withdrawn, and the 82nd Company formed the right of the battalion, extending into the woods from the southeast corner. The 83rd Company was placed on the left. Behind the left flank with orders to cover its advance, were 2 platoons of the 80th Company (2/6), now attached to the 3/6, and with them a detachment of the 2nd Engineers. The remaining two platoons of the 80th Company, with another detachment of the 2nd Engineers, were in battalion reserve, alone the ravine in rear of the center. A detail of Engineers was told off to extend along the eastern edge of the wood as the attack progressed, there being as yet no liaison with Bouresches.[379] The 84th and 97th Companies of the 3/6 were in Bouresches and in supporting positions south of the town, under the order of Major Holcomb.[380]

To prepare the attack, the Stokes Mortar Platoon of the 6th Regiment,

---

378 *War Diary, 4th Brigade,* 7-8 June.
379 History 3/6, pg 23-26. Adjutant, 6th Regiment.
380 Hist. 3/6, pg 19-26.

Headquarters Company, was sent up, and opened fire within the wood. Arrangements were completed by 3:00 am. The attack started at 4:00 am.[381]

The two attacking companies were formed in waves. They went forward, finding that the Stokes Mortar bombardment which preceded them had been ineffective: the brush was very thick and there was no possibility of accurate spotting. A great volume of machine gun fire assailed them, and the Germans of the 461st Regiment defended their positions with rifles and hand grenades, from the rocky ledges in the center. Four machine guns were captured, at a heavy cost in casualties. The combat went on, some progress being made, until 8:30 am. The Marines found that as soon as they took a machine gun, fire was opened on it from another in a flanking position.[382]

The first reports received by Brigade Headquarters were encouraging. Wounded coming back said that the machine gun positions were being enveloped and destroyed.[383] Captain Zane, in Bouresches, could hear the yells of the Marines fighting in the wood, and stood by to fire on the east edge of it, above Bouresches, if targets offered.[384] But at 10:27 Major Sibley reported to Lieutenant Colonel Lee: "They are too strong for us. Soon as we take one machine gun, another opens." Unable to get ahead, and finding his ground untenable, he withdrew his companies in good order, the 83rd covering the 82nd as it fell back, and then in turn joining it. The line was reestablished in the positions held the night before.[385] One platoon of the 97th Company was sent up as reinforcement.[386]

At 12:30 pm, General Harbord directed Major Sibley to withdraw his battalion to cover in the south edge of the woods, so that artillery could shell the Germans out: and Major Sibley would report the hour by which this withdrawal could be accomplished.[387] At 2:30 he received Major Sibley's reply; the battalion would be in the ravine, about 125 yards from the south edge of the woods, by 3:00 pm. He added that his men were much exhausted and in need of food.[388] Both American and German artillery were now firing heavily on the wood.[389] The first battalion of the 6th Marines was available from reserve, and at 6:22 pm General Harbord advised Major Hughes, commanding the 1/6, that he was relieved from Corps reserve, and would enter the line to relieve the 3/6, in the south edge of the Bois de Belleau.[390] In a note to Major

381 Hist. 3/6, pg 6-23.
382 History 3/6, pg 23-26.
383 Adjutant, 6th Regiment to 4th Brigade, 5:45 am, June, Vol. 5.
384 Adjutant, 6th Regiment to 4th Brigade, 6:58 am, June, Vol. 5.
385 Sibley to 4th Brigade, 10:27 [am,] 8 June, Vol. 5.
386 History 3/6, pg 26.
387 Harbord to Sibley, 12:30 pm, 8 June, Vol. 5.
388 Sibley to Harbord, 1:55 pm, 8 June.
389 War Diaries, American and German, 8 June.

Holcomb, the 2/6, the General advised that there would be no relief for the 2/6; that Sibley was coming out of the Bois de Belleau, and that 50 batteries would play on that wood; also that Bouresches must be held, and that arrangements had been made to place fire upon all approaches to the village in the case of an attack by the Germans.[391] At 9:40 pm, General Harbord informed Major Hughes that the Sibley Battalion would be withdrawn from the wood without relief, and the 1/6 was directed to make a reconnaissance of the wood southeast of Lucy where the 2/6 had certain of its supporting elements, with a view to placing one company there. The remainder of the 1/6 would go into the Mon Blanche wood, southwest of Lucy.[392] At 9:45 the commanding officer of the 6th Marines was notified of these arrangements.[393]

Meantime, at 8:30 pm, Major Sibley was advised that 1/6 would relieve him. Later he was ordered to withdraw without relief, and during the night he proceeded with three companies, the 97th, 83rd, and 82nd, to the Bois Platerie, going into Corps Reserve. In the Bois Platerie the 3/6 received a replacement of 6 officers and 128 men, and had its first hot food since 31 May. Its casualties, to date, had been 42 percent of its officers and 40 percent of its enlisted men, a loss of about 400 officers and men, killed, wounded, and missing.[394] Its 84th Company remained in the Triangle-to-Bouresches area until the night of June 9–10, with the 2/6.[395] The 1/6 came up, and lay in the Bois de Chatel, from which place it was reported to 4th Brigade by Lieutenant Colonel Lee on at 12:15 pm, 9 June.[396] All available artillery opened on the Bois de Belleau, and the wood was shelled steadily through the night of the 8th, on the 9th, and until the 10th.[397]

3rd Attack on Bois de Belleau

At 6:30 pm on 9 June, the 4th Brigade issued Field Order 3, which directed a third attack upon the Bois de Belleau.[398] The 1/6, Major John A. Hughes, was designated to make the attack; it then lay in the Bois de Chatel, and had

390 Harbord to Hughes, 6:22 pm, 8 June, Vol. 5.
391 Harbord to Holcomb, 9:15 [pm], 8 June, Vol. 5.
392 Harbord to Hughes, 9:40 pm, 8 June, Vol. 5.
393 Harbord to Lt. Col. Lee, 9:45 pm, 8 June, Vol. 5.
394 History 3/6, pg 27 and 30.
395 History 3/6, pg 26.
396 Lee to Harbord, 12:30 pm, 9 June, Vol. 5.
397 War Diary, 4th Brigade, 8-10 June, Vol. 6.
   Note: The Adjutant and Inspector, USMC, records the following casualties for 3/6: on 6 June, 6 officers and 126 men killed and wounded. Casualties of 2/6 on 6 June were 5 officers and 194 men killed, wounded, and gassed.
398 4th Brigade Field Order #3, 6:30 pm, 9 June, vol 2.

received, at 2:40 pm, that day, instructions from the 3rd Brigade Commander to move, after dark, to an attack position facing the south edge of the Bois de Belleau.[399] There were further adjustments within the 4th Brigade area: the 3/5, which had rested and received replacements, and was now under Major M. E. [Maurice E.] Shearer, was ordered to send one company to the woods southeast of Lucy, as regimental reserve, 5th Marines, and with the other three, after dark, to relieve the 2/6 in the line Triangle-Bouresches.[400] The 2/6, on relief, was to proceed to the wood southwest of Lucy, on the Rue Gobert.[401] On this day, also, a German prisoner was brought in who told of the relief of the 10th Division by the 28th, and of new troops in the Bois de Belleau.[402] The 167th Division on the left captured prisoners of the 5th Guards Division which had relieved the 197th Division.[403] When night fell, the 1/6 moved to its assault position without incident, reporting in place at 2:35 am.[404]

The objective assigned to the 1/6 was a line running east and west across the wood, at about the center, (X — line 261.70). The wood had been subjected to artillery fire, more or less continuously, since 6 June, 28000 75s and 6000 155s having been fired into it.[405] Twelve guns of the 6th Machine Gun Battalion were detailed to support the attack, and to lay a barrage along the eastern face of the wood from the direction of Bouresches. Four-thirty am, 10 June, was zero hour.[406] Six guns of B [23rd] Company, 6th Machine Gun Battalion, were detailed to advance with the infantry.[407]

The 1/6 started promptly: a message from Lieut. Colonel Lee at 3:50 assured Brigade Headquarters that all was in readiness.[408] The Brigade Liaison Officer with the 6th Regiment reported to the same effect at 4:29, adding that Major Cole, commanding the 6th Machine Gun Battalion, had gone forward from his PC to observe the situation with the assaulting troops.[409] At 4:51 Major Hughes, commanding the attack, reported that the barrage was effective and requested that it now fire on the machine guns which covered the line of advance.[410] At 5:20, 6th Regiment reported to 4th Brigade that all had gone well: few machine guns were firing, and the action in the wood was

---

399   *Harbord to Hughes, 2:40 pm, 9 June, Vol. 4.*
400   *Harbord to Shearer, 2:42 pm, 9 June.*
401   *Harbord to Holcomb, 2:43 pm, 9 June.*
402   *[1st] Lt. [LeRoy P.] Hunt to 4th Brigade, 9 June.*
403   *Compte render XXI CA, 9 June.*
404   *Hughes to Harbord, 2:45 am, 10 June.*
405   *Operations, 2nd FA Brigade, [Brig.] Gen. [William] Chamberlaine, Vol. 9.*
406   *FO 3, 4th Brig., 9 June, Vol. 2.*
407   *War Diary, 6th Machine Gun Bn, 10 June.*
408   *Lee to 4th Brig., 3:50 am, 10 June, Vol. 4.*
409   *[1st. Lt. William B.] Moore to Harbord, 4:29 [am], 10 June, Vol. 4.*
410   *Hughes to Harbord, 4:51 [am], 10 June, Vol. 4.*

deemed finished;[411] the assault had suffered no losses up to entering the wood.[412] From 5:20 to 5:45 other messages were received which indicated that the Bois de Belleau had been cleared, almost without resistance; but at 5:47 machine gun fire began in about the center of it.[413] At 5:50 Lieutenant Colonel Lee reported the capture of a minenwerfer 300 yards east of Hill 161;[414] later, men were sent up from the regimental reserve to bring in this minenwerfer.[415] At 6:50 Brigade Headquarters received its first report direct from the 1/6; Major Hughes, at 5:12, reported his 75th Company, Captain [*Edward C.*] Fuller, on its objective.[416] At 6:58, he reported contact with 3 machine guns in the northeastern third of the wood—(176.1–262.3).[417] Captain Fuller was attacking them, with assistance from Major Cole. At 7:34, he sent 2 stokes mortars to the 75th Company to deal with these guns.[418] At 7:56 Brigade received a report, relayed through the 6th Regiment headquarters, that Major Cole had been badly wounded in the hand and face by a machine gun.[419]

In the previous attacks on the Bois de Belleau, as in this one, Major Cole had, after disposing his guns for the problems in hand, gone forward personally and maintained observation of the stages of the fight. The earliest definite reports of the attack on the afternoon of 6 June were sent by him from the Bois de Belleau. He was on the front 8 June, with the 3/6. When he was shot on 10 June, fatally, as it developed, he was engaged in reconnoitering on the western edge of the wood, ahead of the attacking Marines His activities during his participation in the engagements around the Bois de Belleau were characterized by the greatest energy and ability.

The 1/6 reported that the artillery had blown the Bois de Belleau to mincemeat.[420] It reported also the achievement of its objective line before 8 o'clock; after that time the Bois de Belleau was characterized as quiet. It reported 32 casualties, 8 killed and 24 wounded.[421]

The records of the 237th Division note an attack on their left neighbor, the 40th Regiment, at this time,[422] which did not involve them. The 28th Division notes an attack on its 40th Regiment within the wood, and

---

411 6th Regt. to 4th Brig., 5:20 [am], 10 June, Vol. 4.
412 Hughes to Harbord, 7:12 am, 10 June, Vol. 4.
413 Lee to Harbord, 5:47 am, 10 June, Vol. 4.
414 Lee to Harbord, 5:50 am, 10 June, Vol. 4.
415 Lee to Harbord, 7:15 am, 10 June, Vol. 4.
416 Moore to Harbord, 6:50 am, 10 June, Vol. 4.
417 Moore to Harbord, 6:58 am, 10 June, Vol. 4.
418 Hughes to Harbord, 7:45 am, 10 June, Vol. 4.
419 Hughes to the 6th Regiment to the 4th Brigade, 7:56 am, 10 June, Vol. 4.
420 Hughes to the 4th Brigade, 7:12 am, 10 June, Vol. 4.
421 24 hour report, 8:00 pm, 9 June, 8:00 pm, 10 June, 4th Brigade to 2nd Div., Vol. 6.
422 War Diary, 237th DI and annexes, 461 RI, 10 June.

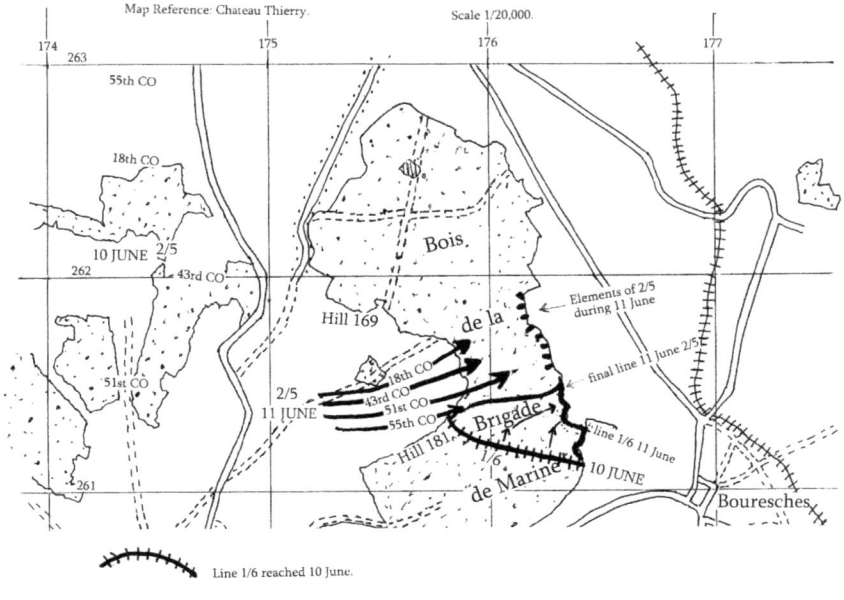

Map 7

describes the artillery and machine gun fire proceeding the attack, from which it suffered.[423] But the 40th Regiment, it asserts, lost no ground and repulsed the attacking Americans.[424] The German lines are shown in the same trace for the 10th June: on 11 June, the next day, they show the lines broken there.[425] There is no record of capture of prisoners or machine guns by the 1/6 on 10 June other than 2 minenwerfers; the weight of the evidence is that on 10 June the 1/6 succeeded only in re-occupying the old lines of the 3/6, vacated by that battalion on 8 June.

4th Attack on Bois de Belleau — 2/5 Marines

The 2/5, Lieutenant Colonel Wise, established, on 2 June, a line from Hill 142 to the northeast edge of the Bois de Veuilly, covering Les Mares Farm. Between 2 June and 5 June, the position, strengthened by the Headquarters Company, 5th Marines, and by the 1/5, as well as guns of the 6th Machine Gun Battalion, was under continuous artillery fire, and was in

---

423 *War Diary, 28th DI and annexes, 40 RI, 10 June.*
424 Ibid.
425 *Situation maps, 28th DI, 10 -11 June.*

action at long ranges with Germans of the 197th Division. At least one contact was made, on 5 June, by a patrol of the German 28th Jager Battalion, which advanced to feel the Marine position at Les Mares Farm. The casualties of 2/5 during this period are not given separately but there was a steady wastage in the command.[426] On the night 5–6 June 2/5 was relieved by the French 116th Infantry Regiment of the 167th Division, and proceeded to the Bois du Chatel, just north of the 5th Regimental Headquarters at La Voie du Chatel, being allotted to Brigade reserve. Early on 6 June, one company, the 51st, was detached by the regimental commander and sent to Major Turrill to assist the 1/5 on Hill 142. Batteries of the 12th Field Artillery were emplaced in the Bois du Chatel, and the woods came under heavy German fire during the morning. In the course of the day, 2/5, less its 51st Company, was moved forward into the Bois de Champillon, behind the line of 3/5, and remained in reserve during the evening attacks of 6 June.[427]

During the closing hours of the day, Brigade considered the employment of 2/5 on the left of Lieutenant Colonel Feland's force, for the 2nd phase of the Bois de Belleau attack. At 10:25 pm, however, with the definite abandonment of the 2nd phase, General Harbord directed Lieutenant Colonel Feland to use the Wise battalion to establish contact with the left of the Berry battalion, presumed to be near Hill 133, and the north end of the Bois de Belleau."[428]

Lieutenant Colonel Wise reports that he started at 2:00 am, 7 June, to carry out the order,[429] moving from the Bois de Champillon to the Lucy-Torcy road, and proceeding northward along the road. Dawn found his leading companies in the open, directly between the old 3/5 positions on the ridge to the west, and the Germans in the unshaken face of the Bois de Belleau to the east. A platoon of the first company, the 55th, was thrown forward as advance guard, and this group very quickly drew fire, both from the Germans in Belleau Wood, and from the Marines of 3/5, each side believing that it was

---

426 [First] Lieutenant W.[illiam] R. Mathews, USMC, Bn. Intelligence Officer, 2/5, says 2/5 lost about 25% of its strength prior to 11 June, 2nd Div. file.

427 Harbord to Feland 10:25 pm, 6 June, 4th Brig., Vol. 4.

428 Ibid. Operation Report 2/5-2 -16 June incl.-18 June, 5th Regiment, Vol. 7. See Field Messages-Larsen to Neville, Neville to Harbord, and Lee to Harbord as to situation 3/5 between 8:00 pm and 12 midnight 6 June to 2:15 am, 7 June 4th Brigade, Vol. 4.

429 Wise in O.P. 2/5-2-18 June incl.-18 June, 5th Regiment, Vol. 7 refers to "Brigade Order #83." This order is not available. [Several handwritten notes appear below this note, referring to the very existence of Brig. Order # 83. The first was by Mathews "The order did exist. I held the flashlight while Col. Wise read it. Harbord omits all reference to it in the brigade War Diary. Why?" This was followed by a note written by Harbord which rebuts Mathews. He clearly states that there was "No number 83, that it was Field Order # 3 issued on June 9th [and] referring to a third attack on Bois de Belleau. Field Order No. 4 was of June 10th." Frankly, from the available records, it appears that Harbord's memory was more substantial than either Mathews or Wise. GBC].

attacked. The company commander of the 55th Captain [*John*] Blanchfield, and his command were hit, the Captain mortally. Other casualties occurred. Two/5 was halted, its advanced elements withdrawn, and, the companies conducted to the shelter of the ridge west of the road, along which it presently extended, taking over those positions of the 3/5 which faced east. During the day, the Brigade Commander withdrew the remnants of 3/5 for rest and reorganization, the last company to be relieved being the 45th, Captain Conachy, which was replaced by the 55th, under [*First*] Lieutenant [*Elliott D.*] Cooke, [*USA*],[430] immediately after Captain Conachy had taken the square woods east of Hill 142, late in the evening of the 7th.[431]

Two/5 remained in the old 3/5 positions for 3 days, its 51st Company being returned to it on the 10th. The battalion commander reports heavy shelling, machine gun fire, and some gas. Meantime, the 3/6 made its second attempt in the southern end of the wood, and was withdrawn; and after a prolonged artillery preparation, on 9 June and during the night 9–10 June, 1/6, Major Hughes, attacked at daylight or the 10th and re-occupied the positions reached by Major Sibley.[432] Following the attack by 1/6, on the 10th, General Harbord believed that the wood was in his possession generally to the X–line 261.7 — that is to say, Hill 181 and the southern third, with a German machine gun nest protruding in his line on the eastern side.

Under this impression, 4th Brigade Headquarters, at 5:45 pm, 10 June, issued Field Order 4.

The objective given was the northeastern edge of the Bois de Belleau and Hill 153, and, the 2/5 was designated as the attacking force, with 12 machine guns in support, as assigned by the Commanding Officer of the 6th Machine Gun Battalion, and 2/6 in the woods southwest of Lucy, constituting Brigade Reserve. The sector limits for the attack were eastern, 175.4–261.7 to 176.3–262.3; and western 175.0–261.9 to 175.5–263.0. Lines projected through these points are slightly divergent, and enclose the northern third of the woods, Hill 169 lying in the right center of the approach, and, the right flank passing along the deep traversing ravine that entered the Bois de Belleau east of Hill 169. The left sector limit coincided throughout its length with the Double-Tree Road, which came down from Belleau to the Lucy-Torcy road near Hill 169. Machine guns of the Bouresches group

---

430 Succeeded Captain Blanchfield. [*Army officer Cooke rendered excellent service while with the 4th Brigade and remained with the Brigade after being wounded at Soissons. For some reason his name had consistently been spelled "Cook," without the letter "e" but all have been corrected to "Cooke." He would become a general officer in WWII. GBC*].

431 See 45th Co., 7 June.

432 Records of the 237th DI and 28th DI do not indicate that they discovered the withdrawal of Sibley. They were making a relief [*of their forces*].

would fire, for half an hour after the beginning of the assault, a barrage on the Bouresches-Chateau Belleau road east of the Wood. Artillery preparations ordered by the 2nd FA Brigade, and aviation by the French XXI Corps. Zero hour was 4:30 am, 11 June. Its objective attained, 2/5 would establish liaison on the right with 1/6, which would advance its left to conform with the progress of attack paragraph 4 of F.O. 4 directs that the objective be at once organized and held against counter- attack, with the left flank slightly refused, along the Lucy-Chateau Belleau Ravine. The last is confusing. There is no Lucy-Chateau Belleau ravine. It is possible that the road to Belleau, which branches off the Lucy-Torcy road near Hill 169, is meant.[433]

The old positions of 3/5 will be remembered: 2/5 held them unchanged, except that the 55th Company occupied the square woods east of Hill 142. During the evening of 10th June, the 20th Company of 3/5, Captain [*Richard N.*] Platt, took over the north edge of the Bois de Champillon and the liaison with 1/5 on Hill 142. The 51st Company, Captain [*Lloyd W.*] Williams, had rejoined from the west side of Hill 142. The battalion regrouped its 4 companies west of the Lucy-Torcy road, and there was a conference with the company commanders. Lieutenant Colonel Wise had already conferred with General Harbord and Colonel Neville. The attack was to be made on a 2-company front, each company in 2 waves, the 43rd, Captain Dunbeck, on the left, and the 51st, Captain Williams, on the right. The 18th, Captain [*Lester S.*] Wass, and the 55th, Lieutenant Cooke, in artillery formation (half-platoon columns), were to follow the 43rd and 51st. The general plan was to drive through to the east edge of the woods, then turn north and roll up the Germans in the west face.[434] The attack was to be a direct frontal assault, delivered across the open ground between Lucy-Torcy road and the Bois de Belleau.

---

433 Field Order #4, 4th Brigade, 5:45 pm, 10 June, Vol. 2. [*When Hughes and 1/6 went back into the southern edge of the woods, their total advance was much less than the ordered "X-line" objective. When progress was reported Hughes, unintentionally perhaps, misled Harbord with his message acclaiming success. Harbord assumed that 1/6 had reached up into the middle of the woods (at approximately 261.5-176). In fact Hughes was barely within the woods. This would cause numerous and ruinous problems in the days ahead. GBC*].

434 These details are from the notes of Lieut. W. R. Mathews, battalion intelligence officer, present at the conference. They are confirmed in essential points by statement of Lieutenant E.C. Cooke, USA, Inf., 55th Co. "Battle of Belleau Woods," 2nd Division File. No official reports exist which give the battalion order of battle, or the detailed plan of action. It is impossible to reconcile the notes of either Mathews or with Field Order 4, 4th Brigade, which directed an attack astride Hill 169, northeastward, with the left flank on the Double-Tree Road and the right flank about the traversing ravine. Yet all evidence shows that the attack was actually delivered as Lieutenants Cooke and Mathews say it was planned. The German records are entirely definite as to where the Marines struck their lines. In this connection, it may be mentioned that, in "Told by a Marine," Wise and Frost [ghost writer], cont. pg 134

Lieutenant Colonel Wise received Field Order 4 at about 10:00 pm.[435] The artillery preparation, by the 12th and elements of the 17th Field Artillery Regiments, began at 3:30 am.[436] The companies were in position at dawn facing due east and advanced promptly on zero hour, 4:30 am. A heavy mist lay in the low ground between the wood and the Lucy-Torcy road, favoring the attacking Marines, so that they covered most of the open area before the Germans machine guns came into action. Once discovered, however, they were brought under fire, and the leading waves shot to pieces, the volume of fire coming from the right front in the angle of the woods. The support companies merged quickly with the assault, and the Marines forced their way into the woods, coming to close combat with the German infantry and machine gunners.[437] When the 2 support companies came into line, the front was already much disorganized by losses and by the natural obstacles encountered at the edge of the woods, but the 18th Company seems to have swung generally to the left, extending the line to the north, while the 55th came up on the right of the 51st, making contact with a platoon of 1/6 which had been in position on the edge of the woods west of Hill 181.[438]

434 pgs 215-218, Lieutenant Colonel Wise writes that he was given a free hand by General Harbord in the planning of the attack: that he drew up a plan for an enveloping advance on the northern end of the wood by way of the wooded area north of Hill 169 (his description is vague, but north of Hill 169 lay the only sheltered approach): that he discussed with his company commanders and looked over the ground: that the Brigade Commander, in the afternoon of 10 June, approved his plan: that he made all arrangements for it: that about midnight, he received a written order from General Harbord, directing him to attack across the open ground opposite the southern half of the Bois de Belleau, a frontal attack, which he desired to avoid in drawing up his own plans: and that he made the attack as ordered by the Brigade Commander in his written order. Study of the map shows that the attack Field Order 4 directed was not delivered as therein prescribed. The advance ordered by General Harbord would have taken the battalion across Hill 169, in the woods almost all the way from the positions west of the Lucy-Torcy road to the Bois de Belleau proper. It approximates, so far as it can be ascertained from Colonel Wise's rather vague locations, the movement which he planned, and which he says he was not allowed to make. That it followed—as laid out in Field Order 4—the logical approach to the western side of the Bois de Belleau, cannot be disputed. Study of the German records (461st RI of the 237th DI) is interesting by way of speculation. Facing Hill 169, across the sector limits prescribed for 2/5 in Field Order 4, was not more than one company (2/462). The weight of the German defense lay southward, exactly where the Marine attack struck the line.

435 War Diary, 4th Brigade, 11 June.

436 Ibid and two groups of French 75's and 1 of 155's were under the orders of the 2nd Division. It is assumed that they took their part in all artillery work: but official reports of their activities do not exist, except in the data for 10 June, and 25 June, and 1 July.

437 The report of 1/461 RI, Major von Hartlieb, says there were two distinct shocks; the first repulsed, and the second successful, rolling up the left flank of his battalion. He says the mist made it possible for the Americans to approach his line. There may have been an interval between the stopping of the first wave and the arrival of the 2nd. (War Diary and annexes, 237th DI, 11 June.)

Bouresches and Bois de Belleau

The progress of the action may be traced in part from the messages sent to regimental and brigade headquarters in the hours following. At 5:00 am, Brigade was advised that all was going well.[439] At 5:45 Lieutenant Colonel Lee reported an advance of the Germans on Bouresches;[440] and at 5:55, Major Shearer, who, with elements of 3/5, now held Bouresches, requested a barrage: the Germans were advancing along the railroad track, infantry and machine guns.[441] At 6:00 am, Major Shearer reported that the Germans were attacking him: the matter was referred to the artillery.[442] At 6:11 am, the 43rd Company of 2/5 reported on its objectives.[443] and at 6:33 the 6th Regiment reported to Brigade that 2/5 had taken all its objectives; that the German attempt on Bouresches had been broken up by machine gun and artillery fire, and that the machine gun group with Major Shearer had caught the Germans retiring from the east edge of the Bois de Belleau and slaughtered them.[444] These reports were at once forwarded to Division Headquarters.

As a matter of fact, the records of the German 28th Division indicate no designs against Bouresches on 11 June: the Germans reported by Major Shearer were, in all probability, the local reserves of the battalion of the 40th Regiment in the Wood. They were stationed east of the Belleau-Bouresches road, and attempted to move forward to reinforce the front line. Their reports show that flanking fire from Bouresches, and the enemy artillery, dispersed them and drove them back to cover; and fugitives from the Wood suffered in the same way.[445]

Up to 6:33 am, all reports were encouraging: the next group is not so favorable. The companies of 2/5 had been impressed with two things for the conduct of their movements: they must drive through the woods to the other side, and they must keep touch to the right, where they expected to find 1/6. This they had endeavored to do. Now, the 51st Company sent word to 4th Brigade that machine guns were causing damage in right rear: it requested a company be sent to clear them out; this was at 6:50. Major Hughes retorted, through Lieutenant Colonel Lee at 7:05 that machine guns were holding up the 2/5, and that he was not in touch with Lieutenant Colonel Wise on the flank.[446] But prisoners began to come in: 60 were then at 6th Regimental Headquarters.[447] At 8:38 Lieutenant Colonel Wise reported

---

438 Lieutenant E.C. Cooke, 55th Co., 2nd Div. file.
439 [Captain Charles C.] Gill to 4th Brigade, 5:00 am, 11 June, Vol. 4.
440 Lee to Harbord, 4th Brigade, 5:45 am, 11 June, Vol. 4.
441 Shearer to 4th Brigade, 5:55 am, 11 June, Vol. 4.
442 Ibid, 6:00 am.
443 Dunbeck to 4th Brigade, 6:11 am, 11 June, Vol. 4.
444 6th Regt. to 4th Brigade, 6:33 am, 11 June, Vol. 4.
445 War Diary and annexes 28th DI, 11 June: see reports 40th Fusilier Regt.

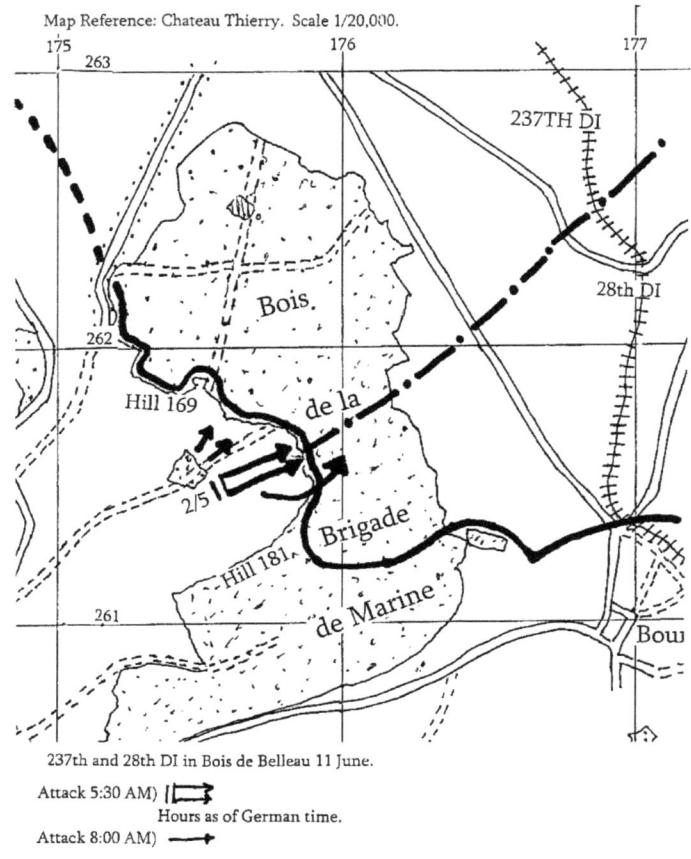

Map 8

to Colonel Neville that he needed a barrage on the northeast end of the woods; that his losses were heavy, and that there was still no contact with Major Hughes.[448] Again, at 9:25, Wise reported that there was no liaison between 2/5 and 1/6, some prisoners accompanied the bearer of this message to Colonel Neville, and it was requested that the prison-chasers be sent back, as they were needed.[449] At 10:55 the 55th Company reported that it had reached its objective;[450] and at 10:30 Colonel Neville asked for 2 companies of engineers for consolidation work.[451] The request was relayed to

446 Hughes to Lee, 7:05 am, 11 June, 6th Regt., Vol. 5.
447 Lee to 4th Brigade, 7:05 am, 11 June, Vol. 4.
448 Wise to Neville, 8:55 am, 11 June, Vol. 4.
449 Ibid, 9:25 am, 11 June, Vol. 4.

Division, and the Chief of Staff started the engineers forward at once.[452] At 10:40, there were prisoners to the number of 2 officers and 169 men at Division Headquarters.[453] Then, at 10:45 am, Lieutenant Colonel Wise reported to Colonel Neville that he was in contact with 1/6 on his right.[454] Ten minutes later an artillery liaison officer reported to Lieutenant Colonel Wise, who had established, his PC in the north edge of the woods, just west of Hill 181, and who now wrote that his positions were organized and in perfect liaison with 1/6 although he had lost many officers and men.[455] At 11 o'clock Colonel Neville reported to 4th Brigade that the situation was satisfactory in the Bois de Belleau.[456]

What had actually happened must be constructed from a number of sources, among which the German reports are noteworthy. In the first place, 1/6 had been no where as far forward as Brigade Headquarters believed it to be, and the line of the 40th Regiment ran unbroken, east and west across the Wood, on about the X — Line 261.3. One/6 lay south of it. The contact point with the 461st Regiment, holding the western face was also the German divisional boundary, and it was strengthened, by a liaison detachment of the 461st Regiment. Striking this point, 2/5 met strong resistance, and the weight of the battalion drew in to overcome it. The 51st Company, and then the 55th, swung south of the original direction of the advance.[457] Every man and officer had in mind the injunction to guide right, and the other companies inclined right in turn. The expected Hughes battalion was not met: the right of 2/5 found, instead, the line of the German 40th Regiment, which it overran from the flank.[458] At least one large group of prisoners from the 40th was brought out, through the west face of the woods, by Marine Gunner [*Michael*] Wodarzeck [*sic* Wodarczyk] of 2/5.[459] A little later, 1/6, advancing, fell upon the 40th from the front, making contact first with the German line on the east face of the woods, where the going was easiest, and, the lines in closest contact.[460] Under such pressure, the two companies of the 40th were torn to pieces, and their heavy machine gun defense bro-

---

450 55th Co. to 4th Brigade, 10:15 am, 11 June, Vol. 4.
451 Neville to 4th Brigade, 10:30 am, 11 June, Vol. 4.
452 Chief of Staff, 2nd Div. to 2nd Eng., 10:40 am, 11 June, Vol. 4.
453 War Diary, 2nd Div., 11 June, Vol. 4.
454 Wise to Neville, 10:45 am, 11 June, Vol. 5.
455 Wise to 4th Brigade, 10:55 am, 11 June, Vol. 4.
456 Neville to 4th Brigade, 11:00 am, 11 June, Vol. 4.
457 Notes of Lieutenant Mathews and Cooke, 2/5, 2nd Div. file.
458 Ibid.
459 Ibid. [Wodarczyk would become a flying officer and earn a Navy Cross in Nicaragua. GBC].

ken up. The support and reserve companies, approaching from the east were caught in flanking fire from Bouresches, and stopped. The developments anticipated by the 461st Regiment, when von Hartlieb turned over his east-and-west line to the 28th Division, were all realized.[461]

The 461st Regiment, which had, received the frontal attack of 2/5 fared hardly at first, but had the enormous advantage of well-placed reserves, and an energetic commanding officer.

Charging straight in through machine gun fire, the Wise Battalion overwhelmed the right of the German line, entirely destroying the 1st and 4th Companies, which, with their commanders were killed, wounded, or led away captive. The 8th Company — the liaison detachment — was forced away from the flank of the 40th Regiment and driven back through the woods, together with the 3rd Company, in support, and the German line, from Hill 181 to the traversing ravine at about X — line 261.7, was swept out of existence. Fugitives of the 40th Regiment, mixed with elements of the 8th and 3rd Companies, which maintained their integrity, retired northeastward through the woods.[462] But the Marine companies, now much reduced by the stubborn German fighting, held eastward, instead, of following north. One after another, they reached the eastern face of the wood opposite the points of entrance, casting down to the right for contact, and reported on their objectives, variously, from 6:11 am (43rd) to 10:15 am (55th), and from these reports, at 10:55, Lieutenant Colonel Wise advised Colonel Neville that he was organized on his objectives, and in liaison with Major Hughes. During the fighting, Captain Williams of the 51st Company had been killed, and many of the experienced company officers wounded.[463]

Shortly before the last company reports came in, the Headquarters Company of the 5th Marines, Captain [*Alphonse*] de Carre, following the assault, had moved to the left, near Hill 169, and come upon a body of Germans, who surrendered. Examining the ground, Captain De Carre found

---

460 Note that at 6:50 am, 2 hours and 30 minutes after the attack started, the 51st Co. of 2/5 then forcing its way across the woods, reported machine guns firing on its right rear, and that at 7:05 Major Hughes advised Lieutenant Colonel Lee [that] 2/5 had passed the machine guns on its right flank. This indicates that elements of the 40th on the front of 1/6 held out for some time. 51st Co. to Brigade: 6:50 am, Vol. 4., and Hughes to Lee, 6th Regt., 7:05 am, Vol. 5. [The real story was that 1/6 had barely entered the woods and remained pretty much where they began. That left the 2/5 right flank wide open to German machine guns and, especially, the 51st Company, which was literally wiped out. For further details see Clark, G.B. "Devil Dogs, Fighting Marines of WWI" pages 145-155. GBC].

461 War Diary, 237th and 28th DI, 11 June: reports 40th and 461st RI.

462 War Diary, 237th DI: report 461st RI, 11 June.

463 5th Regt. and 4th Brigade annexes, 11 June, Vol. 5, and 4: also notes Mathews and Cooke, 2/5, 2nd Div. file.

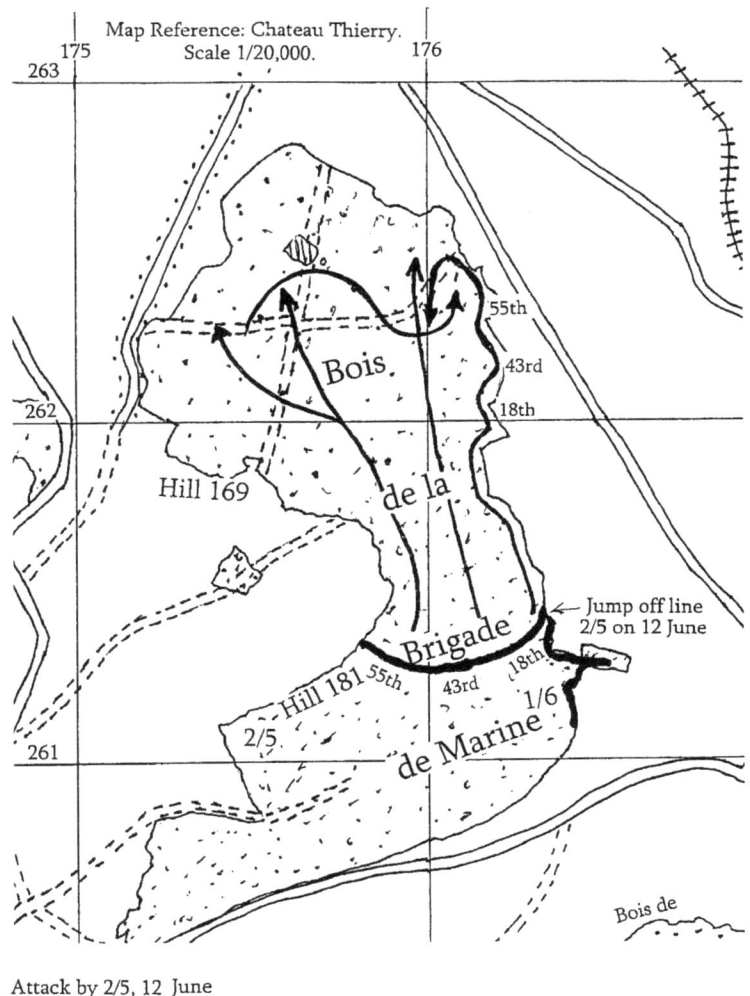

Attack by 2/5, 12 June

Map 9

neither Marines nor at the time, Germans, and he advised, Lieutenant Colonel Wise that the left of the woods was open. The Battalion Intelligence Officer, Lieutenant Mathews, was sent forward to reconnoiter. He worked to the north, a little past the trail of wounded that marked, the advance of the left companies, found nobody except casualties, and, pushed east to the edge of the woods. There, on the, wood road, that traverses the Bois de Belleau, emerging near X–line 262, he came upon the 3 surviving company commanders, Captains Dunbeck and, Wass, and Lieutenant Cooke. He states that they located themselves, by the map, on the north face of the woods, and oriented, themselves by the town to the north, Belleau, which they took to be Torcy, and, the town to the south, Bouresches which they took to be Belleau They considered that the mass of woods behind them had been overrun, and was safe Lieutenant Mathews reconnoitered again to the north, and realized, that the flank was wide open, and exposed to any movement the Germans cared to make. He returned to the Battalion Commander and reported his observations: but his statements were not accepted by Lieutenant Colonel Wise, who insisted that his company commanders had correctly described the situation. It was then between 11:00 and noon, and confirmation of Lieutenant Mathew's report came from an unexpected source. A Marine, who had gone back with prisoners, and, was rejoining his company over the route they had followed, came upon a German hospital corpsman, and, brought him in to the battalion PC. He told the Marines that the Germans were already returning, through the north end of the woods.[464]

At 11:45 Lieutenant Colonel Wise informed Brigade that his left flank was weak,[465] and 1/6, at the same time, discovered some more machine guns which had remained in the southern end of the woods, and was obliged to deal with them.[466] By personal reconnaissance, Lieutenant Colonel Wise then ascertained that his men were on the east side of the woods instead of the north, and that his flank was in the air.[467] About noon, he drew his 55th Company from the right, and moved it to the left of his line, 1/6 extending to maintain the contact. Reconnaissance by the 55th Company to the left drew heavy fire: the Germans were in force to the north, and presently they began to filter southward towards their old positions, past the flank of the Marines. A platoon of 1/6 was sent up by Major Hughes, to reinforce the 55th Company,[468] and as the afternoon passed, the situation slowly clarified itself for Lieutenant Colonel Wise. His line along the east edge of the woods had extended to about X — line 261.6, and steady pressure developed on the flank. Runners, sent across the woods to battalion PC, were captured, or killed, or they returned to their organizations saying that Germans were across the rear. On the suggestion of the battalion commander, some German-speaking Marines worked out from the left flank and called invitations to surrender, on promise of good treatment, but they were driven in by prompt rifle and machine gun fire. The Marine left, as finally

---

464 Lieut. Mathews, 2/5, 2nd Div. file.
465 Wise to 4th Brigade 11:45 am, 11 June, Vol. 4.
466 Hughes to Lee, 6th Regiment, 1:20 pm, 11 June, Vol. 5.
467 Lieutenant Mathews, 2/5 notes, 2nd Div. file.
468 Ibid and Lieutenant Cooke, 2/5 Notes, 2nd Div. file.

stabilized, reached the north side of the large clearing in the eastern face of the woods, at about X–line 261.6, and about dark, local preparations were made to form front to the flank and push northward, from this clearing: but the battalion commander considered that the enterprise was not feasible,[469] and he withdrew his left, forming a line east and west across the wood, approximating X–line 261.4, the right on the south side of the large clearing, and the left east of Hill 181. One/6, detaching certain elements to reinforce the weakened companies of 2/5, occupied the east face of the wood and the old line across Hill 181.[470]

As for the Germans, they had been active during the day. Major von Hartlieb, in the forenoon, as soon as he could collect the shattered formations which had held his front line, incorporated them with his local reserves and led them back down the western edge of the Wood. He found the positions of the 1st and 4th Companies empty: the Marines had taken out those companies and swept straight on. He pushed southward, and at 12:15 pm (1:15 French time), located his left flank at a point 100 metres north of Hill 181. A battalion of the German 110th Regiment was sent in by the 28th Division to replace the 40th, and the German line was traced from the rocky ridge south of the Pavilion in the north end of the woods, traversing down to the point north of Hill 181. Until night a steady bickering kept up, between the Marines and the Germans who were filtering down behind them. After dark, Germans strayed into the Marine lines and American runners were lost in the same way. The Germans worked forward until the lines were within 50 feet of each other.[471]

The day's fighting had been of the closest and most savage description. The woods were so thick that all action was local and individual. The Germans had posted snipers and machine gunners in trees, and every path and clearing was commanded from masked positions. Rocky knolls and small depressions, hidden from view by the dense foliage, offered endless ambushes for the defense. So heavy was the forest growth that the effect of field artillery was minimized, and accurate observation of fire impossible. The German system of defense, an outpost zone defended by light machine guns, tacked by a main line of infantry and heavy machine guns in mutually covering emplacements, exacted a heavy toll from the attackers. There were further difficulties in orientation, all directions looking the same under the trees and in the bushes. Also, the woods were larger

---

469 Ibid.
470 Lieutenant Mathews, 2/5 notes, 2nd Div. file.
471 War Diaries, 28th and 237th DI's and annexes: reports of 40th and 461st RI's. The movements and dispositions of the Germans on 11 June are elsewhere considered in detail.

than indicated by the French hachured map then in use, and the map conveyed no hint of its physical features. When Lieutenant Colonel Wise organized his line at the end of the day, he thought that the small depression, east of Hill 181 was the large traversing ravine in the upper third of the western side, and so reported his position. He did not know, nor did his staff, that two-thirds of the woods were yet before him. Finally, the entire battalion was much exhausted. It had been under fire since 2 June, and there had been no issue of hot food since the 5th Regiment left the Chaumont-en-Vexin area. The nearest water was in Lucy, and the men suffered for it: the weather was very hot. There were very many wounded, and German prisoners were impressed to carry them out, across Hill 161 and up the Lucy-Bouresches ravine to the dressing station under the culvert at the edge of Lucy.[472]

The casualties of 2/5, on 11th, were 6 officers and 176 men killed and wounded.[473]

The action of 1/6 during 11 June is obscure. Its general mission seems to have been to advance in conformity with 2/5, but the burden of maintaining liaison was laid on 2/5. It reported, during the morning, that [First] Lieutenant [Macon C.] Overton with the 76th Company captured 7 heavy machine guns in the south of the woods.[474] Elements of the battalion reinforced the left of 2/5 during the day. The prisoners it took were not counted separately, but were included in the general total. Its opponents, 2 companies of the German 40th Regiment, state that their line across the woods was first penetrated from the right flank, and afterwards attacked on the left front, which would indicate that 1/6 made contact with them after 2/5

---

472 *Operations report, 2/5, 2 -16 June-18 June, 5th Regt., Vol. 7.*
473 *Adjutant and Inspector, USMC.*
474 *War Diary 4th Brigade, 11 June, Vol. 6: Losses of the Overton company in this exploit are given here as 3 killed, 16 wounded, and 3 shellshock. Deduction from total casualties of 47 above leaves 23 casualties for the rest of the battalion. From the same source, the 76th Company is credited with clearing out the whole machine gun nest which had stopped 1/6 on 10 June, the total number of guns not given. [Overton's company was that which was detailed to accompany the right flank of 2/5 in its entrance and wheel northward in the woods. It didn't and Overton's excuse was vaguely that he didn't see them until after they had passed. GBC].*

A story of 2/5, taken from the diary of Major J.[oseph] D. Murray, then Captain and second-in-command of 2/5, is worth repeating. Attached to 2/5 was a Frenchman of the Interpreter's Corps, one Courtois. As the battalion Headquarters group moved forward behind the assault, Lieutenant Colonel Wise said: "Courtois, I don't think we'll need any interpreting done where we are going. You might as well report to Regimental Headquarters-no use in your coming along. Courtois said: "Colonel Wise, I have been with the 2nd battalion since it landed in France, and I think this is a very strange time for me to be leaving them. I will stay." And he stayed, rendering excellent combat service.

Captured German officer

had already involved their positions. The final line of the 1/6 was cited along the eastern face of the wood, from the southeast corner northward to the right flank of 2/5. The casualties of 1/6 for the 11th were 1 officer and 46 men, killed and wounded. Compared with the casualties of 2/5, the figures do not indicate heavy action.

The 4th Brigade report for the 24 hours ending at 8:00 pm, 11 June, shows the impression formed at headquarters, from the sum of the combat messages received. It states that the artillery preparation started at 3:30, the attack by 2/5 at 4:30, and that, by the middle of the forenoon, the north half of the Bois de Belleau was taken and the line established on the northeast side. The total of prisoners was estimated at 400, of whom 301 had been received at Brigade Headquarters and some 50 were, when the report was made, working in the Bois de Belleau under Lieutenant Colonel Wise, removing wounded. Three or more minenwerfers were captured, and about 30 machine guns. The southern half of the wood had been cleaned out by Major Hughes, the 1/6, who reported 60 prisoners, included in the total of 400. Liaison existed between Bouresches and Major Hughes at the southeast corner of the wood, and Lieutenant Colonel Wise prolonged the line to the northwest corner of the wood, his left, lying near Hill 133, being slightly refused. Under the authority of the Division Commander, 3/6 had been replaced as Corps reserve by 2/6, 3/6 receiving orders to move into the woods northwest of Lucy.[475]

On 10 June, General Harbord had invited the attention of the Division command to the physical condition of the 4th Brigade, which had then been under fire for 10 days, and was considered to be approaching exhaustion. In the 11 June report, this condition was again referred to: as approximating complete physical exhaustion.

---

475   *24-hour report to 8:00 pm, 11 June, War Diary, 4th Brigade, Vol. 6. It is not necessary to point out, in view of the foregoing, that this report was based on incorrect data in its most vital points. It was, however, the basis for future orders and operations.*

The prisoner captured (see ante) late on 11 June and interrogated by Colonel Wise, gave information of Germans in the northwest corner of the wood: his statement is considered in the 24-hour report for 12 June, but its full significance was not appreciated.

Fifteen

237th and 28th Divisions (German): 10–11 June

The reports and comments of the German 237th Division on the fighting in the Bois de Belleau are detailed and voluminous. It is to be inferred that they were ordered to submit estimates of the American assault tactics and reports on the fighting value of American troops, for some of their regiment's papers are unmistakably of this nature. Also, controversy developed between the 237th Division and their left neighbor, the 28th, as to the responsibility for the loss of the Belleau Wood position on 10–11 June.

On 9 June, it will be remembered, the 237th held a line across the southern third of the wood, running east and west just north of Hill 181 to the western edge; thence along the western and northwestern faces of the wood to Hill 133. This was the sector of the 461st Regiment, Major Bischoff. From Hill 133 westward to Torcy, the 462nd Regiment prolonged the line. The third rifle regiment, the 460th, was in support and reserve. The 40th Fusilier Regiment of the 28th took over with 2 companies, the east and west line through the Bois de Belleau. The sector of the 461st Regiment was then narrowed to the western and northwestern perimeter of the wood. This line was held by the 1/461, Major von Hartlieb, with 2 companies of 2/461 in reserve, one company, the 8/461, acting as contact company between the flank of the 40th Regiment and von Hartlieb's left.[476]

On 10 June, when 1/6 attacked in the south of the wood, the 461st Regiment was not engaged.[477] The 28th Division reported that its 40th Regiment was attacked in the wood, lost no ground, and repulsed the attackers.[478]

---

476 War Diary, 237th DI, 9-13 June, and annexes, 461 RI.
477 War Diary, 237th DI, 10 June.
478 War Diary, 28th DI, 10 June.

At 3:30 am, on 11 June following a night of harassing artillery fire on the approaches to the front and on the rear areas, a violent barrage fell on the German lines in the wood.[479] At 5:30 am, (4:30 French time) the 40th Regiment was attacked: the 461st heard heavy rifle and machine gun fire from that direction. Then the 8th Company of the 461st, the company attached for contact with the 40th Regiment, was attacked on its front and left. It lost contact with the 40th Regiment, asked for and received a platoon from the 3rd Company of 1/461, and maintained touch with the 461st Regiment. The left front of 1/461 was then attacked; that part of it held by the 1st Company. This attack was repulsed, and 50 dead Americans were counted in front of the 1st Company. On the right of the 1st Company were the 4th, then the 2nd. The 3rd was battalion reserve. At 8 o'clock, a new assault developed. The enemy appeared on the front and flank of the 1st and 4th Companies, 461st, and then in their left rear. The 8th Company was rolled up and driven back. The 1st and 4th Companies were overrun and disappeared with all their officers. Fragments of the 3rd and 8th Companies retired hastily towards the northern end of the woods.[480]

The German local command post was at the Pavillion where one company, the 5th, of the regimental reserve was stationed: the other reserve company was in Belleau. While these were being hurried forward, Major von Hartlieb collected his scanty local reserves and such men from the routed companies as could be reformed, and personally led them in a counterattack.[481] They pushed down the western side of the wood, and found their old positions unoccupied. The Americans had gone right through the line and kept on going with their prisoners. Those positions were reoccupied; and patrols pushed to the left in search of the 40th Regiment; but they could not find the 40th Regiment. The 5th and 7th Companies were led up, and placed in line back across the woods in a northeasterly direction to the commanding knoll south of the Pavillion, since there was nothing else to base the left flank upon. Now the only company remaining intact in the 1/461 was the 2nd Company, in the northwest edge of the Bois de Belleau: it does not seem to have been involved at all. The 1st and 4th Companies had disappeared. Major von Hartlieb reorganized his line with his 2nd Company, fragments of the 3rd, and the 5th and 7th Companies of 2/461. This was at 10:00 am, (11:00 am, French time).[482] There was discussion with the 28th Division as to the flanks, and at 12:15 pm (1:15 French time) the left flank

---

479 *War Diary, 237th DI, 11 June.*
480 *Ibid, and annexes, 461st RI.*
481 *237th DI annexes to W.D.: 461 RI, 11 June.*
482 *Report 461st RI to 244 Inf. Brigade, 1-15 June.*

of the 237th was verified, on the spot, by Major von Hartlieb and staff officers of the two divisions, at a point 100 metres north of Hill 181. (German map 1/25000 BI 61 Epaux-Bezu).[483]

The new line of the 461st Regiment rested its left on the rocky knoll just south of the Pavillion, ran southeasterly through the wood to the point 103 metres north of Hill 181, and lay in its old trace along the western face of the wood to its junction point with the 462nd Regiment to the west. During the afternoon, elements of the 40th Regiment, with reinforcement from the 110th Regiment of the 28th Division, reentered the wood from the north and took up their old positions through which the Americans had passed, but patrols found the Americans holding the eastern face of the wood, as far up as the square wood that thrust out to the Bouresches-Belleau road.[484]

During the remaining hours of the 11 June, the Germans were not further molested, although there was some sniping activity on both sides, and Marines on the extreme left of the 2/5 fired at Germans filtering past them to the south. Plans were drawn up for a concerted counter-attack by the 28th and 237th Divisions to recapture the wood. On this day, 244th Infantry Brigade of the 237th Division had present for duty 47 officers and 1482 men.[485]

The reports of the 25th Division differ from those of the 237th Division. They state that the enemy, attacking the Bois de Belleau on 11 June, penetrated the positions of the 237th Division, on the right, and delivered an enveloping attack on the 40th Regiment; but, following a successful counterattack by this regiment, the lines were restored to their old trace. On 12 June the 40th Regiment was again attacked in the woods, the enemy coming upon its rear through the lines of the 237th Division, and it became necessary to withdraw the 40th Regiment from the wood, establishing its flank on the road Chateau Thierry-Belleau.[486]

These reports were brief and not detailed. In view of the very light organization of the 40th Regiment, it is more probable that their lines were first breached in the in the fighting of 11 June, while those of the 237th may have held for a while. Certainly the 40th Regiment was crowded out of the wood, and large numbers of fugitives were accounted for among the artillery positions north and east of the wood upon which they retired early on the morning of 11 June. Their reported loss in missing is 55, about the number

---

483   Annexes to W.D. 237th DI, 11 June.
484   War Diary and annexes, 40th DI, 11 June.
485   War Diary and annexes, 237th DI, 11 June.
486   War Diary, 40th DI, 9-17 June.

of 40th and 110th Regiment men captured by the Marines; but the loss of the 237th in prisoners was more than 200, which lends color to the plea of an enveloping attack. It is possible that some elements of the 28th worked back into the wood from the north the afternoon of the 11th: but the Marines record nothing like a counter-attack in the eastern and southern portion of the wood, and the Marine line was solid along the eastern edge as early as the forenoon of 11 June. Further, the reserve companies of the line in the woods were east of the wood, and would have come under the fire from Bouresches group machine runs, as they went on to counter-attack: these guns fired effectively on Germans retiring from the wood at this time: none entered it from the east. The weight of the evidence is that the 40th Regiment made no effective defense within the wood, and never reestablished its lost lines to any purpose after it had lost them. After 12 June, the maps of the 28th Division show a battalion of the 110th Regiment holding its flank outside of the wood; the 2/40 had disappeared from the front.[487]

487   Ibid.

Sixteen

5th Attack on the Bois de Belleau, 12 June — 2/5

During the night 11–12 June the Bois de Belleau was relatively quiet, both Germans and Americans, lying in close contact, devoting their efforts to reorganization and improvement of their positions.[488] Two/5 received 2 companies of engineers and about 150 Marine replacements, the latter being distributed to the companies. The reports of 2/5, together with the information received from German prisoners, gave Brigade the impression that the enemy still clung to the northwestern edge of the wood, and at a conference held by General Harbord during the morning of the 12th at which the regimental commanders and Lieutenant Colonel Wise were present, Lieutenant Colonel Wise said that, with same artillery preparation, he thought he could dislodge the Germans in the afternoon. Orders were issued accordingly, the 12th Field Artillery being directed to take the supposed enemy line under fire.[489] The 2/5 was to advance at 5:00 pm, and for an hour before jump-off time, the northern section of the Bois de Belleau was heavily shelled.[490] Just before 4:30, however, Lieutenant Colonel Wise sent word, from his PC, that preparation was not sufficient, and he requested another hour of shelling, which was given him.[491] The German reaction does not seem to have been impressive, although the IV Reserve Corps, realizing that the situation in the sector of the 237th Division was critical, held the artillery groups of the neighboring 5th Guards and 28th Divisions in

---

488 *Operations report, 2/5, 2-16 June, inclusive 18 June, 5th Regiment, Vol. 7*, and *War Diary and annexes, 237th DI*.
489 *War Diary 4th Brigade, 24-hour report to 8:00 pm, 12 June, Vol. 4*.
490 Ibid.
491 *Wise to Harbord, 4:30 pm, 12 June, Vol. 4*.

readiness for emergencies.[492] As a matter of fact, the artillery directed by the 4th Brigade was ineffective for the German front line was far to the south of where the Brigade believed it to be, and the few and scattered reserve companies of the 431st and 110th Regiments in the shelled area were protected by the thick forest growth, which localized the bursts of the shells.[493] In course of the preparation, artillery observers noted a concentration of about 400 German infantry near the woods south of Etrépilly, and dispersed it by fire. But this had no visible influence on the action in the Bois de Belleau.[494]

At 5:30 pm the 2/5 rose out of its holes and attacked straight north through the woods, in order of companies from the left, 55th, 43rd and 18th. Elements of 1/6 moved up behind the right flank, covering the portion of the east face of the woods which 2/5 had held, and these details did not come forward in time to relieve the 51st Company, which, consisting only of 1 officer and a handful of men, followed later in the track of the assault. The Marines encountered the Germans within 50 feet of their jump-off line, and [the Germans] developed a stubborn resistance at once. The German advanced positions were overrun, and the main line of heavy machine guns, behind them, was broken. German supports lay across the low ground just south of X–line 262, and were organized along the traversing ravine on the western side, and fought savagely where they stood. The shrunken companies of 2/5 had started from the narrowest part of the woods, and the Germans exacted a heavy price for the ground they lost, so that the Marine formations became thinner and thinner as the woods widened and the company commanders endeavored to remain touch with each other, and, at the same time to sweep through the woods from left to right. In the wide northern third of the woods the Germans had the same[495] difficulty, and their units were forced apart and broken up, under fierce pressure. The companies of 2/5 became separated, and during the closing hours of the day there was no semblance of organization anywhere in the north end of the Bois de Belleau. Small groups, scattered across the woods, independent of each other, followed such officers as were not shot down, and some of these groups reached the north edge of the woods. Marines of the 55th, the left company, came out on Hill 133 with Lieutenant Cooke. Marines of the 43rd Company followed 2nd Lieutenant [Drinkard B.] Milner to the Pavillon in

---

492   *War Diary and annexes, 237th DI.*
493   Ibid.
494   *2nd F.A. Brigade to 2nd Div., 10:00 pm, 12 June, Vol. 4.*
495   *War Diary 237th DI, 12 June. Operations report 2/5, 2-16 June, Inclusive 18 June, 5th Regiment, Vol. 7. Notes on Chateau Thierry, Lt. Mathews, 2/5, 2nd Div. file. Battle of Belleau Woods, Lt. Cooke, USMC [sic], 55th Co., 2/5, 2nd Div. file.*

5th Attack on the Bois de Belleau, 12 June — 2/5

the large clearing at the north end, and Lieutenant Milner reported that he climbed up in the Pavillion and looked through the edge of the woods down into Belleau and saw the Germans running about the streets. The 18th Company came out on the northeastern edge. For a little while it is certain that all organized German elements were driven entirely from the woods, or so broken as to be ineffective. But the low initial strength of 2/5, and the casualties they sustained as they went forward, made it impossible for them to form a continuous line. The order was still to guide right, and the 55th and the 43rd Companies, as they were reassembled, moved sideways to the right flank, feeling for the 18th, and the 18th dropped back along the east edge of the woods to base its flank on 1/6. Captain Dunbeck of the 43rd had been wounded and evacuated, and Captain Wass of the 18th was the only company commander now surviving.[496]

The field messages show in part the stages of the assault. At 6:15, 45 minutes[497] after the advance began, Lieutenant Colonel Wise sent word that all was apparently going well: his information came from the walking wounded who passed the battalion PC. At 7:30 2/5 forwarded to Brigade a report from Lieutenant Milner, who had reached the clearing in the north end of the wood where the Pavilion was.[498] At 8:00 pm, Major Hughes reported to Colonel Lee that he had relieved the 51st Company, which constituted the slender reserve of 2/5.[499] At 6:40, Lieutenant Colonel Wise advised the 5th Regiment that all objectives had been reached, and that his Marines had taken many machine guns and some prisoners. All this was perfectly true.[500] But there were not enough men left in 2/5 to hold what they had gained.

In the meantime, the organization of the 461st Regiment had been almost destroyed, and the battalion of the 110th Regiment which had

---

496 Operations report 2/5, 2-16 June, Inclusive 18 June, 5th Regiment, Vol. 7. Notes on Chateau Thierry, Lt. Mathews, 2/5, 2nd Div. file. Battle of Belleau Woods, Lt. Cooke, USA, 55th Co., 2/5, 2nd Div. file. War Diary and annexes, 237th DI, see: reports 461st RI, 12 June.

497 Battle of Belleau Woods, Lt., USA, 55th Co., 2/5, 2nd Div. file. War Diary and annexes, 237th DI, see: reports 461st RI, 12 June.

498 Milner 43rd Co to Wise: 7:30 pm, 12 June, 4th Brig., Vol. 4. ["]The 55th Company is also located in this message, in touch with the 43rd.["] This message reached 4th Brigade at 10:55 pm. There is a message from Captain Wass, 18th Co. to Wise (7:35 pm, 12 June, 4th Brigade, Vol. 4.) reporting depleted state of 18th Co., and attached squads of 55th. It asked for reinforcements, material, and a barrage, but does not locate the 18th Co. at the time of sending. At 7:35 pm, 12 June (4th Brig., Vol. 4.) Wise asked for counter-battery work, since he was being shelled heavily.

499 Hughes to Lee, 8:00 pm, 12 June, 6th Regt., Vol. 5.

500 Wise to Neville, 8:40 pm, 12 June, Vol. 4. (received at 8:40) Lt Col Wise had previously reported at 6:15 pm, to Brigade, that he had taken all objectives, but he had heard from the 18th Co only.

152   Chapter Sixteen

relieved the 40th was torn to pieces. Men of the 110th fled back to the battery positions of the 237th Division before they could be rallied, and no elements of the 28th Division ever entered the wood again. The local commander of the 461st, however was on the ground, following every stage of the combat. The Bois de Belleau in the northern third is almost a kilometre wide, and Major von Hartlieb took instant advantage of the lightening of the pressure upon his broken formations, which occurred when the Marine groups filed off to the right. By hard fighting, a few detachments of the 461st had been able to maintain themselves on the rocky knoll south of the pavilion, and these were quickly connected up as the Marines drew away. Local reserves from Belleau, and such fugitives as could be collected, were brought forward, and a new position organized. The Marine flank stabilized on the southwest slope of the knoll, where the[501] unimproved road emerges from the northeastern corner of the wood and passed to the Belleau-Bouresches road — about 176.1 — 262.5. Thence the line passed down the eastern face of the wood, below X–line 262, to contact with 1/6. As darkness approached, the German pressure on the left flank became serious, and the left was sharply refused, along the steep contours of the rocky knoll, forming the position known as the Hook in the Bois de Belleau. Here the Marines and the Germans, at dark, lay in the closest contact, but both were so exhausted that no further aggression was attempted. The line of 2/5 was strengthened by details of the 2nd Engineers, led forward through the barrage which the German guns laid across the center of the wood during the attack, and by details from 1/6. The order of companies remained the same: 55th, 43rd, and 18th, with the 51st in support. The 43rd and 55th were much mingled. As the night went on, the Germans began to filter past the Marine left, into the center of the woods, and the Marine line was annoyed by flares that went up directly behind it, and bursts of machine gun fire in its rear. Further, there was disquieting information.[502]

In the final stages of the attack, while the 2/5 was readjusting itself, an officer and 42 men of the 401st Regiment, cut off in the thickets, surrendered under a white flag. The officer, who was wounded, informed the Marines that the Germans planned a counter attack, for the following morning, jointly by the 237th and 28th Divisions, to recover the woods. His information was forwarded by Lieutenant Colonel Wise to Colonel Neville, and sent quickly to Brigade. This added to the anxiety of the 5th Regiment

---

501   *War Diary, 237th DI, 12 June. See reports.*
502   *War Diary, 237th DI, 12 June. See reports 461st RI. Notes on Chateau Thierry, Lt. Mathews, 2/5, 2nd Div. file. Battle of Belleau Woods, Lt. Cooke, USA, 2/5, 2nd Div. file.*

during the night. To confirm it, a very heavy artillery fire was laid upon the woods, the batteries of the 5th Guards, 237th, and 28th Divisions participating,[503] and reports of 2/5 describe it as the most intense bombardment they ever suffered. It continued unabated through the night, and the American guns in retaliation, harassed the German rear and approach areas and stood by for SOS barrages.

That night the bag of 2/5 in its two-days fight was appraised. The prisoners, officers and men, taken in the wood, mounted above 400, 42 being captured on the 12th, and there were 59 machine guns and 10 minenwerfers.[504] Two/5, on the 12th, had lost 2 officers and 146 men killed and wounded, and Lieutenant Colonel Wise, after the attack, reported that he had available about 300 old men (replacements not included) and about 1 experienced officer per company.[505] One/6 had 1 officer and 53 men killed and wounded,[506] and reported about 700 men fit for duty.[507]

Brigade, on consideration of the information given by the captured officer, asked for and obtained 2/6 from Corps reserve, and ordered it into the woods northwest of Lucy to stand by as a counter attack force. The relief of 1/5 on Hill 142 by 3/6 had been ordered, and 1/5 was directed to the old 2/5 positions west of the Lucy-Torcy road, flanking the Bois de Belleau. About midnight the German artillery activity, including all the 4th Brigade area and extending down the lines of the 23rd Infantry in the 3rd Brigade, attained the weight of serious preparation.[508]

In its report for 12 June, the IV Reserve Corps advised the German 7th Army, and the 7th Army entered in its War Diary: "This day the wildly-fought-for Bois de Belleau remained in the hands of the enemy." Corps, however, at once ordered a counter attack to regain the Woods.[509]

Attack on Bouresches 12–13 June

On 12 June, 3/6 was ordered from Corps Reserve in the Bois Platerie to Brigade Reserve in the woods northwest of Lucy, the 2/6, then coming

---

503 War Diary and annexes, 237th DI, 12 June: see reports 461st RI.
504 War Diary, 4th Brigade, 12-13 June: see 24-hour report to 8:00 pm, 13 June, Vol. 6. Many of the machine guns were put into action against the enemy.
505 Adjutant and Inspector, US Marine Corps.
506 Ibid.
507 War Diary, 4th Brigade, 12-13 June: see 24-hour report to 8:00 pm, 13 June, Vol. 6.
508 Ibid.
509 War Diary, 7th Army, 12 June. War Diary and annexes, IV Reserve Corps. 12-13 June.

154   Chapter Sixteen

out of the Triangle-Bouresches line, replacing it as Corps Reserve.[510] Three/6 was then placed at the disposal of the 5th Regiment and ordered to relieve 1/5 on Hill 142, where that battalion had been in line since the capture of the position on 6 June. The relief began after dark that night, and, was carried out without incident, 1/5 going into the woods northwest of Lucy as Brigade Reserve. Three/6 was given the additional mission of reconnoitering the foreground, south of Torcy, with a view of extending its line eastward towards the Bois de Belleau. This would eliminate the bend in the front of the Marine Brigade, from the brook east of Hill 142 back around the edge of the Bois de Champillon, now held by a company of 3/5, and would flank the northwestern approaches to the Bois de Belleau. Three/6 was ordered to send forward its patrols as soon as it had taken over the position, examining particularly the ravine running northwest from the cross-roads a kilometre south of Torcy, at which point it was desired to construct a strong point for the new line.[511]

In consequence of the information gained from the German officer captured by 2/5 the evening of 12 June, these orders were modified. One/5 was sent from the woods northwest of Lucy to a position west of Lucy-Torcy road, flanking the line of any attack that might be delivered on the Bois de Belleau from the northwest—for it was still believed that the Marines had reached the northern end of that wood.[512] Two/6, Corps Reserve in the Bois Platerie, was returned to the Brigade, and at 12:15 am, 13 June, was ordered to the woods northwest of Lucy, in position for counterattack, should the expected assault develop.[513] It was in position there at 4:00 am; 1/5 was also in its new positions by dawn.[514] Meantime, the German artillery had shelled the Brigade area, and at 1:30 am 1/5 reported that an attack upon their line in the north end of the Bois de Belleau had been repulsed:[515] the German 237th Division reports no offensive movements by the 461st Regiment this night, and the reported attack was most probably some local patrol activity.[516] But at 3:23 am, the German artillery fire became violent on the eastern and southern portions of the wood, and upon Bouresches,[517] the guns of the 237th Division and its neighbors, the 5th Guard and 28th Divisions all firing.[518] In reply the 2nd Field Artillery Brigade fired inter-

510   24 hours report to 8:00 pm, 13 June, Harbord to 2nd Div., Vol. 6.
511   Harbord to CO, 5th Regiment, 12 June, Vol. 5.
512   24 hour report to 8:00 pm, 13 June, Harbord to 2nd Div., Vol. 6.
513   Harbord to CO, 2/6, 12:15 am, 13 June, Vol. 5.
514   Holcomb 2/6 to Harbord, 4:00 am, 13 June, Vol. 5.
515   24 hour report to 8:00 pm, 13 June, Harbord to 2nd Div., Vol. 6.
516   War Diary, 237th DI, 12-13 June.
517   24 hour report to 8:00 pm, 13 June, Harbord to 2nd Div., Vol. 6.
518   War Diary, 237th DI, 12-13 June.

diction barrages.[519] At 3:50 am, the German fire slackened, and Bouresches was attacked, the attack involving also the line of 1/6 in Belleau Wood. At 4:10, the 4th Brigade had a report from the Shearer battalion that Bouresches was taken; a replacement Lieutenant brought the message out.[520] The 23rd Infantry also reported to Division, from Lieutenant Villmuth, 1/23, that Bouresches had been taken, and the 23rd asked the artillery to fire on the town.

Immediately afterward these reports were contradicted: 1/23 sent urgently to cancel the artillery.[521] Fourth Brigade was informed that Bouresches held out.[522] But the artillery of both sides was now firing violently, and the machine guns were going. Fourth Brigade ordered Major Holcomb, with two companies of his 2/6, to proceed to the woods southeast of Lucy, and prepare to counterattack towards Bouresches.[523] At 8:27 am, Major Holcomb reported his 79th and 80th companies in position,[524] for the counterattack. At 4:30, Lieutenant Colonel Wise sent word that 2/5 was under heavy fire, but holding out.[525] At 5:04, 4th Brigade heard from 1/6, though Colonel Neville: Major Hughes had all his men in line, and asked for two companies to reinforce him and two to reinforce the Wise Battalion.[526] At 5:10, General Harbord advised Division that he had sent up two companies of 2/6 in readiness to counterattack, and that he was holding Bouresches.[527] At 5:45 word came from Major Shearer through the adjutant of the 5th Regiment: He had not given up an inch of ground.[528] At the same time, the 5th Regiment reported that 1/6 had lost two company commanders, Captain Fuller killed, and Captain [John F.] Burn[e]s wounded.[529] Later, details came out. Two companies, the 1st and 4th, of the German 109th Regiment had penetrated the Bouresches defense, and the Marines threw them out. They left 15 dead in the streets, and 40 bodies were counted in the fields outside.[530] The report of a platoon commander of the 1st Com-

519   24 hour report to 8:00 pm, 13 June, Harbord to 2nd Div., Vol. 6.
520   Ibid.
521   2nd Div. to 4th Brigade, 5:05 am, 13 June, Vol. 4.
522   Harbord to 2nd Div., 5:10 am, 13 June, Vol. 4.
523   Ibid.
524   Holcomb 2/6, o Harbord, 8:27 am, 13 June, Vol. 4.
525   Wise to Harbord, 4:30 am, 13 June, Vol. 4.
526   Hughes to Harbord, 5:04 am, 13 June, Vol. 4.
527   Harbord to 2nd Div., 5:10 am, 13 June, Vol. 4.
528   Adjutant 5th Regiment to 4th Brigade, 5:45 am, Vol. 4. [Harbord had sent a message to Shearer demanding to know why he had fallen back under German pressure. This was Shearer's negative and angry response. GBC].
529   Ibid. [Burnes died of wounds received on 14 June. He had been "skipper" of the 74th Co and Fuller of the 75th Co. GBC].
530   Int. Off. 6th Regiment to 4th Brigade, 13 June, Vol. 4.

pany, 109th, who entered the town, states that they captured one prisoner and took him with them when they retired.[531] The Germans came from the east; the report of this platoon commander indicates that he expected another force, from the north, to make junction with him in the center of the town; but they did not get in.[532] The line of 1/6 was not approached by the attacking forces of the 28th Division: but their fire may have neutralized the forces expected to enter the town from the north. Two/5 was not involved, except by the artillery fire that fell on the area. 1/6 reported a loss of 20 percent of its effectives from this fire.[533]

This attack was to have been carried out by the 237th Division and the 28th together. But the 28th did not advance its right flank, and for that reason the 237th made no move.[534]

Gas Attack, 13 June

Following the repulse of the enemy in Bouresches, the front of the 4th Brigade gradually quieted down; but the War Diary of the 4th Brigade notes that the German artillery activity had been the most violent so far experienced.[535] During the forenoon officers of the 3/23 reported to Major Shearer, the 3/5 to reconnoiter Bouresches, preparatory to taking it over from the Marines.[536] At noon Major Sibley reported to the 5th Regiment that he had started patrols towards the ravine near the cross roads south of Torcy, as ordered, on entering the line, the night before, but had withdrawn them in consequence of the artillery which came on during the night. They had, however, ascertained that the ravine was occupied by the Germans, and he did not consider the occupation of this ravine possible without artillery cooperation: he also asked for a barrage arrangement to cover the ravine in case the Germans should attack from it. He outlined plans for a more thorough examination of the terrain that night.[537] During the day, orders were issued to the 2/6, directing it to relieve the 2/5 in the Bois de Belleau after dark.[538] In the afternoon the German artillery increased in volume, and towards night, gas shells mingled with their high explosive.[539] After

531 *Annexes to War Diary, 28th DI, report 109th DI, 13 June.*
532 *Ibid.*
533 *Hughes to Harbord, 13 June, Vol. 4.*
534 *War Diary, 237th DI, 12-13 June.*
535 *24 hour 4th Brigade report to 8:00 pm, 13 June, Vol. 6.*
536 *War Diary, 4th Brigade, 13 June, Vol. 6.*
537 *Sibley to Neville, 12:00 am, 13 June, Vol. 5.*
538 *24 hour 4th Brigade report to 8:00 pm, 13 June, Vol. 6.*
539 *Ibid.*

dark, the right portion of the 4th Brigade sector was placed under a heavy Yperite (mustard gas) concentration, involving the area around the Ru Gobert where the 78th and 96th Companies of 2/6 lay, and the lines of 1/6, in the southeastern part of the Bois de Belleau.

At 1:55 am, 14 June, Colonel Lee advised 4th Brigade that Major Holcomb would be late with his relief; there was gas in the Bois de Belleau.[540] At 2:50 Major Hughes reported to 4th Brigade that his battalion was being gassed.[541] [Lieutenant] Colonel [Hiram I.] Bearss was sent to investigate the 2/6 and he reported 160 men of the 78th and 96th Companies gassed; most of the men were sent out through the 9th Infantry positions in CR 201.[542] Meantime Major Holcomb got up what men he could, suffering further losses as he entered the Bois de Belleau, both from the gas which now permeated the wood, and from shelling, which continued through the area; he reached 2/5 about daylight with less than two companies; and Lieutenant Colonel Wise did not consider this sufficient force to hold the lines, and the relief was not carried out. The 80th Company, which had suffered the lightest casualties, went into position on the extreme left of 2/5, prolonging the refused left towards the south: fragments of the other companies strengthened the weakened companies of 2/5 in position.[543] By 3:50 in the afternoon, 378 men had been evacuated from 2/6, including the commanding officers of the 78th and 96th Companies;[544] and 1/6 had evacuated 185.[545] Deaths were estimated at about 10%, from 2/6,[546] and there were 60 or 70 shell casualties. One/6 wore its gas masks for 6 hours.[547]

During the night 13–14 June, the 23rd Infantry relieved the Marines in Bouresches.

On 12 June, following a memorandum from 2nd Division, the 3rd Brigade issued Field Order 14. This order announced the taking over, by the 3rd Brigade, of that portion of the 4th Brigade line running from Triangle Farm to Bouresches, inclusive. To do this, the 23rd Infantry extended

---

540 *Lee to Harbord, 1:55 am, 14 June, Vol. 5.*
541 *Hughes to 4th Brigade, 2:50 am, 14 June, Vol. 5.*
542 *Hughes to Harbord, 5:20 am, 14 June, Vol. 5.* [Bearss was 2nd in command of the 6th Marines. He had once briefly commanded the 4th Brigade and before that the 5th Marines. GBC].
543 *Op. report 2/5, 2-16 June, Vol. 7.* (dated 18 June)
544 *Adjutant 5th to 4th Brigade, 3:50 pm, 14 June, Vol. 5.*
545 *Lee to Harbord, 5:37 pm, 14 June, Vol. 5.* [Gas had devastated 2/6 and also hit 1/6 badly, consequently, Hughes was in bad shape as was much of his battalion. GBC].
546 *Adjutant 5th to 4th Brigade, 3:50 pm, 14 June, Vol. 5.*
547 *Lee to Harbord, 5:37 pm, 14 June, Vol. 5.* Note: The Adjutant and Inspector, USMC, gives the following gas casualties for the 1/6 and 2/6 on this occasion: 1/6-1 officer, 84 men; 2/6-3 officers, 377 men.

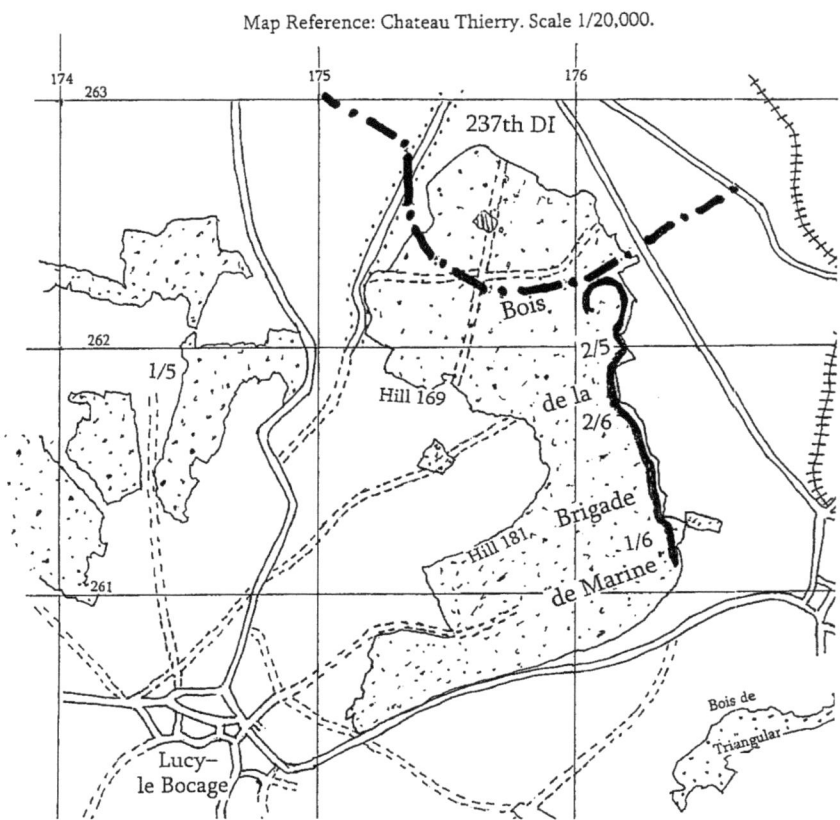

Lines in Bois de Belleau 14 June.

Only fragments of 2/6 were in line as of 2/5.

| •▬ ▸ ▬ ▸ | German line. |
| ▬▬▬▬▬▬ | U.S. Line. |

Map 10

its left, and the 9th Infantry extended also, taking over a company front north of the Paris-Metz road, which had hitherto been the regimental boundary. The line from Triangle Farm through Bouresches had been held by 3 companies of Marines; at this time, the 3/5, less its 20th Company, was in position. The relief was ordered for the night 13–14 June.[548] Reconnaissance was reported complete at 10:30 pm, 12 June.[549]

---

548 F.O. 14, 3rd Brigade, 12 June, Vol. 2.
549 Moore to 3/23, 10:30 pm, 12 June, Vol. 5.

These reliefs were without incident, other than some loss from shelling. B Company of the 9th Infantry came north of the highway, taking over from E Company of the 23rd, which then passed to regimental reserve.[550] The 3/23 replaced the 3/5, and H Company, 23rd, relieved B Company, 23rd, south of Triangle Farm, B Company, 23rd, going to Division reserve.[551] M Company, 23rd, was caught in the open by shell fire, waiting for the Marines to get clear, and suffered some loss.[552] K Company, 23rd, constituted the Bouresches defence.[553] The 3/23 was involved in the gassing of the Gobert area, and evacuated 1 officer and 142 men from gas.[554] The relief was reported finished at 5:05 am, 14 June.[555]

13 June

Fourth Brigade issued, at 4:50 pm, on 13 June, Field Order 5, making dispositions for its shortened front, which now ran from Bouresches, exclusive, through the Bois de Belleau to the Champillon Brook. This front was divided into two regimental sectors. The 5th Marines, Colonel Neville, had the sector from Bouresches to a line running north and south through point 175.9–262.9. The 6th Marines, Lieutenant Colonel Lee, had the sector from that point to the Charmpillon Brook. In this order, the relief of 2/5 by 2/6, 2/5 to go on relief to Division reserve, was ordered; but 2/6 was gassed on its way in the night of 13–4, and the relief was not made. Two/5 strengthened by fragments of 2/6, remained in position. Three/5, on relief by the 23rd Infantry, was ordered to the woods northwest of Lucy. The machine guns of the Marines would remain 24 hours in Bouresches, and then rejoin the 6th Machine Gun Battalion.[556]

On 14 June General Harbord placed Lieutenant Colonel Feland in command of all forces in the Bois de Belleau, now the 2/5, the 1/6, and fragments of the 2/6. He established his command post with Lieutenant Colonel Wise, the 2/5, near Hill 181, at about 3 pm, Major [*Ralph S.*] Keyser going with him as second-in-command of 2/5. Major Keyser at once made a reconnaissance of the lines in the wood, and the fact that the Germans were still in force in the northern end was verified. It was not realized that their

---

550 *War Diary, 23rd Inf., 13 June, Vol. 7.*
551 *Report of activities, 3/23, 14 June, Vol. 7.*
552 *Three/23 to CO 23rd Inf., 7:35 am, 14 June, Vol. 5.*
553 *Report 14 June, K Co., 23rd Inf., Vol. 7.*
554 *Report of events, 3/23, 14 June, Vol. 7.*
555 *CO 23rd to 3rd Brigade, 5:05 am, 14 June.*
556 *F.O. 5, to Brigade, 4:30 pm, 13 June, Vol. 2.*

line extended also down the western face.⁵⁵⁷ Plans were drawn up by the 2/5 for a third attack, but it was decided to try other methods, since an assault on the rocky knoll above the flank of 2/5 promised to be very costly.⁵⁵⁸ During the afternoon, the southern and eastern part of the wood being saturated with gas, General Harbord ordered 2/5 to withdraw three companies to high ground around Hills 181 and 169, leaving the battalion front on the eastern face of the wood held by one company; the Germans would not, the Brigade Commander considered, attempt the occupation of a wood newly gassed.⁵⁵⁹

17th Company of 1/5 in the Bois de Belleau: 13–16 June

Following its relief by 3/6 on the left of the 4th Brigade front, during the night of 12–13 June, 1/5 went into position west of the Lucy-Torcy road, in approximately the old line of departure of the 2/5 with the mission of flanking the anticipated German counter-attack. Brigade Headquarters believed that the Woods was almost entirely cleared of Germans, and the situation sketch annexed to the 4th Brigade War Diary for 5:00 pm, 13 June, shows that it believed the 2/5 to be occupying all the northern portion of the Wood, except for a very narrow strip on the northwestern edge, paralleling the Double-Tree Road. No contact, however, existed between 1/5, west of the Wood, and 2/5, within it.⁵⁶⁰ After daylight on 13 June — the exact time is not a matter of record, but reports of the 17th Company indicate that it was after the violent artillery activity centering around Bouresches had died down — the 17th Company, Captain Winans, was ordered to establish contact between the Bois de Champillon and the left of Lieutenant Colonel Wise.⁵⁶¹

The directions given for the location of the 2/5 flank were vague, and Captain Winans sent a small patrol under [First] Lieutenant [Robert] Blake to find the line of the Wise Battalion and. to examine the approaches to the new position. The patrol crossed the Lucy-Torcy road at the fork where the Double Tree Road branches off to Belleau noting many dead men on the open ground to the right, and proceeded through the scattered trees around Hill 169, where they found a Corporal of 2/5 with a few men, who had been dropped off on the 11th to cover the battalion left, and who had been out

557 *Major Keyser, 2nd Division file.*
558 *Operations report, 2/5-2-16 June, Vol. 7.*
559 *24 hour report, 4th Brigade to 8:00 pm, 14 June, Vol. 6.*
560 *24-hour report to 8:00 pm, 13 June, 4th Brigade War Diary, Vol. 6.*
561 *The 20th Co, 3/5, held the north edge of the Bois de Champillon. 24-hour report to 8:00 pm, 13 June, 4th Brigade War Diary, Vol. 6.*

of communication ever since. From Hill 169 the patrol entered a small ravine which led into the west face of the wood, north of X–line 262, where there was the wreckage of a machine gun nest with dead Germans and dead Marines.[562] North of the ravine, the patrol found a road running eastward across the wood, and along the road it encountered Germans, who opened fire. No Marines were seen, anywhere — except the dead, but the Germans were numerous. The patrol returned to Captain Winans in the Bois de Champillon and reported.[563]

Captain Winans then put his company in motion, the leading platoons in advance guard formation, and worked across Hill 169 into the Bois de Belleau, following the general route of the patrol, to the ravine which the patrol had passed. The company was halted on the ravine and scouting parties were pushed to the front and to the right, in search of the Wise Battalion. A little later a German plane came over, his undercarriage brushing the treetops, and Captain Winans deduced that artillery would follow. He called in his reconnaissance parties and retired to the woods west of Hill 169, just beyond the Lucy-Torcy road, where he halted, organized, and dug in, and immediately an intense bombardment visited the area he had vacated. Only 1 casualty was incurred in the operation, and it had been ascertained, that, wherever the flank of 2/5 lay, it was nowhere near the west side of the Woods and that a very wide gap existed in the western part of the Woods through which the Germans were free to move. The promptness with which his reconnaissance drew artillery attention showed also that the Germans were on the alert. Two Marines were then sent from the 17th Company around the southern end of the Wood, to locate the Wise Battalion from the rear, and Captain Winans reported the results of his movements to Major Turrill, remaining in position through the remainder of 13 June and through 14 June.[564]

On 14 June, Lieutenant Colonel Feland was sent into the Bois de Belleau to take command of all troops within it — then the 1/6, 2/5, and fragments of 2/6.

In the meantime, Major Turrill and Captain Winans conferred with Lieutenant Colonel Feland, and Captain Winans considered that, with some assistance from special weapons, he could connect up with 2/5 on the other side of the wood. Lieutenant Colonel Feland directed that the 17th Company proceed with the movement on the 15th, and 1-pounders, trench mortars, and some machine guns were promised. During the afternoon of 14

---

562 Captain Winans, to 2nd Div. Hist. Sect. file. Captain R. Blake, to 2nd Div. Hist. Sect. file.
563 Captain R. Blake, to 2nd Div. Hist. Sect. file.
564 Captain R. Winans, to 2nd Div. Hist. Sect. file.

June, Lieutenant Colonel Feland and Captain Winans made a personal reconnaissance of the woods and decided on details.[565]

The 17th Company entered the woods again at daylight on the 15th, supported by position fire from 4 machine guns. A sharp resistance developed at once, and the German advanced forces south of the rocky knoll on which their main line ran were driven in and forced aside. The 17th Company fought its way across the woods, forming a front to its left flank as it advanced, and between 7:00 and 8:00 its leading elements made contact with the left of the Wise battalion, where it found fragments of 2/6 acting with 2/5. A line was established, in liaison to left and right respectively, from about 176.1–262.4 to 175.0–262.0. During the operation, Captain Winans was wounded and evacuated, and Captain [*Thomas*] Quigley was sent up from the 49th Company of 1/5 to take command of the 17th, bringing with him, as reinforcement, a platoon from the 49th and a platoon from the 66th Companies.[566] The left platoon of the 17th made an attempt to drive forward along the western face of the wood, its flank on the Double Tree Road, but it was stopped in its tracks by the Germans.[567] Contact was made with the right of the 20th Company, in the near corner of the Bois de Champillon, and the position across the Bois de Belleau securely tied in.

The casualties of the 17th Company, from 13 June through 15 June, amounted to 1 officer and 40 men, killed and wounded, 22 casualties occurring on the 15th.[568]

The importance of the operation is obvious. The left flank of 2/5 had been in the air ever since it left its line of departure west of the Bois de Belleau on the 11th, and it was now secured by the 17th Company. Continuously, since the 2/5 drove through to the east face of the Wood in its first attack, all the western section of the Wood had been open to the Germans, as far south as Hill 181; now the gap in the Brigade line — a kilometre at its widest — was definitely closed. German patrols were no longer free to filter past the Hook and pick up runners, and to fire into the backs of the Marines in line.

The situation in the Bois de Belleau, from 11 June to 15 June, had been more precarious for the Marines than Brigade Headquarters realized, especially on the 13th and 14th. It is hard to see how 2/5 extended in a thin line along the eastern edge, could have avoided a disaster if the German tactics had been aggressive. Certainly a thrust down the woods from the northwestern third would have been serious, for the Marines were at no time able

---

565 *Ibid.*
566 *Captain Quigley to Colonel Neville, 8:20 am, 15 June, 5th Regt., Vol. 5. Major Turrill to Colonel Neville, 7:15 am, 15 June, 5th Regt., Vol. 5.*
567 *Captain R. Blake, to 2nd Div. Hist. Sect. file.*
568 *Adjutant and Inspector, USMC.*

Map Reference: Chateau Thierry. Scale 1/20,000.

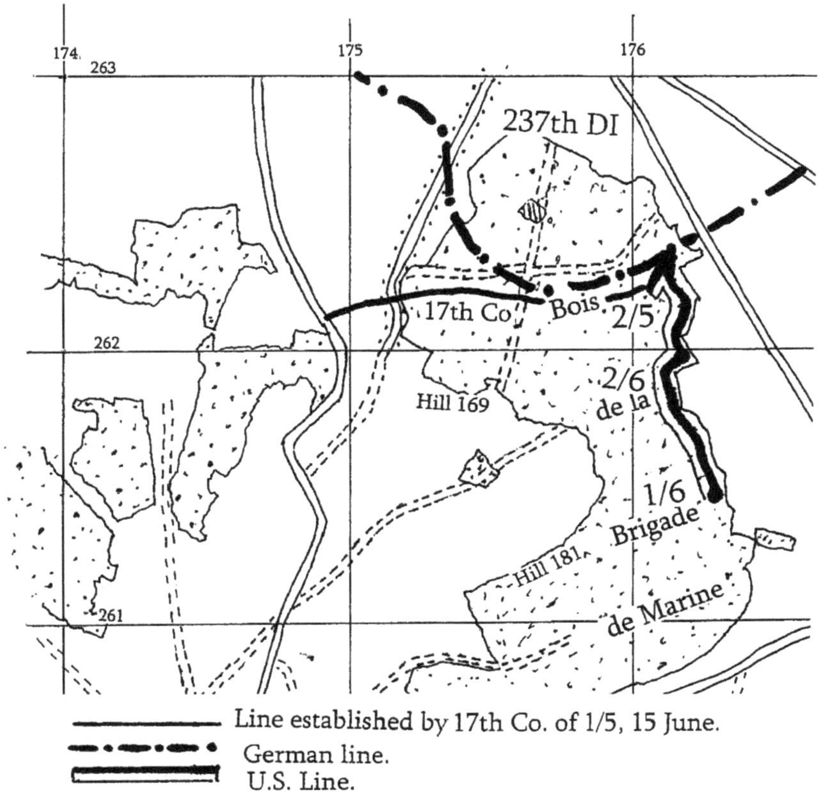

———— Line established by 17th Co. of 1/5, 15 June.
—•—•—• German line.
▭▭▭▭ U.S. Line.

Map 11

to create a defensive organization, with zones of outpost, of support, and reserve, for their line of resistance. But, while the Germans held to their ground with extreme tenacity, and took quick advantage of every opportunity to reoccupy 10st areas, they made no serious attacks on forces in position. Their reports indicate that the location of the Marines was known, and their patrols moved freely through the Woods. The strength reports of the 237th Division may contain the answer: on 11 June the Division was holding a 3-kilometre front with 47 officers and 1462 men, and influenza was prevalent among the troops, both in the line and out of it. On the 13th, the infantry problem was so acute that the division command combed out all orderlies, liaison agents, and odd[569] details serving in the rear areas, pri-

569 War Diary, 237th DI, 11-15 June.

A Marine corporal walking

vates and non-commissioned officers, to number of 340, and sent them to the front. The neighboring divisions had their hands full. The 5th Guards, fighting from Bussiares to the west, was losing 50 per cent of its effective strength, holding the Clignon line against Degoutte's Frenchmen[570] and the 28th already exhausted when it relieved the 10th, appeared incapable of aggression. No fresh divisions were allotted to the Conta Corps.[571]

    570 *History of the German Divisions, G-2, GHQ, AEF, 1919.*
    571 *War Diary, IV Reserve Corps, 1-22 June.*
    Note: This operation of the 17th Company, 13-15 June, is not mentioned in the War Diary of the 4th Brigade. Field messages referring to it are found in the 5th Regiment, Vol. 5. Captain Winans and Blake, have reported it in detail to the BMC and to the 2nd Div. Historical Section.

Seventeen

Relief of the 4th Brigade by the 7th Infantry

After the attacks of 11–13 June, within the Bois de Belleau, it became apparent to the command of the 2nd Division that the Marine Brigade must be given a period of rest and recuperation. General Harbord had been insisting on a relief, temporarily, at least, since 10 June.[572] Every Marine Battalion had been in action and the battle casualties of the Brigade had, by 15 June, amounted to more than 50 per cent of its effectives in officers and men.[573] These losses had been to an extent made good by replacements, but the replacements, in many cases, fresh from the United States and without advanced training in France, had been incorporated with companies on the line under conditions which made sound reorganization impossible.[574]

It was the opinion and the desire of the French Corps Commander — now General [*Stanislaus*] Naulin, who had succeeded General Degoutte, that the matter could be handled within the 2nd Division, by a distribution of the battalions of the 3rd Brigade on the front line, the Marines acting as support and reserve while they rested and reorganized. The Division command, however, refused to entertain the idea. From the entry of the Division into the sector, it had been resolved that only one of the infantry brigades was to be engaged at a time, the other being held intact to meet unforeseen emergencies. The situation towards the Ourcq was still threatening, and attack divisions held the front of the German XXV Corps on Conta's left. General Bundy and Colonel Brown, therefore, refused to dissipate the strength of the 3rd Brigade on the Bouresches-Vaux line.

572   *War Diary, 4th Brigade, 10-14 June,* Vol. 6.
573   *Adjutant and Inspector, USMC.*
574   *War Diary, 4th Brigade, 10-14 June,* Vol. 6. History 3/6: see other unit histories also *War Diary, 2nd Division.*

The 3rd U.S. Division, regulars, lay on the right in the area, of the French XXXVIII, Corps, not engaged as a divisional unit. Certain of its regiments, notably the 7th Infantry, were in the rear along the Marne unemployed. The 2nd Division command suggested that the 7th Infantry was available for the temporary relief of the 4th Brigade, without in any way disturbing the permanent sector arrangements. After some argument, in which General Bundy threatened to exercise his seniority as ranking American Officer present in the 2nd and 3rd U.S. Divisions, and to assume command of all American troops, for such purposes as he saw fit, General Naulin yielded and issued orders for the 7th Infantry to relieve the Marine Brigade.[575]

7th Infantry Regiment in Bois de Belleau

On 15 June XXI Corps, now commanded by General Naulin, issued Ordre d'Operations No 2065, placing the 7th Infantry Regiment of the 3rd U.S. Division provisionally at the disposal of the 2nd Division in order to give adequate rest to the regiments of the 4th Brigade.[576] The 3rd Division was at this time in the XXI Corps area, and the 7th Infantry Regiment was billeted along the Marne south of Montreuil.[577]

On the same day, Field Order 6 of the 4th Brigade, issued at 2:30 pm, announced the temporary detail of the 7th U.S. Infantry Regiment to the 4th Brigade; and announced further that the French 167th DI would take over the ridge running north from Hill 142, and the line as far east as the brook running east of the ridge. The relief of 3/6, then in line on Hill 142, would take place the night of 15 June; the 3/6 would then go to Division reserve. The relief of 2/5 was ordered by the 1/7th Infantry; the 2/6 was directed to the Bois Gros Jean on the Paris-Metz road. The 2/5 would retire to Mery. It was provided that each Marine battalion relieved by the 7th Infantry would exchange billets, kitchens, and water carts with the battalion making the relief.[578]

On this day Colonel [*Thomas M.*] Anderson, [*Jr.,*] commanding the 7th, was directed by the Chief of Staff, 2nd Division, to designate a battalion to enter the trenches that night, and to report at once to 2nd Division Headquarters, with the designated battalion commander and his captains.[579]

575 *Notes on Chateau Thierry; Maj. Gen. P. Brown. File.*
576 *Orde General d'Operations No. 2065, 15 June of XXI CA.*
577 *Operations of the 7th Inf. in Belleau Wood, 3rd Div. file.*
578 *F.O. 6, 4th Brigade, 2:30 pm, 15 June, Vol. 2.*
579 *Chief of Staff, 2nd Div. to CO 7th Inf., 15 June, Vol. 1., 2nd Div. records.*

Relief of the 4th Brigade by the 7th Infantry 167

In accord with this arrangement, at 2:30 pm 15 June, the 4th Brigade issued Field Order 6, providing for the first relief's of Marine battalions by the assigned Infantry: in general, battalions relieved in the line were to exchange stations with the relieving battalions.[580] Administrative memorandum 33 of the 2nd Division directed that each incoming battalion would exchange transportation and supply details, including kitchens and water carts with the organization it replaced.[581]

In obedience to orders, Colonel Anderson of the 7th, with Lieut Col [*John P.*] Adams, the 1/7, and his company commanders, reported to 2nd Division Headquarters, and the 1/7 was brought from Mery-sur-Marne to Montreuil. The regimental and battalion commanders proceeded to 4th Brigade Headquarters, where they arrived shortly after noon; and they were sent on to the PC of Colonel Neville, 5th Marines.[582] Lieut Col Adams and his officers then made a reconnaissance of the positions held by 2/5 and 2/6 in the northern part of the Bois de Belleau; they had been informed by General Harbord that the Marines had suffered very heavy losses and must be given a period of rest, and that the mission of the 7th Infantry was to hold the wood at all costs.[583] The reconnaissance was completed at about 8:00 o'clock, the battalions meantime marching up from Montreuil, and entering the wood after dark. The relief was completed before daylight,[584] with minor losses.[585] During the relief, it was reported that two German attacks were repulsed in the northern end of the woods;[586] but it is probable that these were, if anything, enemy patrols; the Germans were making a relief in the same place, and attempted nothing on the Americans, although the 461st Regiment also reports an attack upon its lines while the relief was taking place.[587]

The 1/7 placed all four companies in line, in order, from right to left, A, C, D, and B. A company connected with 1/6 near X–line 232.0; C prolonged the line to the north; D was around the angle now called the Hook, and B Company extended the left south-westerly across the wood toward

---

580   *F.O. 6, 4th Brigade, 2:30 pm, 15 June, Vol. 2.*
581   *Records of the 3rd Inf. Div., and the 7th Inf.*
582   *24 hour report to 8 pm, 15 June, 4th Brigade War Diary, Vol. 6.*
583   *Report Operations Belleau Woods 1/7: 3rd Div. file.*
584   Note: *There is a conflict between (5) and (6) as to the date of this relief: Lt Col Adams says it took place the night [of] 16-17 June.(8) General Harbord's 24 hour reports are substantiated by 2nd Division order to 7th Inf, and by 6th Regiment Field Message, Lee to Harbord, 12:55 pm, 16 June, Vol. 5., and by Wise, 2/5 Operations Report, Vol. 7. Lt Col Adams, in view of these records, is in error.*
585   *Report Operations Belleau Woods 1/7: 3rd Div. file.*
586   *24 hour report to 8:00 pm, 16 June, 4th Brigade War Diary, Vol. 6.*
587   *War Diary, 237th DI, 15-16 June.*

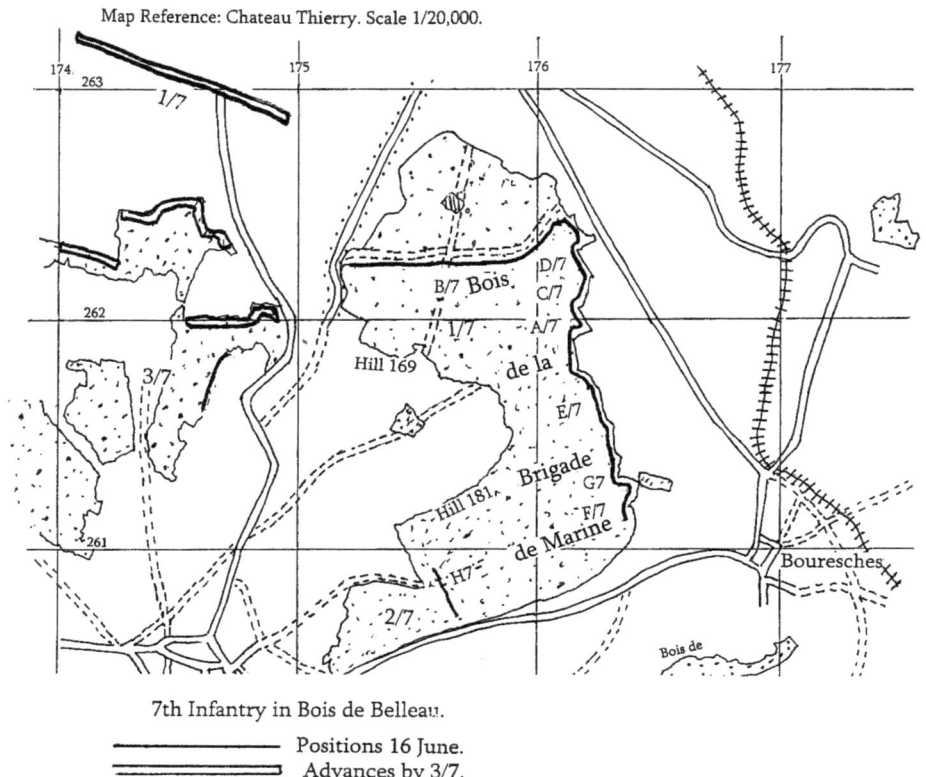

7th Infantry in Bois de Belleau.
——————— Positions 16 June.
═══════ Advances by 3/7.

Map 12

its western face, in the positions established by the 17th Company of 1/5 the morning of 15 June. One platoon of A Company was held out as battalion reserve, and each company posted one platoon in support. There was no second line proper.[588]

The general plan for the reduction of the German positions remaining within the wood had been discussed with Lieut Colonel Adams by General Harbord, who believed that the Germans could be gradually encircled and captured or dislodged without assault; and Lieut Colonel Adams was in accord with this plan.[589]

Two/5 withdrew to Mery-sur-Marne and 2/6 to Bois Gros Jean on the 16th.[590] During the night 3/6 was relieved by the French 167th Division, and

588 Operations report 1/7 in Belleau Wood; 7th Inf., 3rd Div. file.
589 24-hour report to 8:00 pm, 15 June, 4th Brigade War Diary, Vol. 6.
590 Operations report 2/5, June 1918, Vol. 7.

marched to Bois Platerie.[591] The night was generally quiet on the Brigade front.[592]

Sixteen June was quiet, marked only by aerial activity: a French balloon was shot down.[593] Reconnaissance was made by officers of the 2/7, Captain P. J. Hurley, U.S.A., in the southern part of the Bois de Belleau, and after dark that battalion relieved the 1/6, the relief passing quietly.[594] One/6 had begun the wiring in of the east face of the wood,[595] since no further advance was contemplated here. The 2/7 carried on this work: it also did some work towards burying the dead, and collecting and sending out the abandoned war material, German and American, scattered through the wood.[596] Liaison was maintained with the 23rd Infantry in the ravine between the southeast corner of the Bois de Belleau and Bouresches. No other activity was required on the part of this battalion. It had in line 3 companies, in order from the left, F, G, and E. H Company was battalion reserve: on 21 June, after the attack by 1/7, two platoons of H Company reinforced the right of the battalion, since its flank company had been weakened by casualties.[597]

The 17th [of] June was without incident, other than marked activity on the part of the German gunners and airplanes. One/7 reported an attack by the enemy during the night of 16–17; 4th Brigade considered this attack to be only patrol activity on the battalion front: the Germans report no attack made by them.[598] After dark, the 3/7, Major [Jesse] Gaston, entered the line, relieving 1/5 in the positions west of the Lucy-Torcy road, and on the north edges of the Bois de Champillon. Three companies, I, K, and L, took up positions: N remained in the vicinity of battalion Headquarters as reserve. The relief was accomplished with minor losses.[599] With the entry of 3/7, all of the 7th Regiment was now in line. Colonel Neville retained command of the 5th Regiment sector, with Lieut Colonel Feland local commander in the Bois de Belleau. Lieut Colonel Lee was relieved of responsibility, and was directed to devote his energies to the reorganization of his battalions.[600] The commanding officer of the 7th Regiment was present but

---

591 History 3/6.
592 War Diary, 4th Brigade, 15-16 June, Vol. 6.
593 24-hr Operations report 2/7 in Belleau Wood, 3rd Div. file. Our report to 8:00 pm, 16 June, 4th Brigade War Diary, Vol. 6.
594 Operations report 2/7 in Belleau Wood, 3rd Div. file.
595 Lee to [2nd Lt. John I.] Conroy, 11:38 am, 14 June, Vol. 5.
596 Operations report 2/7 in Belleau Wood, 3rd Div. file.
597 Ibid.
598 24-hour report 8:00 pm, 17 June, 4th Brigade War Diary, Vol. 6. War Diary, 87th DI, 16-17 June.
599 Operations report 3/7 in Belleau Wood; 7th Inf., 3rd Div. file.
600 Harbord to Lee, 16th June, Vol. 5.

exercised no command. The machine guns and supply echelons of the 4th Brigade remained in place, only the infantry being withdrawn.

On the night 18–19 June 1/7 made its first movement towards clearing its front; B Company attempted to move forward to straighten its line across the woods. It was brought at once under fire from the rocky ridge in front of it, and fell back to its original line with a loss of 5 killed and 16 wounded.[601] The battalion had begun to wire its position with the assistance of the 2nd Engineers: it was enjoined by Brigade not to wire in its east and west line across the wood, since it was desired that steady pressure be exerted in that direction.[602] One/7 reported to 4th Brigade that it had taken under fire and killed 12 Germans in the fields outside the wood.[603] During the 18th Major Gaston, the 3/7, determined by reconnaissance that his left company, I, just west of the Lucy-Torcy Road, was ineffective: he swung it north and established it in an east and west line along X–line 262.0, with its right on the Lucy-Torcy Road. After dark he sent a patrol towards the ravine a kilometre south of Torcy: enemy movement was observed along the Torcy-Belleau Road, but no contact was made with the enemy, and no identifications were secured.[604] Nineteen June was uneventful; plans were drawn up for the 3/7 to advance its left, in furtherance of the general scheme for the envelopment of the Bois de Belleau.[605]

On the morning of 20 June 1/7 made the first of two attacks upon the enemy positions in front of it. A force was made up of two platoons from B Company and one platoon each from companies A and C; this force advanced against the Germans in the northern end of the woods, but was beaten back with a loss of 11 killed, 45 wounded, and 7 missing. The detail from D Company did not get into position promptly, and seems to have taken no actual part in the operation; the thrust was delivered by only two platoons.[606] German patrols of the 87th Division later identified the 7th Regiment from casualties that fell into their hands.[607]

---

601 *Operations report 1/7 in Belleau Wood, 7th Inf., 3rd Div. file.*
602 *War Diary, 4th Brigade, 18 June, Vol. 6.*
603 *24-hour report 4th Brigade to 8:00 pm, 19 June, Vol. 6.*
604 *Operations report, 3/7, Belleau Wood, 7th Inf., 3rd Div. file.*
605 *Ibid.*
606 *Operations report, 1/7 in Belleau Woods, 7th Inf., 3rd Div. file. 24-hour report to 8:00 pm, 20 June, 4th Brigade War Diary, Vol. 6.*
Note: *The dates given for the first attack by the 1/7 conflict: Lt Col Adams says he attacked the morning of 19 June. General Harbord, in his 24-hour reports places it on 20 June. Major Gaston, 3/7, agrees with Lt Col Adams; but the report of 3/7 confuses events of 19 June with events of 21 June. Field Messages, Harbord to Adams, and Adams to Harbord on 20 June confirm the Harbord reports; as does 2nd Div. War Diary.*
607 *War Diary, 87th DI, 20 June.*

Relief of the 4th Brigade by the 7th Infantry

One/7 made no further move on 20 June, but that night the 3/7 advanced 3 platoons of I Company to the ravine at the cross roads a kilometre south of Torcy, where a position was organized from about Y–line 174.0 eastward to the road at 174.6–263.2. The 4th Platoon of I Company was behind the left flank in the small square woods on X–line 263.0, in liaison with the French. The movement was unopposed, and was affected without loss.[608] It will be remembered that the 3/6, before its relief on 15–16 June had reconnoitered this area with a view to occupying it, but had found it held in force.[609] Since that time the 237th Division had also been relieved, and the 87th Division does not seem to have retained its force there.

During the night 20–21 June, 3/7 established 2 platoons of I Company in line extending the right of I Company from the crossroads towards the Bois de Belleau, to 175.0–262.7. There was no opposition, and no loss was suffered.[610]

Following the failure of the attempt of 1/7 in the woods, General Harbord advised the battalion commander that he was to have one more chance to dislodge the enemy; that if he succeeded, credit for clearing the Bois de Belleau would be freely given to him, and that the 7th Regiment could not afford to fail: the battalion was to be relieved the night of 21–22. A second attack was ordered to take place on the 21 June.[611] Acknowledging these orders, Lieut Col Adams wrote that arrangements had been perfected for the attack to be made by A Company, Lieutenant Helm, at 3:15 am on 21 June. He felt, however, that such an attack without extensive artillery preparation would be unsuccessful; he considered it necessary to withdraw all troops from the line in the north end of the wood and subject the German positions to thorough shelling before assailing them. He presented these views to Lieutenant Colonel Feland, who referred them to General Harbord.[612] General Harbord acceded to his suggestion. At 7:45 pm Lieutenant Colonel Adams received an order from the Brigade Commander, signed at 6:00 pm, directing him to withdraw his companies south of X–line 262.0. After midnight, irregular harassing fire would be placed around the area to prevent the Germans from filtering into the vacated positions, and from 2:00 am the guns would make a thorough preparation of the German line. He would then attack.[613]

---

608   Operations report, 3/7 in Belleau Woods, 7th Inf., 3rd Div. file.
609   Sibley to CO 6th Marines, 11:00 am, June 14, Vol. 5.
610   Operations report, 3/7 in Belleau Woods, 7th Inf., 3rd Div. file.
611   Special report CG, 4th Brigade, to CG, 2nd Division, 21 June, 4th Brigade, WD, Vol. 6.
612   Operations report, 1/7 in Belleau Woods, 7th Inf, 3rd Div. file. Special report CG, 4th Brigade, to CG 2nd Division, 21 June, 4th Brigade, WD, Vol. 6.
613   Ibid.

Lt Colonel Adams dictated his orders to his company commanders for these movements at 9:40 pm. The attacking force was composed of A and B Companies in two waves each, with Company C in support of the attack and Company D as battalion reserve. The withdrawal from the forward positions began as ordered at 11:45 pm and was accomplished by 2:30 am 21 June without mishap.[614] The artillery preparation proceeded as ordered.[615] The reports of 1/7 indicate, however, that the fire of preparation, and the barrage placed on the objective at 2:00 am were light in volume and ineffective.[616] At 3:15 the assaulting troops moved forward. A and C Companies reached the enemy positions and delivered an attack: B Company lost direction in moving up and did not get into the fight. A Company went in alone, seeing nothing of B, which was expected on its left flank. C Company, in support about 150 yards to the rear, moved up into line and was engaged, but not so heavily as A. The German positions were not penetrated; A Company was repulsed with a loss estimated at 140 to 150 killed and wounded: C Company had about 30 casualties. D Company was not engaged.

A German counter barrage fell upon the area after the attack started, and all companies were somewhat dispersed, but A, C, and D were back in their original positions by 7:30 am.[617]

Company B, which had been directed to place its left in the west edge of the woods when it advanced, placed its right in that trace, had no contact with the rest of the battalion, and turned up after the attack behind the right company (M) of 3/7.[618]

Fourth Brigade Headquarters received no reports from this attack until 7:00 am, when a message came in from Lieut Col Adams stating that "all is not going well."[619] At 8:20 am a report was received from Major Gaston, commanding 3/7: he advised that the Lieutenant commanding A Company had turned up at the PC of 3/7, without his men, stating that A Company was shot to pieces.[620] On receiving this, General Harbord ordered the command-

614 Ibid.
615 *Special report CG, 4th Brigade to CG, 2nd Div., 21 June, Vol. 6.*
Note: *All battalion commanders of the 7th Inf. join in describing the artillery preparation given the 1/7 on 21 June as light and ineffective. It was delivered by the 12th and 17th FA Regiments, and the records of the 17th indicate nothing beyond routine harassing fire the night of 20-21 June; no shelling of the Bois de Belleau is recorded. The 75's of the 12th were not effective in dense woods. "Operations report 1/7," ascribes the failure of 1/7 to the lack of adequate artillery preparation more than to any other cause.*
616 *Operations report, 1/7 in Belleau Woods, 7th Inf, 3rd Div. file.*
617 Ibid.
618 Ibid. *Special report, CG, 4th Brigade to CG, 2nd Div., 21 June, Vol. 6.*
619 *Operations report, 1/7 in Belleau Woods, 7th Inf., 3rd Div. file. Special report, CG, 4th Brigade to CG, 2nd Div., 21 June, Vol. 6.*
620 *War Diary, 87th DI.*

ing officer, A Company, forwarded to 5th Regiment PC, and went to that place to meet him. Immediately afterward, a second message came from 3/7: Major Gaston reported that B Company of 1/7 had appeared in the rear of his right (H) company, on the Lucy-Torcy road just northwest of Hill 169, and that they reported firing within the woods to their right rear.[621] This indicated that the Germans had pushed south again in the woods, and the 47th Company of 3/5th Marines was at once marched to Hill 169 to investigate. Reaching there, it found no Germans;[622] the German 347th Regiment had contented itself with holding its positions and made no attempt to advance, although the area was held under heavy fire from small arms and artillery.[623]

Colonel Anderson was then at the 5th Regiment PC, and General Harbord sent him into the woods to report on 1/7. At 11:30 am he sent word that the attack had failed, with the loss of 170 officers and men, and that Companies C and D were then in their former positions.[624] Lieut Col Adams reported that by 7:30 am A, C, and B Companies were reassembled and in their original lines and that B Company returned to its lines by 3:30 pm that afternoon. Two platoons of H Company, battalion reserve, were sent by 2/7, and took over a part of the line of A Company. The loss reported by 1/7 for this attack was later fixed at 16 killed, 70 wounded, and 13 missing.[625] During the forenoon, officers of 3/5 began the reconnaissance of the lines of 1/7, and after dark the relief of 1/7 by 3/5 was carried out, 1/7 withdrawing without incident.[626]

The casualties of 1/7, from the night 15–16 June to the night 21–22 June were 2 officers and 34 enlisted men killed; 3 officers and 157 enlisted men wounded, and 38 enlisted men missing; a total of 5 officers and 229 enlisted men casualties from all causes. The 1/7 reported two machine guns captured from the Germans and 2 machine guns destroyed.[627] When relieved, they turned over their lines intact as they had received them; but no gains were made by this battalion in the woods,[628] nor is there any evidence of any aggressive attempts against them by the German 347th Regiment which was on their front.[629] They took no prisoners and secured no identifications.[630]

---

621   Ibid. *[I wonder why the German division would be reporting on an American unit in the woods? It doesn't make any sense, but that is what the note states. GBC].*
622   Special report, CG, 4th Brigade to CG, 2nd Div., 21 June, Vol. 6.
623   War Diary, 87th DI. Operations report, 1/7 in Belleau Woods, 7th Inf., 3rd Div. file.
624   Special report, CG, 4th Brigade to CG, 2nd Div., 21 June, Vol. 6.
625   Operations Report, 1/7 in Belleau Woods, 7th Inf., 3rd Div. file.
626   Ibid.
627   Ibid.
628   Ibid.
629   War Diary, 87th DI.
630   Operations Report, 1/7 in Belleau Woods, 7th Inf., 3rd Div. file.

Three/7 planned, during the night 21–22 June, to extend the line established by L Company the previous night to the patch of woods at 175.0–232.5; 2 platoons of H Company were in readiness to move up into this position. But a patrol sent forward to reconnoiter drew heavy fire from the edge of the Bois de Belleau about 200 metres distant, and the movement was not carried out.[631] Three/7 made no further movements in its sector. 22 June and 23 June were uneventful, and the night of 23–24 June it was relieved by 2/5, Major Keyser, without incident or casualties.[632]

Two/7 continued its work in the south half of the Bois de Belleau, and the wiring in of the east face of the wood was about completed by 23 June.[633] Two/7 was relieved by 3/6, Major Sibley during the night 22–23 June.[634] Two/7, while in this sector, reported a loss of 6 killed, 49 wounded, and 2 missing.[635]

The 7th Infantry was with the 4th Brigade from 15 June to 24 June, and during the period 17–22 June it held the entire front of the 4th Brigade. Its 2nd battalion performed the work required of it, suffered some loss from shellfire, and was not otherwise in action. Its 3rd battalion advanced the line west of the Bois de Belleau materially, but met no opposition and was at no time engaged. The 1st Battalion held its lines intact, but was unable to advance them. The regiment enabled, however, the six exhausted Marine battalions to rest and recuperate for the final clearing of the Brigade front.

Doughboy hiking

    631 *Operations report, 3/7 in Belleau Woods, 7th Inf, 3rd Div. file.*
    632 *24-hour report 4th Brigade to 8:00 pm, 24 June, Vol. 6.*
    633 *24-hour report 4th Brigade to 8:00 pm, 23 June, Vol. 6.*
    634 *Hist 3/6, pg 28.*
    635 *Operations report, 2/7 in Belleau Woods, 7th Inf., 3rd Div. file.*

Eighteen

Final Attacks in Bois de Belleau by 3/5

Reconnaissance of the northern end of the Bois de Belleau was carried out by the battalion commander and company commanders of the 3/5 on 21 June, following the last attack by 1/7. After nightfall 3/5 took over the positions. During the night a German deserter came into the American Lines, and gave information regarding the enemy dispositions which was verified through a personal reconnaissance by Lieut Col Feland. For the first time since the attacks of 10–13 June, Brigade Headquarters realized that the German line was solid and organized across the northern end of the wood; and that all previous impressions as to the possibility of enveloping the German positions within the wood had been erroneous. Major Shearer was informed that, with the forces at his hand, he would clear the woods forthwith. No other troops would be sent him, since the space did not permit the deployment of a larger force. Nor did the Brigade Commanders consider it practicable to make further artillery preparation. VB rifle grenades and trench mortars were to be used before the attack, and hand grenades were provided for the assault. Snipers in pairs were sent out through 22nd June, and, it was believed, had good results.[636]

It may be noted that harassment in the northern end of the woods, where the lines were in close contact, by snipers and rifle grenadiers, was considered most effective by the Germans of the 461st Regiment, who suffered from these methods during the last days of its duty in the woods. (12–15 June). A man could not show himself without drawing fire, they record. They had severe losses in Von Hartlieb's force before they were relieved.[637]

636 *24-hour report 4th Brigade to 8 pm, 22 June, Vol. 6.*
637 *Annexes to the War Diary, 237th DI.*

On 22 June, Major Shearer submitted plans for his attack, and they were approved. Twenty-three June was quiet until about 7 pm, when 3/5 went forward. The line of the 3/5 was held, from left to right, by the 45th, 16th, 20th, and 47th Companies, with a reserve posted in rear of the right center, about behind the Hook.[638]

The attack started at 7:00 pm, with the 16th Company, Captain [Robert] Yowell, plus 1 platoon 47th Company on the left, and the 20th Company, Captain Platt, plus 50 men of the 45th Company on the right. When these companies moved clear of the Marine line, the 45th Company extended its right, and the 47th Company its left, to close the line behind them. Combat groups were thrown forward in advance armed with hand and rifle grenades, and these quickly made contact with the enemy, and developed resistance from numerous machine guns, which they assaulted by bombing, the skirmish lines of riflemen following them. It was observed, that as soon as a German machine gun was involved, its crew fell back, taking with them the gun and any casualties that had occurred, while flanking fire was at once opened on the lost position. The volume of their fire did not slacken, and the casualties suffered by the Marines were out of proportion to the ground they gained. Contact was lost between the 16th and 20th Companies.

At 8:00 pm Major Shearer reported to the 4th Brigade that he was making progress slowly.[639]

The 20th Company, which lay at the start in the closest contact with the enemy, was able to get forward only about 20 yards, to the top of the rocky knoll just north of the hook; but the knoll was immediately made untenable by machine guns beyond it, and although this company cleaned out three machine gun positions, the enemy got away with his machine guns and his wounded. The 16th Company advanced further, but was unable to dig in or to organize new positions, and lost heavily. Eventually both companies fell back to their old lines, the 16th reporting an estimated loss of 1 officer and 75 men, and the 20th, 26 men. The 45th and 47th Companies suffered in position from the German artillery reaction.[640] At 11:20 pm a report from

Brigade to the effect that the attack was held up, and would proceed in the morning.[641] During the night 2 platoons of the 83rd Company was sent forward to reinforce the 16th Company; these joined Captain Yowell

---

638 *Shearer to Harbord, 24 June, Vol. 5.*
Note: No artillery preparation is mentioned in the records of this attack.
639 *Shearer to 4th Brigade, 8:00 pm, 23 June, Vol. 4.*
640 *Shearer to 4th Brigade, 11:00 am, 24 June.*
641 *Neville to Harbord, 11:20 pm, 23 June.*

in his old line. The attack had failed completely: no ground was gained, no prisoners taken, nor machineguns captured. In the opinion of the battalion commander, his captains did the best possible, and their withdrawal was regarded as justifiable and wise by him it was the further opinion of Major Shearer that the tactics used were the only ones which would succeed at this place, but that the infantry alone could not dislodge the enemy.[642]

On 24 June a conference was held, regarding further efforts in the Bois de Belleau. General Bundy, General Harbord, General Chamberlaine, and the regimental and battalion commanders concerned were present, and it was decided to give the artillery a free hand in the preparation of the woods for assault It was agreed to withdraw the 3/5 to positions south of the X–line 262.0, while all the divisional artillery shelled the woods, and the approaches to the German positions in the northern end.[643] Prior to this, only the artillery assigned to the 4th Brigade had been used to prepare the way for the successive infantry attacks. The movement of 1/6 on 10 June had been the only effort preceded by fire from all the divisional artillery. Orders for the withdrawal of the 3/5, to be effective by 3:00 am 25 June, were issued to Major Shearer during the day.[644]

The night of 23–24 June, 2/5, Major Keyser, had relieved 3/7 west of the Bois de Belleau, and on the 24th it was directed to extend its right eastward to the Double-Tree Road, which passed along the edge of the wood from Lucy to Belleau.[645] This was effected during the night of the 24 June, and 2/5, from its advanced positions, was able to observe the movements of the Germans in the north end of the woods and along the approaches from Belleau.[646] In the meantime, the German 347th Regiment had effected its last relief in the woods: the night 22–23 June the 1/347th relieved the 2/347th, placing its 2nd, 3rd, and 4th Companies in the front line, where 1/347 had maintained two companies only, and leaving the 1st Company in support in the northern tip of the woods. These dispositions had effected the repulse of the first attack of 3/5, on 23 June, with no great effort.[647]

The 24th passed quietly, with some patrol activity along the front of the 2/5.[648] At 2:53 am 25 June Major Keyser reported the line of 2/5 continuous from the French 147th Regiment on Hill 142 to a point on the dou-

642   Ibid.
Note: The casualties of 3/5 on 23 June were 104 men killed and wounded;
Adjutant and Inspector USMC.
643   24 hour report 4th Brig., to 8:00 pm, 24 June, Vol. 6.
644   4th Brig. to 3/5, 24 June (no time), Vol. 5.
645   4th Brig. to 2/5, 12:00 noon, 24 June, Vol. 5.
646   Keyser 2/5 to 4th Brig., 2:30 am., 25 June and subsequent 2/5 messages, Vol. 5.
647   War Diary, 87th DI, 23-25 June.
648   Ibid.

bletree road at about X — line 262.4.[649] The withdrawal of 3/5 was carried out. At 3:00 am the artillery preparation began, 2 batteries of the 12th FA and 4 batteries of the 17th FA concentrating on the northern end of the woods, and the remainder of the Divisional guns covering the areas to the year [rear?].[650]

From 3:00 am to 5:00 pm on the 25th, the gunfire fell upon the Bois de Belleau, continuous for 14 hours.[651] Towards 4:00 on it reached its greatest intensity, and the companies of 1/347 suffered many casualties. The records of the German 347th Regiment mention especially trench mortar shells that fell upon their positions about 5:00 pm (6:00 pm German time) bursting in the trees and raining down with shrapnel effect. In this fire the officer commanding the 4th Company was killed, and the commander of the 3rd Company mortally wounded, and severe losses were inflicted in the ranks.[652] This fire involved also the contact companies of the neighboring battalions, the 5th Company of the 2/347, west of the wood, and the right flank of the 1/3rd Reserve Ersatz Regiment.[653] At 5:00 pm the artillery lifted to the area north of the wood, and the 3/5 advanced, with the 16, 20th, and 47th Companies in line, left to right, the 45th following in reserve, Heavy fire was laid upon them as they started, but very little of it was from machine guns: these were silenced.[654] Their objective was the north edge of the woods.

The German 347th Regiment received the impact of this attack at 5:30 pm, (6:30 pm German time) and the 1/347th immediately yielded ground. Half an hour later, at 6:00 pm (7:00 German time) the battalion commander, Captain of Cavalry von Kaulbars, realized, that it was serious. He sent his 1st Company up to the line from the north tip of the woods, distributing it among the remnants of the 2nd, 3rd, and 4th Companies, which had survived the artillery, and at 7:00 pm (8:00 pm German time) he called by wireless for reinforcements. The Regimental Commander of the 347th alerted the 3/347th, which was resting in the rear of the regimental area; but this battalion was allotted to Division reserve and could not be used. Instead, 2 companies of the right regiment, the 3rd to Reserve Ersatz, were sent over to the 1/347th, one arriving in the area at 11:00 o'clock and the other at 2:00 am, (12:00 am and 3:00 am German time) when they were too

---

649   Keyser 2/5 to 4th Brig., 2:30 am, June and subsequent 2/5 messages, Vol. 5.
650   Operations 2nd FA Brig., Gen Wm Chamberlaine, 25 June, Vol. 19. [sic-Vol. 9.]
651   Operations 2nd FA Brig., Brigade General Wm Chamberlaine, 24-25 June, Vol. 9.
652   War Diary, 87th DI, 25 June. Note: no trench mortars used: and for the first time, the woods were shelled extensively with 155's.
653   Ibid. War Diary and annexes, 347th RI, 25 June.
654   Shearer to 4th Brigade, 5:55 pm, Vol. 4., and a second message at 7:00 pm, 25 June, Vol. 5.

Final Attacks in Bois de Belleau by 3/5

late to do more than reinforce the shattered line, then reestablished near Belleau.[655]

At 8:40 pm 4th Brigade received a message from Major Shearer, despatched from the fight at 7:00 pm; The 47th Company had gained its objective, and was with the 20th, digging in. The 16th Company was still advancing against resistance. Major Shearer estimated 150 prisoners already in hand, who were being utilized to carry out the wounded. He asked for reinforcements, since all his force would be needed to hold the new line, and a counter attack on the 47th Company was reported. He also requested that the artillery keep the northern approaches under fire.[656]

At about this time, only the 2nd Company, the left company of 1/347th, retained its original line. The 3rd and 4th, with elements of the 1st, had been forced to the extreme northern tip of the woods. They noted an increase in the enemy's artillery, shells of the heaviest calibre — the 155's of the 17th Field Artillery, probably, and of the French 333rd — falling on and behind, them. Soon afterwards, the Marines penetrated this line, between the fragments of the 3rd and 4th Companies, and rolled up the 2nd Company on the left and the 5th Company of the 3rd Reserve Ersatz Regiment on the right. There were held at this point in the German line a few men of the 3/5 who had been captured in the opening phase of the assault; from these the 5th Marines had been identified: they were now recaptured by their comrades. At 9:15 pm (10:15 pm German time) the 1/347 began to organize a new position along the Torcy-Belleau road, entirely out of the woods and to the north of it. It was here some hours later, that the reinforcement from the 3rd Reserve Ersatz reported.[657]

Long after this, however, small detachments of Germans within the woods held out. The 16th Company was still fighting at 9:30 pm, machine guns being active on their front. It was reported that a number of Germans on the front of the 47th Company were trying to surrender, but one of their own machine guns kept them pinned to the ground, firing on them when they rose to run across to the Marines. Major Shearer considered that he had most of the woods, but his casualties had been so heavy that a counterattack, he thought, would be fatal.[658] There was the possibility that the companies had passed some of the Germans in the wood, but 3/5 had no

---

655 War Diary and reports, 347th RI, 25 June, Vol. 5.
656 Shearer to 4th Brigade, 7:00 pm, Vol. 5. [See above note. Same message. GBC].
657 War Diary and Annexes, 347th RI, 25 June.
658 Shearer to 4th Brigade, 9:30 pm, 25 June, Vol. 5.
Note: The losses of 3/5 on 25 June were 4 officers and 119 men killed and wounded. On 24 June, an inactive day, 3/5 lost 1 officer and 37 men. The total for the period 23-25 June was: 5 officers and 260 men. Adjutant and Inspector USMC.

men to patrol to the rear, and heavy enemy shellfire was now laid upon the battalion. Major Sibley, the 3/6, had extended his line to cover the east edge of the woods, since all of 3/5 was in line: further reinforcements to clean up behind the battalion were requested.[659] This message was received by the 4th Brigade at 11:12 pm; at 11:20 Colonel Neville was directed to make use of the 3/6 to cover the northeastern edge of the woods, and Major Keyser was ordered to connect up with the west side of the woods, and to send a platoon around his right rear to reinforce the 16th Company on the left of 3/5. Meantime, the artillery would proceed with counter battery work.[660]

The small individual combats in the wood continued through most of the night, but the 347th Regiment contemplated no counterattacks. They rebuilt their line along the Torcy-Belleau Road.[661] By dawn of 26 June the companies of 3/5 were in position around the edges of the woods: 3/6 was connected up on the right and 2/5 had contact on the left. At 10:50 am, 216 prisoners, including four officers, had passed through 4th Brigade Headquarters, and numerous wounded prisoners had passed through the dressing stations with some 250 wounded of the 3/5.[662] There was one lot of 78 prisoners which had surrendered to a single Marine, Private [*Henry P.*] Leonard [*sic Lenert*]. More wounded Germans lay in the Bois de Belleau, and many dead.[663] The total of prisoners rose finally to 7 officers and 302 men, including 22 wounded evacuated through the dressing stations.[664] The 16th Company reported 10 heavy and 8 light machineguns taken; the 20th, 5 light and 1 heavy.[665]

As to the German losses, the 347th Regiment reports 2 officers and 64 men wounded and 5 officers and 369 men killed and missing.[666]

Major Shearer reported to General Harbord: "Belleau Woods now U.S. Marine Corps entirely."[667]

---

659 Shearer to 4th Brig., 7:00 pm, 25 June, Vol. 5.
660 CG, 4th Brig. to CO, 5th Regt., 11:00 pm, 25 June, Vol. 5.
661 War Diary, 347th RI, 25 June.
662 24 Hour report 4th Brig., to 8:00 pm, 25 June (supplement), Vol. 6.
663 Ibid. [The story of Lenert's exploits went up the line, from Harbord to Chaumont, where the AEF officials ridiculed the story as more "Marine hokum." His reward was a Silver Star citation (later a medal) and a French Croix de Guerre, Palm, and a trip to Paris on 4 July on which he went AWOL for a couple of weeks and had a grand time. GBC].
664 Ibid.
665 Ibid.
666 Report of prisoners 5 pm, 25 June, HQ, 2nd Div., Vol. 4.
667 24 Hour report 4th Brig., to 8:00 pm, 25 June (supplement), Vol. 6. [More than twenty-five days in the doing. GBC.]

Note on Attack of 25 June

The 3/5 attacked on 25 June the same positions which had repulsed two attacks of 1/7, held against 1/7 by 3/347, and against 3/5 by 1/347. The enemy dispositions were slightly different, 3/347 having two companies in the front line and two companies in reserve, and 1/347 having three companies in the front line and one in reserve. Unlike Major Von Hartlieb of the 237th Division, whose command post was in the woods about 200 metres behind the front line, and in the line when necessary, the command post of 1/347 was in Belleau. The attack delivered by 3/5 on 23rd June was repulsed without difficulty by the Germans. The attack of 25 June was deliv-

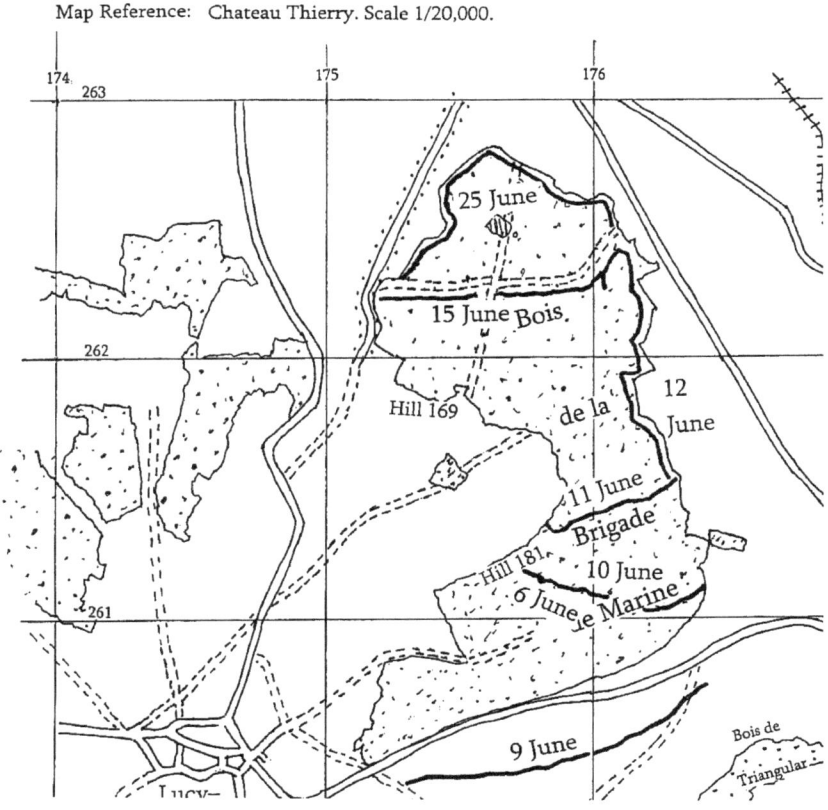

Successive lines in the Bois de Belleau 6 – 25 June.

Map 13

ered by about the same number of men; a third company had been inserted — the 47th — to make up the strength lost by the 16th Company on the 23rd June. The attack followed the same method as the previous one. But by the German accounts, they were much shaken by the 14-hour bombardment which preceded it, and their companies had suffered grave losses before the infantry advanced to the assault. No other attack on the woods was so thoroughly prepared as this one. The only preparation approaching it in scale was the bombardment which preceded the attack of 1/6 on 10 June, but the 1/6 does not seem to have done more than make a contact with the German line in the woods on that occasion, and the fire was distributed over the whole woods, a depth of nearly two kilometres. On the 25th, it concentrated on a relatively small area approximately 600 metres square.

The 87th Division was an Eastern Front formation, brought west in 1918. It was rated 4th class in a classification of four, and was certainly no better than the 237th Division. In performance, it did not show the devotion and energy which characterized the 461st Regiment. But it did well enough on the 10th and the 21st of June, and well enough on the 23rd, against the 3/5. As to the 3/5, it had been more roughly handled than any battalion in the Marine Brigade. On 6 June it had been repulsed in its first attack with heavy losses, including the battalion commander.

It had reentered the line at Bouresches, and sustained there the most determined, of the German efforts to regain that town. It made no gains on 23 June: one of its companies lost very heavily then. It attacked again over the same ground, and was successful on the 25th. The conclusion is inescapable that the powerful artillery preparation preceding its movement on 25 June was largely responsible for its success; and there is no evident reason why the same artillery could not have been utilized earlier in the month of June against the Germans in the Bois de Belleau.

Note on 87th Division Prior to 23 June

The 87th Division, on relieving the 237th, placed the third battalion of the 347th Regiment in the Bois de Belleau: the 345th Regiment prolonged the line to the west, and the 3rd Reserve Ersatz Regiment was east of the wood, maintaining liaison with the 28th Division. The 3/347 described its new position as consisting of individual rifle-pits, the front line being within 70 metres of the Americans.[668]

It reported a patrol in contact with its outpost line the evening of 17

---

668   *War Diary, 87th DI, 16 June.*

June, the patrol being driven off.⁶⁶⁹ On 20 June, at 4:15 am (5:15 French time) it was attacked, in the woods, the blow falling on the 10th and 11th Companies. These companies held their lines and beat off the enemy, who retired, leaving his dead; one wounded American fell into their hands, and they collected two automatic rifles and some arms and equipment from the bodies on their front.⁶⁷⁰

On 21 June, in the early morning, after some artillery and trench mortar fire on their front line, the enemy advanced again. In all, four attacks were made, and repulsed; although at one time the enemy was against the main line of resistance. A rumor went back that the position had been penetrated, and the regimental commander sent forward the 2/347, another company, and a platoon of machine guns to restore the situation; but they were not needed and were withdrawn to reserve. Three/347 noted that the Americans came forward impetuously and without fear, but their attacks were delivered in an amateurish manner. Their dead were left on the German front, and wounded men were captured and sent back. The 3/347 reported a loss of 15 wounded.⁶⁷¹

Gassing of 3rd Brigade

During the night 23–24 June, the front of the 3rd Brigade was severely gassed, the weight of the concentration falling to north and south of the Paris-Metz road near Le Thiolet. By 10:10 pm 24 June, the gas evacuations came to 152 from the 9th Infantry, 162 from the 23rd Infantry, and 25 from the 5th Machine Gun battalion, a total of 339.⁶⁷² By 6:00 am on the 25th, the total had risen to 414.⁶⁷³

Regimental Sectors, 4th Brigade

The first sector limits laid down within the 4th Brigade allotted to the 6th Marines that part of the line from Triangle Farm to Lucy-le-Bocage, inclusive, and to the 5th Marines the line from Lucy through the Bois de Champillon to the ravine running west of Hill 142 which was also the left

---

669   Ibid, 17 June.
670   Ibid, 20 June.
671   Ibid, 21 June.
672   Report, 3rd Brigade to 2nd Division, 10:10 pm, 24 June, Vol. 4.
673   Report, Div. Surgeon, 24 hours to 6:00 am, 25 June.

Shells began to drop into the trench

Divisional Boundary. This was communicated by General Harbord to the Regiments on 5 June, following the withdrawal of the French on the 2nd Division front.⁶⁷⁴ Headquarters of the 6th Marines were established at La Maison Blanche, a farmhouse on the Paris-Metz road, and the 5th Marines located at La Voie du Chatel, a group of buildings on the Lucy-Marigny road, southwest of Champillon. Colonel Catlin and his successor Lieutenant Colonel Lee of the 6th Marines, and Colonel Neville, commanding the 5th Marines, maintained themselves at these command posts through the subsequent actions, until 25 June. [*Not so. Neville had previously taken up a position in a quarry about three miles to the west of the lines. GBC*]. On 13 June the 23rd Infantry of the 3rd Brigade extended its left to include the

---

674 *Harbord to CO's, 5th and 6th Marines, 5 June, Vol. 2.*

line from Triangle Farm through Bouresches: and the regimental limits within the 4th Brigade area were altered To the 5th Marines was given the sector Bouresches-Bois de Belleau, to a point just west of the wood (175.9–262.9), and to the 6th Marines the line from that point to the Champillon Brook west of Hill 142.[675] The Regimental command posts remained in place, Lieutenant Colonel Feland of the 5th Regiment establishing himself in the Bois de Belleau in command of troops in the wood, on 14 June.[676] The area of the 6th Marines was materially shortened by the taking over of Hill 142 by the French, which moved the left boundary of the Brigade to the brook east of that hill. On the relief of the 6th Marines by the 7th Infantry, Lieutenant Colonel Lee, then commanding the regiment, had no duties on the front until the return of his battalions to the line;[677] but Colonel Neville retained command of the Bois de Belleau and the troops west of it. The order for the relief of the 7th Infantry, issued on 21 June, gave the 5th Marines the Bouresches-Bois de Belleau line as far as the double-tree road west of the wood, and the 6th Marines the line from that point to junction with the French at Hill 142 (Y–line 174), and this division of sectors became effective the night 23–24 June.[678] On 24 June, for greater convenience in handling their commands, the regimental commanders were ordered to exchange command posts, which change was effective on 25 June.[679]

---

675 *F.O. 5, 4th Brigade, 4:30 pm, 13 June, Vol. 2.*
676 *Statement [of] Major Keyser, 2nd Div. file.*
677 *Harbord to Lee, Vol. 5.*
678 *Harbord to CO's, 5th and 6th Marines, 5 June, Vol. 2.*
679 *Statement Major Keyser, 2nd Div. file.*

Nineteen

4th Brigade, 25 June–5 July

After the Bois de Belleau was cleared of the enemy, on 25 June, the lines of the Marine battalions were consolidated around its edges, from the liaison point with the 23rd Infantry off its southeastern corner, to the northeastern face of the wood, where, on the double-tree road at about point 175.2-262.65, there was contact with the 2/5 to the west. On 26 June 2/5 was ordered to straighten this line, so that it ran direct from the road-fork south of Torcy at point 174.75-263.1 to the double-tree road at 175.4-262.7. This movement was effected the night of 26–27 June without difficulty.[680] The night of 26–27 June 3/5 was relieved by 2/6, and withdrew to rest in the Bois Gros Jean.[681] The 28th June was without incident. On 29 June General Harbord visited the wood, and recorded that "No one who has never visited that wood can comprehend the heroism of the troops which finally cleared it of the Germans."[682] Certain relief's were ordered for the night of 29–30 June: 1/6, which had moved into the woods northwest of Lucy on 26 June as Brigade reserve, relieved 3/6, which went to Bois Gros Jean; and 1/5 moved from Bois Gros Jean to the woods northwest of Lucy on 27 June, remaining in Brigade reserve until 30 June. That night it took over the line from 2/5, and 2/5 replaced it in Brigade reserve.[683]

On 30 June instructions were issued, pursuant to the orders of the Division Commander, for all front lines to be held more lightly; and 4th Brigade informed the regiments that 2/6, when taken out of the Bois de Belleau, would not be replaced: 1/6 would extend its lines from the south

680 24-hour Report, 4th Brig., to 8:00 pm., 27 June-Vol. 6.
681 Ibid.
682 Ibid, 29 June-Vol. 6.
683 Ibid, 30 June-Vol. 6.

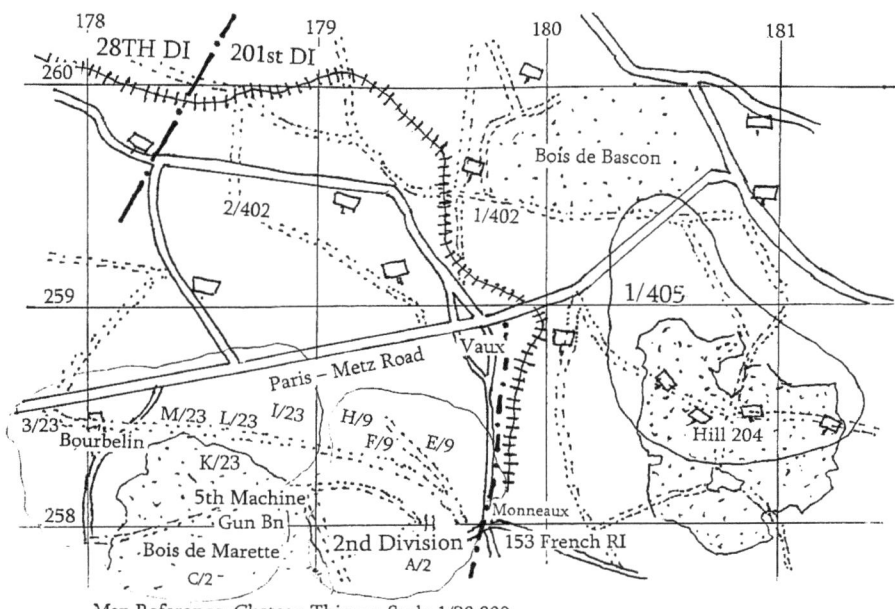

Dispositions before Vaux, 1 July 1918.

Map 14

and hold the wood alone. The relief of 2/6 was ordered for 2 July.[684] Thirty June was the final day of preparation for the 3rd Brigade attack on Vaux, and 3/5 and 3/6, in the Bois Gros Jean, were placed at the disposal of Division Headquarters in case they should be needed in that attack.[685] On the relief of 2/6, the 4th Brigade front was held by two battalions only: the 1/6 in the Bois de Belleau; and the 1/5 from the Bois de Belleau to the French on Hill 142, with two companies in line and two in the wooded area to the rear. Two/6 and 2/5 lay in the woods northwest of Lucy, and 3/5 and 3/6 in the Bois Gros Jean. The guns of the 6th Machine Gun Battalion, supplemented by the 4th Machine Gun Battalion, remained in place, with two companies out of the line.[686]

The night of 4–5 July, Lieut Col Bearss, with an officer and 25 men of the 67th Company of the 1/5 made a raid on the German positions south of Torcy, killing two Germans and capturing two.[687]

684 Ibid.
685 Harbord to CO's, 3/5 and 3/6, 12:00 am., 30 June-Vol. 4.
686 Harbord-4:40 P.M., 30 June-Vol. 4.
687 24 Hour report, 4th Brigade to 8:00 P.M., 5 July-Vol. 6.

Marine with a pistol

On 4 July two companies of Marines paraded in Paris, in connection with the Independence Day celebration there: they were formed from selected officers and men of the 4th Brigade on 2 July.⁶⁸⁸ On this day also, officers of the 52nd Infantry Brigade of the 26th Division reconnoitered the Brigade front, and on 5 July the relief of the 4th Brigade began.⁶⁸⁹

688   Ibid, 2 July-Vol. 6.
689   Ibid, 5 July-Vol. 6.

Twenty

Vaux: XXI CA, 12 June

On 12 June, the reduction of Vaux was first mentioned in orders.

This date, the French XXI Corps d'Armee, Degoutte, issued Ordre General d'Operations 2.031/3, which analyzed briefly the situation on the Corps front: The 167th Division was on the south bank of the Clignon, and in Bussiares; the 2nd American Division was organizing its gains in the Bois de Belleau and held Bouresches; the Corps would continue its offensive operations. The line of the 2nd Division, it pointed out, from Triangle Farm to the right flank halfway between Vaux and Monneaux, formed a reentrant angle, the apex of which was Le Thiolet. In order to reduce the number of troops necessary to hold this front, and to organize in depth the defensive works in the Le Thiolet region, it was desired to flatten out the reentrant angle. To this end, the 2nd Division would carry forward its line to the general front: Triangle, road from Hill 182 to 192, small wood, northeast of Hill 192, Vaux. This was to be accomplished, by a series of small operations, well prepared by artillery, looking to the occupation of:

> small woods between the Bois des Clerembauts and Hill 192,
> envelopment of Hill 192,
> occupation of road 192 to Vaux,
> envelopment of Vaux.

All movements on the right flank of the 2nd Division would be carried out in close liaison with the 10th Colonial Division in the Corps on the right.[690]

On 14 June, General Degoutte, just appointed, to command of the French 6th Army, and General Naulin, succeeding Degoutte in command

---

690 *Ordre General d'Operations XXI CA 2.031/2, 12 June 18.*

of' the XXI Corps, called at 2nd Division Headquarters and discussed an attack on Vaux,[691]

On 17 June the 2nd Division received Ordre General d'Operations 2090/3 of the XXI CA, directing the Corps to continue to prepare for the operation against the Vaux-La Roche line, as outlined in the Corps Order of 12 June In this order (17 June) the 2nd Division was further enjoined to reduce the forces holding its front lines, and to organize a defensive system in depth; when the 4th Brigade returned to the front and the 7th Infantry was withdrawn, Hill 142 would be connected directly with the north end of the Bois de Belleau, economy of forces being applied in the new line.[692]

Four days later, on 21 June, the XXI Corps, General Naulin, was relieved by the III Corps, General [*Léonce M.*] Lebrun, the XXI Corps going to the Champagne.[693]

On 25 June, III Corps issued Ordre General d'Operations 1091/3. The III Corps would attack the line 192-La Roche-Vaux-Hill 204, in conjunction with the XXXVIII Corps on the right. The attack would be made by the 2nd American Division and the 39th French Division. The 2nd Division would move forward its right, as far as Vaux: south of Vaux the 39th Division would take Hill 204, as far as the dirt road running southeast up the hill from Vaux. For this movement, the group of 155 mm guns of the 164th French Division were allotted to the 2nd Division, and the light heavy artillery of the XXXVIII and III Corps were united under the command of the III Corps artillery officer. The attack would take place with the least possible delay: the division commanders concerned would immediately arrange details.[694]

By 26 June, the Bois de Belleau had been disposed of, and the mission assigned to the 4th Brigade by the French Corps was accomplished. Everywhere on the Brigade front the German line was thrown back beyond the Clignon Brook. The 2nd Division was ready to undertake a new operation. The 3rd Brigade had been held in place for 3 weeks, enduring the steady wastage of position warfare, and enjoying no opportunity to strike back. The spirit of the infantry was angry and ardent.

While the Division command had refused to engage more than one of its Brigades at a time, the Staff had proceeded through the month with work on the 3rd Brigade front, and the Divisional G-2, Colonel A.[*rthur*] L. Conger, had, collected the most minute and exact information about Vaux, its surroundings, and its garrison.

 691 General Wm. Chamberlaine, *Operations, 2nd FA Brigade, 14 June* (also WD, 2nd Div., Vol. 4).
 692 *Ordre General d'Operations, 2090/3, 17 June, XXI CA.*
 693 *Ibid, 2127/3, 21 June, XXI CA.*
 694 *Ibid, 1091/3, 25 June, III CA.*

Vaux first appeared in the German dispatches about 2 June, when the 10th Division, advancing from the northeast, rested its left flank on the village, in contact with the 231st Division, which, between 31 May and 2 June, occupied Chateau Thierry and Hill 204.[695] Vaux seems, at first, to have been an unoccupied point in the German outpost zone, patrolled by both Germans and Americans at night, and left open during the day. Later in June, it was garrisoned by the German 231st Division.[696]

This unit was relieved by the 201st Division, orders for the relief being issued on 15 June, and the movement carried out between the nights 17–18 June and 19–20 June, without incident. The command passed to the 201st at 9:00 am 19 June.[697]

The 201st Division was, like the 231st and the 237th, a 1916 formation, rated 3rd class in a classification of 4.[698] It came to the Marne salient from St. Mihiel, after having made 5 moves in the first 2 weeks of June. Upon entering the Vaux-Chateau Thierry line, it found that no sector organization work had been done by the 231st Division. For the remainder of June it devoted its energies to new entrenchment and the improvement of old defensive positions. Prisoners captured by the 2nd Division during this time told of a rumored attack in the sector, but nothing in the nature of offensive operations was attempted by the Germans, nor do their divisional records mention aggressive plans.[699]

On 21 June, General of Infantry von Conta, with his Corps Headquarters, was detached to the other side of the Marne Salient, and General Schoeler, the VIII Army Corps, relieved the IV Reserve Corps.[700] Certain changes were instituted by the new command.

On 23 June, its Corps advised the 201st Division that the right neighbor, the 28th Division, which had been in the Belleau-Bouresches-Vaux line since 8 June, would be withdrawn without replacement, and its sector would be covered by the extension of the Divisions to the right and left — the 201st and the 87th. There would be, on the retirement of the 28th, an additional 800 metres for the 201st to take over, on its right, and there would also be a slight re-adjustment of the left off the 201st, which was now the left division of the VIII Corps: the 10th Division would assume a portion of the 201st's area in the town of Chateau Thierry.

---

695 *War Diary, 10th DI,* 2 June.
696 *War Diary, 231st D.I., 1-15 June. Patrol Reports and Intelligence Data, 9th Inf.,* Vol. 8.
697 *War Diary, 201st D.I.,* 15-20 June.
698 *History, German Divisions, G-2, GHQ, AEF.,* 1918.
699 *War Diary and annexes, 201st DI.*
700 *War Diary, German 7th Army.*

Accordingly, the right elements of the 201st occupied 800 metres of the front of the 28th Division on the night of 26–27 June, and the 10th Division extended its left in Chateau Thierry the following night. The effect was to shorten the line of the left regiment, the 403rd, and to lengthen the front of the 402nd Regiment, on the right of the Division. The new flank rested just northeast of Hill 192, where contact with the 110th Regiment of the 28th Division was maintained.[701]

At the end of June, this was the situation of the 201st Division: it had the 3 regiments of its infantry brigade in line, from left to right, the 403rd, in Chateau Thierry, the 401st, across Hill 204, and the 402nd, from the northern slope of Hill 204 through Vaux and the Bois de la Roche to the Bois de Cote 192. Each regiment had 2 battalions in line and support, and 1 battalion resting. Of the disengaged battalions, the resting battalion of the 402nd Regiment was the farthest from the front. It was, on 30 June, at Bezu St. Germain, 8 kilometres north of Vaux. The 3 regimental sectors were known, respectively, as Stadt, Höhe, and Wald. Höhe and Wald — Hill 204 and Vaux-la Roche — were the sectors which interested the Americans.

Hill 204 was the most strongly held portion of the Division front, and the divisional records indicate that its possession was regarded as vital. In line through the woods on the crest of the Hill was a battalion of the 401st Regiment. It was closely supported by a battalion east of the Hill, and the third battalion lay immediately to the north at la Colombier Farm, in the artillery line.

Vaux-La Roche was occupied by 2 battalions of the 402nd Regiment. The 1/402, on the left, had 1 company east of Vaux, between the last houses and the woods on the crest of the Hill, and 1 company, the 2/402, in the village. One company was in the edge of the Bois des Rochets, near Bascon-le-Bas, on the railroad, and the remaining company was farther within the Bois des Rochets. To the west, the 28th Division, the 2/402 prolonged the line to the contact point with the 28th Division, having 1 company on an outpost line near the Bois de le Cote 192, 2 companies in the Bois de la Roche, and 1 company just north of the same woods. A company of the

---

701 These dispositions, from the War Diary and Annexes of the 201st Division, are given in detail, because, when the Vaux attack was made, the only force assigned to counter attack was the 3/402, which was 5 miles distant when the attack opened. A similar instance of the handling of reserves is noted in the 87th Division following the last attack on the Bois de Belleau, 25 June. The German system seems to have been rigid. It is possible, however, that the holding of Hill 204 was considered so important that all reserves immediately on the ground were allotted to its defense or held in readiness to counter-attack in case it was lost. War Diary and annexes, 201st DI, 15 June-2 July. [This same note was utilized three times. See the word "note" and read this same number, for this same text. GBC].

110th Regiment was north of Hill 192. The 3/402, as has been seen, was at Bezu-St. Germain.

Vaux was a town, in normal times, of 82 houses and 250 inhabitants. It was built along the Paris-Metz Highway, just northwest and at the foot of Hill 204. East of the town the highway curved sharply northeast, to encircle the Hill, and where the highway bent southward again, towards Chateau Thierry, was Hill 187. East of the town also, at the last group of houses, the metre-gauge railroad running from Essomes, Monneaux and Vaux northward to Bouresches and Belleau and the Clignon Valley, passed by a viaduct under the highway. The railroad, north of the town, crossed the eastern part of the Bois de la Roche. Entering Vaux from the north was the macadamized road to Bouresches. Another road led south to Monneaux, and 200 metres out of Vaux this road crossed a ravine, at which point the right flank of the 9th Infantry had contact with the left of the French XXXVIII Corps. The ravine, which came down from Vaux, paralleled the road to Monneaux, and another ravine branched off it, leading westward to Bourbetin, and covering the front of the Bois de la Marette. The forward positions of the 9th Infantry were based on these ravines, but they were dangerous places, because the German observers on Hill 204 looked directly into them, and held them continually under fire. The ground rose between Vaux and the Vaux-Monneaux ravine, and rose also to the west and north, so that the town lay in a hollow, invisible from the American lines, and well covered from all except high-angle artillery fire. The Bois de la Roche blanketed the approach from the north, and scattered trees and orchards, set among the open fields, hid it from the west. South, west and east, it was protected by belts of wire, strongest on the east. There was a tank trap on the Monneaux road, and barriers of logs and iron gates blocked the roads within the edge of town.[702]

G-2 of the 2nd Division had at its disposal a mass of information compiled from the reports of observers and of the nightly patrols sent out by the infantry regiments, and from the examination of prisoners, and from aerial reconnaissance with the cooperation of the French Corps, former inhabitants of Vaux, now refugees in the back areas, were brought up and interrogated. Among the refugees was the old stone mason of the village, who was able to give specifications as to the thickness of the walls of the houses and gardens, and the depth of the cellars in which the Germans sheltered themselves. The G-2 special maps of 25–26 June, prepared and issued to the troops, showed every building in the place, with cellars, alleys, and

---

702 2nd Div. G-2, Information Bulletin, Vaux-29 June-AGO File. G-2, 2nd Div., Special Map, Vaux-La Roche-25-26 June-Vol. 10.

gardens, by which it was possible to direct squad leaders in the assault battalions to the very dugouts they were to bomb, and signalmen and liaison agents to the exact holes where they were to set up their telephones. Obstacles of every kind, fortified shell-holes, enemy observation posts and machine gun positions, were also located in and around the village. The map showed the headquarters of Lieutenant Adamson, commanding the 2/402, which consisted of 2 officers and 137 men; and the station of the minenwerfer detachment —1 officer,[703] 30 men, and 4 minenwerfers— maintained for defense in the eastern edge of Vaux. Nine machine guns were located. Much was known, also, of the German dispositions in the Bois de la Roche, but since the German lines were sited in the woods, the information was neither as detailed nor as definite as that regarding the village.[704]

The area over which Vaux-La Roche must be approached was quite familiar to the companies of the 9th and 23rd Infantry. The woods around Hill 192 had been reached and held for some hours by the 3/23, on 6 June. Earlier in June, Vaux had been frequently entered by patrols of the 9th, and all of No Man's Land had been many times traversed by scouting parties in small nocturnal operations. Numerous nocturnal encounters had, taken place around the Bois de Bourbetin and the Bois de la Cote 192. It is safe to say that no other operation of the 2nd Division was so extensively studied and prepared as this one.[705]

Following the receipt of the French III Corps orders of 25 June, preliminary instructions were issued by the 2nd Division, and provisional orders were drawn up by the 3rd Brigade and. by the regimental commanders concerned. Field Order 9 of the 2nd Division, directing the final dispositions for the operation, was issued on 30 June.[706]

The III Corps, announced Field Order 9, attacks the line: Woods northeastern, northern, northwestern slopes of Hill 204; crossing of railway on Paris-Chateau Thierry road east of Vaux, northeastern and northern edges of Bois de la Roche, woods north and northeast of Hill 192, on J day at H hour. The French 39th Division would attack and capture Hill 204, establishing contact with the 9th Infantry at the railway crossing on the highway east of Vaux. The 2nd Division would attack, with 2 battalions of infantry reinforced by special troops and artillery, the Vaux-La Roche line from the railway crossing to the woods north of Hill 192. Sector limits for the troops of the 2nd Division were, on the south, a line running from Monneaux around the base of Hill 204 to Hill 187 east of Vaux, and on the

---

703 *G-2, 2nd Div., Special Map, Vaux-La Roche-25-26 June-Vol. 10.*
704 *2nd Div. G-2, Information Bulletin, Vaux-29 June-AGO File.*
705 *Patrol and Intelligence Reports, 9th and 23rd Inf., 1-30 June-Vol. 9.*
706 *Field Order 9, 2nd Div., 30 June-Vol. 1.*

north, a line projected from Le Thiolet to the northern edge of the woods north of Hill 192. The task was allotted to the 3rd Brigade, and the 2/9 and 3/23 were assigned as assault battalions, supported by the regimental machine gun company of the 9th, and 3 platoons of D Company of the 5th Machine Gun Battalion, acting with 2/9 and 3/23 respectively. Company A of the 5th Machine Gun Battalion was detailed to deliver fire of preparation and support, and A Company and C Company of the 2nd Engineers would follow the attack. The artillery attached to the 3rd Brigade — the 15th and batteries of the 17th Field Artillery Regiments— were strengthened by 2 battalions of the French 37th and 1 battalion of the French 7th Artillery Regiments. Air service was by the French. Two companies of 3/9 and a platoon of C Company of the 5th Machine Gun Battalion were placed in the woods south of Tafournay Farm, at the orders of the Commanding General, 3rd Brigade, and 2 battalions of Marines, the 1/5 and the 3/5, in the Bois Gros Jean, were held in Division reserve. Brigadier General E.M. Lewis, commanding the 3rd Brigade, was placed in command of operations.[707]

On 30 June, also, the 3rd Brigade and the 9th and 23rd Infantry Regiments issued their final orders, although preliminary dispositions had already been made on provisional orders, issued earlier.

The front of the 3rd Brigade was held by the 9th Infantry, on the right, and the 23rd Infantry on the left. The original regimental sector limit had passed through Le Thiolet on the highway, but with the occupation, by the 23rd Infantry, of that part of the 4th Brigade front extending from Triangle Farm through Bouresches, on 13–14 June, the entire line of the 23rd was shifted to the left, and the left flank of the 9th was extended across the highway to a point about 500 metres north of Le Thiolet, at the corner of the Bois des Clerembauts. (177.1–258.9) At the end of June, the 9th Infantry lay from the culvert on the Vaux-Monneaux road, 200 metres south of Vaux, westward to Bourbetin, thence across the Paris-Metz Highway, a short distance east of Le Thiolet, to the northeast corner of the Bois des Clerembauts. The line of departure for the Vaux-La Roche attack lay entirely within the 9th Infantry sector.

Of the two battalions detailed for the assault, one, the 2/9, Major Bouton, was already in place, holding the right of the regimental sector. No preliminary movement on its part was necessary. Provisional Field Order 15 of the 9th Infantry, on 28 June, confirmed by Field Order 15 on 30 June, verified its dispositions. Battalion Headquarters for the attack were established at Monneaux, and around Monneaux were grouped the battalion reserve, G Company, the guns of the regimental machine gun company

---

707   Ibid.

which were to accompany the advance, and A Company of the 2nd Engineers. All troop movements were completed by the night 30 June–1 July.[708]

The designated battalion of the 23rd Infantry, 3/23, Major Elliott, had been relieved from the line Triangle-Bouresckes during the night 26–27 June, and lay at Ventelet Farm. It had been on the front for 13 days, since the 23rd extended its left to Bouresches and took over from the Marines on 13 June. On 25 June the 23rd issued Provisional Field Order 43, confirmed on the 30th by Field Order 43, and Major Elliott received, tentative instructions for his part in the attack in the provisional order. Three/23 had been heavily engaged on 6 June, suffering many casualties, and it had lost heavily in the gas concentrations placed by the Germans in the regimental area on 13 June and on 25 June. Its ranks were filled with replacements, and every effort was made, between the 28th and 30th, to instruct the new men in grenades and automatic weapons, and in the use of the German machine gun. During the 30th, Major Elliott and his company commanders reconnoitered, from the positions of the 9th Infantry, the terrain across which they were to attack. At 6:00 pm, when Major Elliott returned to his battalion, he was informed that the attack would take place on the next day, and he was ordered to move, at 12:30 am, into the Bois de la Marette, in the forward area of the 9th Infantry. Three/23, joined later by C Company of the 2nd Engineers and 3 platoons of D Company of the 5th Machine Gun Battalion, was in place by daylight on 1 July.[709] Major Elliott established his headquarters in the ruined village of Bourbetin, and his troops took over the line vacated for them by the left battalion of the 9th Infantry. One company was placed in the Bourbetin-Monneaux ravine, covering the Bois de la Marette from Bourbetin to junction with 2/9 on the right, and the other 3, with attached troops, lay up for the day in the woods close behind the line.[710]

The mission of A Company of the 5th Machine Gun Battalion was to cover the objective with fire of position, while the attacking troops advanced, and to stand by to deliver a machine gun barrage against emergency, after the objective was attained. Its guns were overhauled by the 2nd Mobile Ordnance Repair Shop, in the rear, on 30 June, and during the night 30 June–1 July, it moved into the Bois de la Marette, from the eastern and northeastern edges of which it was to go into action. Its emplacements had

---

708 Provisional Field Order 15, 9th Inf., 28 June, and Field Order 15, 9th Inf., 30 June, Vol. 3.

709 Provisional Field Order 43, 23rd Inf., 28 June, and Field Order 43, 23rd Inf., 30 June, Vol. 3. Operation Report, 3rd Brigade, 1-2 July-Vol. 6. See also regimental and battalion reports of the 9th and 23rd Inf., Vol. 7.

710 Operations Report, 3/23, 1-2 July-Vol. 7.

to be constructed, and all its equipment, ammunition, and material, moved in by hand before the assault began.[711]

All troops designated for attack, for support, and for reserve, were in position by daylight on 1 July.[712]

The movements of the Americans on 30 June did not entirely escape the German observers on Hill 204. Hostile activity was noted on the front of the 402nd Regiment, and artillery fire was placed intermittently on the 9th Infantry sector. The 402nd Regiment issued orders for increased combat readiness on its front.[713]

On the 30th, at 1:21 pm, 2nd Division communicated the hour for the assault: 6:00 pm, 1 July.[714]

At H-13 hours—that is to say, at 5:00 am, 1 July, the advanced positions of the 2/9 and 3/23 were evacuated, and the artillery preparation began. The guns of the 2nd Division, and of the French 164th and 39th Divisions, batteries moved in by Corps for the operation, opened together.[715] Their fire covered the entire front of the German 201st Division, falling with especial severity on the Hill 204 and the Vaux-La Roche line. From the character of this bombardment, in spite of the fact that none of it seemed to be directed against the German battery positions, the 201st Division deduced that a general attack was coming, and in the forenoon it ordered all front line battalions and supporting guns to assume positions of readiness by 1:45 pm. (12:45 French Time).[716]

At 2:00 pm, (1:00 pm French Time) the shelling on Vaux and Hill 204 amounted to drumfire, and continued so for 5 hours. The 201st Division command was thoroughly alarmed and called for assistance from the neighboring units. The 10th Division, on the left, was asked to fire on Louverny and La Borde ravine, the southwestern approaches to Hill 204. The 28th Division, on the right, was requested to assist in covering the Monneaux-Vaux-Bourbetin ravines, and the Bois de la Marette. The neighbors responded with barrage and harassing fire, which inflicted some casualties in the waiting battalions of the 9th and 23rd,[717] and added greatly to the difficulties of A Company of the 5th Machine Gun Battalion, working on its emplacements in the Bois de la Marette.[718]

711 Operations Report, A Co. 5th M.G. Bn., 1 July-Vol. 8.
712 Operations Report, 3rd Brig., 1-2 July-Vol. 6.
713 War Diary and annexes, 201st DI,-30 June-1 July.
714 Confidential memo, 2nd Div., to all organizations, 1:21 pm, 30 June-Vol. 4.
715 War Diary, 2nd Div., 1-2 July-Vol. 6.
716 War Diary and annexes, 201st DI,-30 June-1 July.
717 See Operations Report, 2/9 and 3/23, 1-2 July-Vol. 7.
718 Operations Report, A Co., 5th M.G. Bn., 1-2 July-Vol. 8.

At 4:00 pm (3:00 pm French Time) the 201st Division began to move forward the supports of the front line battalions. The 3/402 was shifted south from Bezu-St. Germain to Chante Merle. One company of the resting battalion of the 403rd Regiment moved to the Bois de Louaillier, and an hour later the rest of the battalion was moved up to the same woods. Two companies of the 401st Regiment were ordered to the tunnel Bezeut. Thus the German grip was strengthened on Hill 204.[719]

The 401st Regiment, at 6:30 pm — (5:30 French Time) reported the enemy moving in the Monneaux-Bourbetin ravine, south of the highway. It was 3/23 and 2/9, advancing into their line of departure.[720]

Finally, at 6:55 pm — 5:55 by the American Watches in the Assault waves of the 3rd Brigade — the observers of the 201st Division reported a general advance against their front, from the Marne banks to the right boundary. The actual zero hour of the Americans was 6:00 pm; there is a discrepancy of 5 minutes with the German reports.[721]

The German observation had been accurate, and the enemy intention correctly read.[722]

On the right, the French 153rd Regiment assailed the slopes of Hill 204. On the left, deployed along a front of some 1600 metres, more than 2000 American regulars went against the Vaux-La Roche line. At 5:30 pm, as the Germans noted, the guns lengthened their range, and the assault companies of 3/23 and 2/9 filed up from the cover of the Bois d la Marette to the forward positions in the ravine, the support companies, engineers, and machine guns, moving in behind them. A detachment of 1 platoon and 2 machine guns took station on the right flank of 2/9, to insure liaison with the French, and a platoon stood by to follow the left flank of 3/23. Each battalion detailed a half-platoon and a machine gun for interior liaison. Company A of the 5th Machine Gun Battalion, working frantically, completed its emplacements and laid its guns, hampered somewhat by the dust and smoke of the enemy barrage. At zero hour everything was ready.[723] Lieutenant [Hanford] MacNider of the 9th Infantry, sent up from Regimental

---

719 *War Diary and annexes, 201st DI, 1-2 July.*
720 *Ibid.*
721 *Ibid.*
722 Prisoners stated that rumors of an American attack were discussed in the 402nd Regiment on 28 June, and on 30 June special arrangements were made in Vaux to receive this attack-notes on Vaux attack, 9th Inf., 1 July-Vol. 7.
    The mess caterer of 4th Brigade Hq. on 30 June, reported a French vegetable vendor in La Ferte as saying that "the 23rd Infantry will attack soon"-War Diary, 4th Brig., 30 June, Vol. 6.
723 *Operations Report, 3rd Brigade, 1-2 July-Vol. 7.*

Headquarters, pushed along the Monneaux-Vaux ravine in the last minutes before the attack, and received the surrender of 5 Germans on outpost duty just south of Vaux. This was the first contact with the enemy.[724]

It was 6:00 o'clock. The 2/9, Major Bouton now in Monneaux, E Company on the right, H Company on the left, and F Company in support, with G Company, and the attached. company of engineers standing by Monneaux, proceeded swiftly and without losses into Vaux. E Company swept through the town, meeting negligible resistance, and seized its objective, which was the railway east of Vaux, with the right flank on the highway viaduct.[725] The job was done in 20 minutes.[726] H Company, striking north and west of the edge of the village, into the La Roche woods, encountered fighting Germans, who opened fire with 7 machine guns.[727] A section of the regimental machine gun company came into action and bombers worked forward under cover of their fire, and the 7 Maxims were silenced and captured. H Company resumed its advance with a delay of 5 minutes, and went through the La Roche woods to the railroad track. F Company followed E through the town and mopped it up. Vaux was a wreck, for every house had been hit by shells and many destroyed, and only the enemy in the deep cellars survived. There was no fight in these Germans, and they came out to surrender. According to their statements, the artillery had penned them in their holes, so that the minenwrerfer crews had been unable to stay by their guns, and the observation posts for the garrison and for the supporting artillery had been destroyed, and all the communications to the rear had been severed.[728] Two/9 sent back, under guard, 5 German officers and 205 men, from the town and from the Bois de la Roche.[729]

E Company, on the left, threw its platoons east of the railroad and organized a line that connected with the French 153rd Regiment on Hill 204. H Company, digging in at 7:05, had its right platoon (the fourth) east of the railroad, with the left of the company refused along the edge of the La

724 Hanford MacNider to Col. Upton, 9:00 pm, 1 July-Vol. 7.
725 Operations Report, 2/9, 1 July-Vol. 7.
726 Lt. Hanford MacNider to Col. Upton, 9:00 pm, 1 July-Vol. 7.
727 Operations Report, 2/9, 1 July-Vol. 7.
728 Examination of Prisoners from Vaux: G-2 papers, 2nd Div. File. Note on time objective was reached by 2/9: Major Bouton (see note 5) reports E Company on objective at 6:27 pm, and H resuming advance at 6:40 pm after having been held up for 5 minutes. Col. Upton (Operations Report 9th Inf. 1 July) reports E on objective at 6:20 and H at 6:40. Lt. MacNider (see note 4) reports E digging in at 6:20 and finds H on objective at 7:05. He was personally on the ground; Col. Upton and Major Bouton were not. 6:20 for E, and between 6:40 and 7:05 for H, should be correct. Note on 7 machine guns taken (see note 5): Col. Upton reports these guns taken by E, but the movements of H, as well as its casualties, substantiate the statement of Major Bouton, that H took them.
729 Operations Report 2/9, 1 July-Vol. 7.

Roche woods. A platoon of I Company of 3/23 was here with them shortly after 7:00 pm, but the rest of the battalion was not in sight.[730] By 7:30, the outpost signal platoon of the 9th had telephone communication from Vaux to the rear. Two of its linesmen, entering town with the assault, took their gear into a designated cellar to set up their phone, and found 9 German soldiers there. The Germans objected to the installation, but when the linesman shot 2 with pistols, the others surrendered.[731] Two/9 proceeded quickly with organization and consolidation of the new position, setting up captured machine guns to strengthen salient points, and by 6:30 pm, Vaux was cleaned out and the battalion front secured.[732] The battalion lost 10 men killed, 2 officers and 46 men wounded, and 20 men missing, a total of 78, all ranks. The weight of the loss fell in H Company.[733]

Three/23 debauched from the Monneaux-Bourbetin ravine with the Bouton Battalion, but Major Elliott had a longer distance to go, across a more exposed terrain. During the German counter barrage on the ravine and on the Bois de la Marette, which lasted from 4:00 to 5:00 pm (French Time), it suffered some casualties in its position. Its assault companies entered the line of departure at 5:45, and got off, in order from the right, I, L, and M Companies. K Company, Captain Valentine, was in support, with C Company of the 2nd Engineers and 3 platoons of B Company, 5th Machine Gun Battalion.[734] Coming over the crest of' the Hill 175, north of the highway, I Company, Captain [*Charles E.*] Moore, was taken under machine gun fire, but continued to advance, countering with marching fire on the German positions, until 6:18. Then, 100 metres short of the Bois de la Roche, it was forced to halt, and take up a firefight. At 6:20 pm, it resumed the advance, but was checked almost immediately, the intensity of the German fire driving it to cover. Captain Moore, commanding, and his senior [*1st*] Lieutenant [*George W.*] Furbush, [*Jr.*] were wounded. At 7:30, assistance was received from the units on the flanks, K Company of the 9th, and L of the 23rd, which drove inwards from their sectors and enveloped the machine gun nest on I Company's front, and I Company proceeded to the objective.[735] Meantime, Company L, in the center of the Elliott Battalion, had made better progress, reaching the Bois de la Roche and fighting through against stubborn resistance. Its left and center were on the objective at 7:00, and Captain [*Starr S.*] Eaton, commanding, was able to move

---

730 Lt. Hanford MacNider to Col. Upton, 9:00 pm, 1 July-Vol. 1.
731 Upton to 3rd Brigade, 9th Inf, 11 pm, 2 July-Vol. 7.
732 Operations Report 2/9, 1 July-Vol. 7.
733 Ibid.
734 Operations Report, 3/23, 1-2 July, Vol. 7.
735 Operations Report, I Company, 23rd Inf., 1-2 July, Vol. 7.

with a detachment into the sector of I Company and flank cut the Germans who had checked the battalion right.[736] M Company, Captain Green, moved forward and cleared the woods on Hill 192, passing the unburied bodies of Americans who had fallen there on 6 June, and came to the objective without delay.[737] Major Elliott reported on the objective at 8:00 pm, with the battalion line consolidated.[738]

The losses in 3/23, particularly in I Company, on the right, had been heavy, and some disorganization attended the thrust through the Bois de la Roche. The support Company, K, was absorbed into the line or dispersed on carrying details, and at 12:20 am, 2 July; Major Elliott requested support from 1/9, which lay now in rear of 3/23, in line from Bourbetin to the left boundary of the 9th Regimental sector. He received 2 platoons of A/9.[739] The 2/9 now extended from the viaduct on the highway, east of Vaux, along the railway to the Bois de la Roche. In the Bois de la Roche, Major Elliott's line began and passed along the northern edge of the woods, around the Bois Halmardiere to the woods northeast of Hill 192, and Hill 192. The engineers immediately began the wiring of the new positions, and captured German Maxims were turned around and used.[740]

Three/23 sent back 133 prisoners, including 1 officer.[741] The loss in the battalion was heavier than in 2/9. One officer and 23 enlisted men were killed, 4 officers and 143 enlisted men were wounded, and 47 men were reported missing, a total of 218 casualties in all ranks The Brigade loss was 302 officers and men.[742]

Notes on 5th M. G. Bn. in Vaux Operation

This attack was supported by the regimental machine gun company of the 9th Infantry, and by B Company of the 5th Machine Gun Battalion, less 1 platoon, these units accompanying the assault. A Company of the 5th Machine Gun Battalion fired a barrage over the heads of the advancing troops.

---

736 Operations Report, L Company, 23rd Inf., 1-2 July, Vol. 7. This report says that L was on its objective at 6:20 pm; that means that it advanced some 1200 metres against resistance in 20 minutes. It was probably later.
737 Major Elliott to 2nd Div. Historical Section: File.
738 Operations Report, 3/23, 1-2 July, Vol. 7.
739 Ibid.
740 Ibid.
741 Operation Report, 23rd Inf., 1-2 July, Vol. 7.
742 Ibid.

A Company was brought into the Bois de la Marette the night 30 June–1 July, its guns having been overhauled for overhead fire by the 2nd Mobile Ordnance Repair Shop on 30 June. Emplacements had to be built in the eastern and northeastern edges of the Bois de la Marette, and all equipment and material moved in by hand from the rear. By the utmost exertion, this work was accomplished. While the guns were being laid, at about 4:00 pm, 1 July, an enemy barrage fell on the edge of the Bois de la Marette and delayed final arrangements for an hour. The company was ready at zero hour, however, and began its barrage at H plus 2½ minutes, at 300 rounds per minute. From H plus 6 to H plus 8, the rate of fire was 150 rounds per minute; thereafter, from H plus 8 to H plus 52, 75 rounds per minute, except for a few minutes when the enemy was seen running north of the highway. Firing ceased at 6:52 pm, although the expected notice from the infantry was not received.

At 2:10 am, 2 July, the position of A Company was gassed; and at 3:45 the enemy laid a barrage on the Bois de la Marette. From 3:45 to 4:15, A Company was again in action, aiding in repulse of the counterattack on Vaux. At 8:30 am, A Company was relieved by a platoon of C Company of the 5th Machine Gun Battalion. Its casualties were 4 men severely gassed and 40 slightly gassed.[743]

The French 153rd Regiment of the 39th Division, on the right of the Americans, advanced with the 3rd Brigade, and re-occupied without difficulty its old, front line on the lower slopes of Hill 204, evacuated during the preparatory bombardment. Pressing up the Hill the Frenchmen at once developed furious resistance in the edge of the woods on the crest. At 6:40 pm, a plane, observing the progress of the attack, reported that they had reached the dirt road which ran east and west across the Hill, and which was the objective.[744] The German line was sited just south of this road.[745] The liaison detachment of the 153rd Regiment, at 6:45, was in contact with the flank of the 9th at the viaduct.[746] At 7:30, the French attack reported heavy opposition beyond the dirt road,[747] and at 7:40 pm it sent word that it was definitely stopped by machine gun nests.[748]

The 201st Division reports that the Frenchmen crossed the dirt road and involved their forward zone, but made no progress through the main

---

743 *Operations Report, 5th Machine Gun Battalion, 1-2 July, Vol. 8.*
744 *Liaison Officer Gulliver to 2nd Div., 6:40 pm, 1 July-Vol. 4.*
745 *Liaison Officer Gulliver to 2nd Div., 6:45 pm, 1 July-Vol. 4.*
746 *Liaison Officer Gulliver to 2nd Div., 7:30 pm, 1 July-Vol. 4.*
747 *Liaison Officer Gulliver to 2nd Div., 8:40 pm, 1 July-Vol. 4.*
748 *War Diary, 201st DI, 1-2 July.*

line of resistance, and the Germans add that the French, on 2 July, fell back on their old front line, down the hill.[749]

It is certain, however, that the strong German forces of the 401st Regiment on Hill 204 were heavily engaged. This regiment was organized in depth on a battalion front, and the 2 battalions out of the line when the attack started were both moved forward and drawn in. They were so occupied that they were unable to give any assistance to the 402nd, on the right, which was driven on its entire front, and, it appears likely that the French retained, if not the line of the road, a foothold in the southern edge of the woods.

The 201st Division had its last report from Vaux at 7:10 pm (6:10 French Time), when the second company of 1/402 reported that it was attacked. The driving in of 1/402 was reported, but the forces west of Vaux, 2/402, record that they held their front until about 8:00 pm (7:00 pm French Time), when a renewed, artillery fire closely followed by the American assault, overwhelmed their lines, driving them beyond the Vaux-Bouresches railroad, With this, the entire forward position of the 402nd Regiment was lost. At about the same time, the right flank of the 401st Regiment, on Hill 204, gave ground, and the enemy established himself in close contact, within the woods on the crest. All combat companies suffered heavy losses. Division [201st] considered Hill 204 the vital point, to be held, at all costs, but it was apparent that, if the thrust through Vaux-La Roche was not stopped, Hill 204 would be enveloped. The Infantry Brigade of the 201st Division, therefore, ordered, at 8:13 pm (7:13 French Time) an immediate counter attack by the 402nd Regiment, on its lost front line. Two battalions of the 402nd were by now incapable, and the task was allotted to 3/402, which had moved from Bezu-St Germain at 4:00 o'clock, to Chante Merle, and was 4 kilometres on an air line, and further by road, from Vaux. The 10th Company of the 401st Regiment was detailed to assist, and the remaining reserves of the Division were sent to Hill 204. The 28th Division, called on for aid, moved 2 companies down to the western edge of the Bois des Rochets, and placed a battalion in the southwestern end of the same woods. After that, except for confused close combat on the wooded crest of Hill 204, the battle stood still for some hours. The movement of the German reserves was much hampered by the enemy artillery, which continued, to harass the approaches to the front.[750]

749 Ibid.
750 *War Diary and annexes, 201st DI, 1-2 July. See Combat Report Schoeler, 1-2 July. It is evident that the Germans did not realize that the thrust which overran the Vaux-La Roche line was made with a limited objective. They expected the Americans to push eastward and northeastward and envelop Hill 204. By 8:00 pm, German Time, there were only about 6 companies-700 or 800 rifles-which could have resisted, and of these the entire 3/402 was too far away to have gotten into the fight.*

The tale of the German counter attack is briefly told. All night the 2/9 and 3/23 worked, energetically on their new line, covered by their own artillery, and not greatly harmed by the German guns, which, although they fired heavily on the area, lacked definite direction. At daylight, the German infantry advanced, came at once under the American barrages, and was shot to pieces by small arms fire delivered from position. In effect, the Germans ran straight into the arms of the American infantry, and were utterly dispersed, most of them being shot or captured, while the loss of the Americans was negligible. The 3rd Brigade line was never seriously threatened, and most of the losses incurred came, not from the Germans on the Brigade front, but from forces in position on the northern and eastern flank of the Hill, overlooking the Vaux-La Roche area.[751]

The 3/402 had been drilling in the afternoon of 1 July at Bezu-St Germain, when they were ordered to fall in, without packs, given coffee, and marched to Chante Merle, 2 kilometres southwest. This was at about 4:30 pm, German Time. They waited at Chante Merle until 7:00 o'clock, at which time the American attack was developing, and shortly afterward marched south by the Bezu-Chateau Thierry road, to a point east of Vincelles, then cut across the fields to the highway 3/4 kilometre west of Vincelles. The battalion took up position and halted 600 or 700 metres east of the railroad line, and made dispositions for counter attack. The march had been slow, and the approach rendered difficult by the enemy artillery, and it is not probable that they were up before midnight. Orders were given for counter attack on Vaux-La Roche to start at 3:15 am–2:15 French Time, but when zero hour came, there was such a fury of gun fire on the area they were to cross, from both German and American guns, that they waited half an hour, unable to move. Then, in the grey of dawn, they advanced, in groups supported by light machine guns,[752] by rushes. Caught between a barrage behind, and machine guns in front, the battalion disintegrated. All those who reached the American lines became prisoners.[753]

Among the prisoners was a non-commissioned officer commanding a platoon of the 10th Company in 3/402. His company was on the battalion left, in support of the 12th Company, which attacked Vaux. The 9th and 11th Companies, he said, extended towards the Bois de la Roche. He did not see the company of the 401st Regiment detailed to support the battalion. His men went forward by squad rushes at 3:45 am, and were fired on by Americans from the line of the railroad. After 3 of such 15-metre rushes, 2

751 *Operations Report, 3rd Brigade, 1-2 July-Vol. 6.*
752 *Examination of Prisoners, G-2 File, 2nd Div. See statement of Sgt. Oskar Glattowski, 10/402.*
753 Ibid.

Vaux: XXI CA, 12 June 205

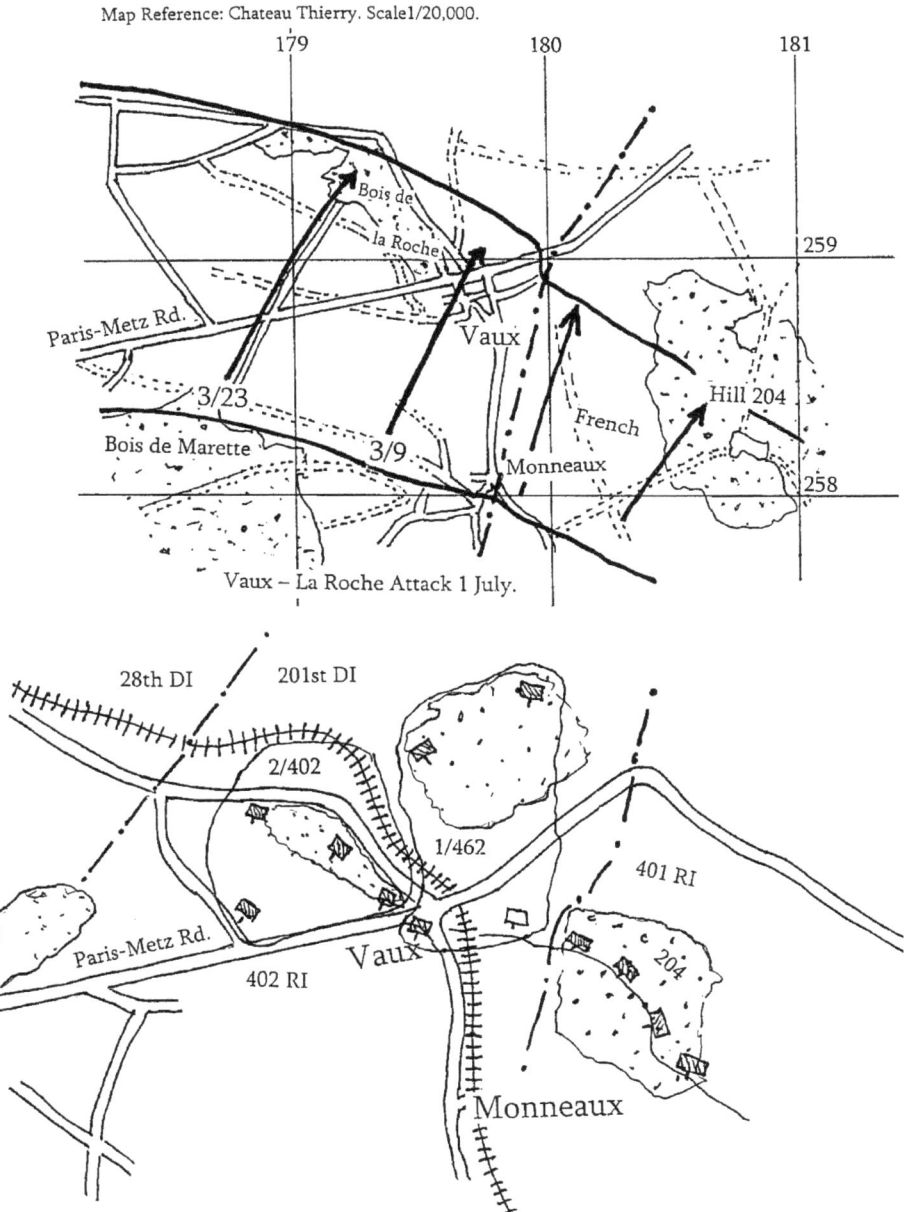

Vaux – La Roche Attack 1 July.

German dispositions Hill 204 - Vaux - La Roche 1 July 18.

Map 15

heavy machine guns were laid upon them, casualties became excessive, and the Germans stopped. This man sent for reinforcements, but battalion headquarters replied that none could be given, and ordered the attack pushed at all costs. The men refused to advance further. The 10th Company became demoralized, and the word was passed for each to save himself. The feldwebel, with 50 or 60 men, took refuge in a nearby cellar, where the American Infantry surrounded them. At about 6:00 am they surrendered.[754]

The German reports assert, however, that they brought their outpost line up to the line of the railroad, organizing their main line of resistance in the western edge of the Bois des Rochets, and the maps of 201st Division show the line so situated on 2 July.[755]

The casualties of the 201st Division for the fighting on 1–2 July, total 17 officers and 1191 men killed, wounded and missing. Of this total, the 402nd Regiment lost 1 officer killed, 5 wounded and 10 missing, 253 men killed, 159 wounded and 500 missing; 925 casualties in all ranks. The casualties of the 401st Regiment, on Hill 204, amounted to 3 officers and 181 men. The remainder of the loss was divided between the 403rd Regiment, which was not heavily engaged, the pioneers and the artillery. The artillery loss was 9 killed and 26 wounded.[756]

The weight of the blow fell on the 402nd Regiment, which sustained the American attack. The prisoners taken by 2/9 and 3/23 numbered 544,[757] and the others, listed as missing by the 201st, were probably killed. The Germans ascribed their excessive loss to the effect of the artillery fire which fell on their positions before and during the attack. The very light loss in the divisional artillery — 9 killed and 26 wounded, bears out the statement that the American artillery, on 1 July, did not seem to be directed against their batteries.[758]

2nd Trench Mortar Battery

The 2nd Trench Mortar Battery, Captain John P. Bonner, received its equipment 2 days before the 2nd Division was ordered, to the sector north-

---

754   Ibid.
755   War Diary and annexes, 201st DI, 1-2 July-See combat report Schoeler.
756   Ibid.
757   Operations Report, 3rd Brigade, 1-2 July, Vol. 6. Journal of Operations, 2nd Div., Vol. 6.
758   War Diary and annexes, 201st DI, 1-2 July-see combat report Schoeler. 1-2 July gives prisoners captured on 1-2 July as 7 officers and 428 men. This includes about 140 taken in the German counter-attack, and does not include about 40 prisoners turned over to the French 153rd Regiment on Hill 204.

west of Chateau Thierry, and remained in the rear for target practice during the first weeks of the action. It was armed with twelve 582 trench mortars of the French type, horse-drawn, and its personnel were unfamiliar with the weapons. It completed target practice and training, and was ordered forward by the 2nd Field Artillery Brigade to participate in the Vaux operation. Plans for its employment were drawn up, in consultation with the 2nd Field Artillery Brigade, and during the night 30 June–1 July its guns were emplaced in the Monneaux-Bourbetin ravine, halfway between the Bois de la Marette and Monneaux. Ammunition was carried forward by hand, and at 4:00 pm on 1 July the battery went into action, at a range of 900 yards, firing on the German defenses in Vaux. The trench mortar projectiles were particularly effective in destroying the wire and other obstacles on the approaches to the village.

The battery was in action during the German protective barrage and artillery reaction following the attack, but no casualties were reported, It fired 450 projectiles.[759]

4th Machine Gun Battalion

Since its arrival in the sector on 4 June, the 4th Machine Gun Battalion, Major [Edmund L.] Zane, had been stationed as divisional reserve in the Bois de Gros Jean not in action, but furnishing working parties and carrying details for the maintenance of the troops on the front line. During the relief of the Marine Infantry battalions by the 7th Infantry Regiment, the machine gunners of the 4th Brigade had remained in line. On 20 June, Company B of the 4th Machine Gun Battalion relieved the 23rd Company of the 6th Machine Gun Battalion in the Bois de Belleau,[760] the 23rd Company retiring to the Bois Gros Jean. On 22 June, Company A went into the line in the Bois de Belleau, replacing the 77th Company of the 6th Machine Gun Battalion,[761] which also withdrew to the Bois Gros Jean in Division reserve. Following this, Major Zane established his command post in the Bois de Belleau;[762] and his companies supported the attacks of 3/5 on 23 June and 25 June, and took part in the final consolidation of the woods, remaining in position until relieved, on 5 July, by the 103rd Machine Gun Battalion of the 26th Division.[763]

---

759 *2nd T M Battery During Attack on Vaux-1 July*, 2nd T M Battery, 2nd FA Brigade, Vol. 6.
760 *Zane to 2nd Div., 8:15 am, 20 June*, Vol. 4.
761 *Zane to 2nd Div., 11:00 am, 22 June*, Vol. 4.
762 *Zane to 2nd Div., 11:00 am, 27 June*, Vol. 4.
763 *Zane to 2nd Div., 8:00 am, 5 July.*

3rd Brigade Regimental Sectors

The first sector assignment of the 3rd Brigade located, its regiments north of the Paris-Metz highway, facing Bouresches and the Bois de Belleau.[764] Owing to the emergencies of 1 June, however, other dispositions were made, and the 9th Infantry, on 1 June, went into line south of the highway, from Le Thiolet to Bonneil, the 23rd Infantry taking station in reserve behind it.[765]

On 2 June the 23rd Infantry, plus the 1/5 Marines and the 5th Machine Gun Battalion, was placed under orders of the French 43rd Division and deployed to the west of the 2nd Division, from the Bois de Veuilly to Bremoiselle. It remained in these lines until the night 4–5 June, when it was relieved by French units and, returned to the Division. During the night 5–6 June, the 23rd entered the 2nd Division line, taking over the front from Le Thiolet, through the Bois des Clerembauts, to Triangle Farm, from the 2/6 Marines. Meantime the 9th had covered the area from Le Thiolet to Bonneil, employing at first 2, and finally 3 battalions. On 4 June command of the 2nd Division area passed from the French to Major General Bundy. Exhausted French elements were replaced by fresh troops, both in the XXI Corps, to which the 2nd was assigned, and in the XXXVIII Corps, on the right of the 2nd, and in the reorganization, the front of the 9th Infantry was contracted from Bonneil to the southeast corner of the Bois de la Marette. By daylight on 6 June the 3rd Brigade Sector, now organized as such, extended from the Bois de la Marette to Le Thiolet (9th Infantry) and through the Bois des Clerembauts to Triangle Farm (23rd Infantry) where it joined the flank of the 4th Brigade.[766]

From this line, in the afternoon of 6 June, the 23rd Infantry attacked, reaching the Bois de la Cote 192, about 1300 metres to its front. It fell back to its original positions in the early hours of 7 June.[767] In the evening of 6 June, the 9th, in liaison with French units on the right, pivoted forward on Bourbetin, establishing its right on the culvert halfway between Vaux and, Monneaux. The new line was in advance of the Bois de la Marette and Bourbetin, and was based on the Bourbetin-Monneaux ravine. The regimental left rested on the highway 40 metres east of Le Thiolet.[768] No further change occurred in the front of the 3rd Brigade until 13 June.

764 F.O. 5, 2nd Div., 7:40 pm., 31 May-Vol. 1.
765 War Diary, 2nd Div., 1 June-Vol. 6.
766 War Diary, 2nd Div., 5-6-7 June-Vol. 6.
767 Operations Report (Special) Col. Malone, 7 June; also, 3rd Brig. Operations Report, 7 June, Vol. 6.
768 Intelligence Reports, 9th Inf., 6-7 June-Vol. 9.

"— began to ascend the long gray slope ahead"

The losses and exhaustion of the 4th Brigade, incident to the prolonged fighting in the Bois de Belleau, made it desirable to shorten the front held by the Marines, whose mission, in the middle of June, was still unaccomplished. Accordingly, the 3rd Brigade extended its left, taking over from the Marines the line from Triangle Farm to and including Bouresches. The relief was made by 3/23, during the night 13–14 June In the redistribution of the 3rd Brigade, accompanying this movement, the 9th Infantry extended its left, placing 1 company (B/1/9) north of the highway, in the former position of E Company of the 23rd. The regimental boundary was in the east face of the Bois des Clerembauts, at about X–line 259.[769] With this readjustment, the Brigade front ran from the culvert on the Vaux-Monneaux road to Bouresches, and it remained in place until the Vaux operation on 1 July.

On 1 July the 3rd Brigade attacked the enemy in the Vaux-La Roche positions. The assault was made from within the regimental sector of the 9th Infantry, south of the highway, 3/23 being moved into the line of the 9th to participate. Two/9 on the right and 3/23 on the left advanced successfully, establishing themselves east of Vaux and on the east and north edges of the Bois de la Roche, and, the north edge of the Bois de la Cote 192. Thence the line followed its old trace, through Triangle Farm and Bouresches, and this front was turned over to the 26th Division on the night 8–9 July, the 51st Brigade relieving the 3rd Brigade.[770]

Headquarters of the 3rd Brigade were established on 1 June at Ventelet Farm, and remained there during the action northwest of Chateau Thierry, closing at 8:00 am 9 July, with the passing of command to the 51st Brigade.[771]

Headquarters of the 9th Infantry were established at Les Aulnois Bontemps on 1 June, and remained in place until the relief of the regiment on 9 July.[772]

Headquarters of the 23rd Infantry were established at Coupru on 1 June, moved to Coulombs on 2 June, returned to Coupru on 5 June, and remained at Coupru until the Brigade was relieved.[773]

The 5th Machine Gun Battalion established Headquarters at Larget Farm on 1 June. On 2 June the Battalion accompanied the 23rd Infantry, Headquarters going to Coulombs. The same day Headquarters returned to Larget Farm. On 4 June Headquarters was moved to Coupru, remaining until 20 June, when it was located in the woods 500 metres west of Larget Farm. It made no further moves until its relief by a machine gun battalion of the 26th Division on 9 July.[774]

769 *Intelligence Reports, 9th Inf., 13-14 June-Vol. 9.*
770 *History of the 3rd Brigade: Hall-2nd Div. File.*
771 Ibid.
772 *History 9th Inf.*
773 *History 23rd Inf.*
774 *Report Operations, 5th MG Bn since leaving Bouconvillers, 31 May-13 Aug.-Vol. 8.*

Twenty-One

Relief of Second Division, 3–10 July

With the storming of the Vaux-la-Roche Line, the last of the tasks assigned to the 2nd Division on its entry into the sector was completed. The French held Bussiares and the Clignon to the West. The Americans had taken Hill 142, cleared the Bois de Belleau, and forced the German line north across the stream. Bouresches was American, and now Vaux and the Bois de la Roche. Only on Hill 204 did the Germans maintain their advanced positions.

The 2nd Division passed to the defensive, assuming a position in readiness, since no further attacks were contemplated. The Allied High Command expected another German drive, and made preparations to receive it. The orders of the 2nd Division reflected this attitude.

On 2 July, acting under instructions of the French 6th Army, and of the French III Corps, Division Headquarters issued a memorandum which set forth the plan for organization within the Divisional area, providing a disposition in depth of three zones of defense.

The Zone of the Advance Posts comprised the present front lines, and covered, in depth, the terrain taken from the enemy, the Bois de Champillon, the woods southeast of Lucy-le-Bocage, the Bois de Vivray, Hill 201, and the ridge of Tafournay Farm.

The Zone of Principal Resistance followed the high ground eastward from Marigny, through La Voie du Chatel, Coupru, Les Aulnois Farm, and Beaurepaire.

The Zone of the Reserves was sited, from Hill 206, through Signal d'Issonge, the woods west of Coupru, La Baudiere, and Domptin, to La Mazure.

The Division sector would be known, the memorandum provided, as the Sector Pas Fini.[775]

Pas Fini was divided into sub-sectors, the right, of the 3rd Brigade, to be called Sub-sector Regular, and the left, of the 4th Brigade, Sub-sector Marine.

Each Brigade front was in turn divided into regimental sub-sectors. Each regiment was distributed in depth from the Zone of the Advance Posts to the Zone of the Reserves. The regimental front was normally held by a battalion of infantry, a machine gun company, a 37mm gun, and 2 Stokes Mortars. A system of strong points, with numerous combat groups and machine gun positions, covered the Zone of the Advance Posts, in which particular attention was given to stream lines and covered avenues of approach favorable to the infiltration tactics of the enemy. No continuous line was manned. Part of the Battalion was held in readiness for counter attack.

Accordingly, 4 battalions were stationed on the Division front, from the railroad crossing east of Vaux to the junction with the French north of Hill 142.

In the Zone of Principal Resistance, each regiment stationed 1 rifle battalion, with a machine gun company, 2 37mm guns, and 4 Stokes Mortars. Two additional battalions were assigned in Sub-sector Regular as the 3rd Brigade Reserve, stationed, one in the woods southeast of Domptin, and one at La Langue, and an engineer battalion was added to them, posted at La Croisette. In Sub-sector Marine, 4th Brigade reserve consisted of one battalion, on Hill 205. The Zone of Principal Resistance was organized in 3 parallels, a parallel of resistance, a parallel of support, and a parallel of redoubts. An extensive construction program, including deep shelters against bombardment, was outlined.

In the Zone of the Reserves, a battalion of Marines lay at the orders of Division in the Bois Gros Jean, Division reserve also including the other Engineer battalion and the 4th Machine Gun Battalion.[776]

The memorandum directed the artillery to make such changes in its dispositions as was necessary to conform to the general defensive plan.[777]

The Distribution of Troops outlined in the Memorandum was par-

---

775 *Memorandum, 2nd Division, 2 July, with annexes: Vol. 1. This is the first official mention of the name "Pas Fini" as applied to the 2nd Division area northwest of Chateau Thierry. It seems to have been used colloquially through the Infantry Regiments during June, but its origin cannot be traced in the records. The legend has it that a retiring Frenchman, on 1 June, as the Americans entered the sector, called out that "la guerre was Fini," and the Americans replied that, on the contrary, "la guerre was pas fini as long as they were in it." But this is legend, nothing more.*

tially in effect when the memorandum was issued, the 4th Brigade having already organized. Sub-sector Marine in depth, on a 2-battalion front, as soon as the Bois de Belleau was cleared of the enemy.

During the night 2–3 July, the 3rd Brigade rearranged its front, relieving 3/23 in the La Roche line with 1/9, and making new dispositions from Vaux to Bouresches.[778]

On 3 July, at 10:00 pm, Field Order 10, 2nd Division, was issued, providing for the relief of the 2nd Division by the 26th US Division (New England National Guard, Major General Clarence Edwards). The relief would begin the night of 4–5 July, to be completed the night 8–9 July. The 2nd Field Artillery Brigade would be relieved by the 51st Field Artillery Brigade; the 3rd Brigade by the 51st Infantry Brigade; the 4th Brigade by the 52nd; the 2nd Engineers by 101st; and, the special services by their opposite numbers in the 26th Division. All movements were to take place between 9:00 pm and 3:00 am. The routine arrangements for sector turnovers would apply between out going and incoming troops.[779]

Officers of the 26th Division entered the 2nd Division area and carried out preliminary reconnaissance. Appended to Field Order 10 were march schedules and Billet lists. Second Division Headquarters were to be established at Nantieul-sur-Meaux, and troops were to be disposed in the region north of the Marne and east of the Ourcq, in the angle formed by the confluence of the rivers. Troop movements would be carried out by marching.[780]

On 4 July the relief of the 4th Brigade began, the rear echelons moving out first. As provided by orders, General Harbord remained in the sector for 24 hours, Colonel Neville assuming command of the outgoing Marine elements. The front was quiet, and the relief's generally without incident.

On 4 July the 2nd Division was assigned to the American I Corps, General Hunter Liggett.[781]

On 5 July, the American I Corps suspended the relief. Information, regarded as reliable, had been received that a German attack was imminent, and Corps stated that sufficiently forceful reasons required that the I Corps retain the full strength of 2 American Divisions in the 1st and 2nd lines of the Corps front.[782] When this order was received, the relief of the

---

776 *Memorandum, 2nd Division, 2 July, with annexes: Vol. 1.*
777 *Ibid.*
778 *Operations Report, 3/23, 3 July, Vol. 7.*
779 *F.O. 10, 2nd Div., 3 July, Vol. 1.*
780 *War Diary, 2nd Div., 4 July, Vol. 6.*
781 *History 2nd Div. (Command and Movements), Army War College.*
782 *War Diary, 2nd Div., 5 July, F.O. 2, 5 July, I Corps.*

4th Brigade was almost completed, only 1 battalion remaining on the front in the Bois de Belleau. The remainder of the Brigade had marched towards its billeting areas in the rear. It was halted, countermarched, and placed in the old positions of the 52nd Brigade of the 26th Division under the command of General Edwards, in what was called the Second Army Line. It rested its right on the Marne, with liaison with the French at Saulchery, and the other flank on the Paris-Metz road, near Montreuil, in liaison with the 51st Brigade of the 26th Division. The 2nd Division retained command of the Sector Pas Fini, with the 52nd Brigade under its orders. Work was commenced on the Second Army Line, the 4th Brigade area of which ran from Le Barre (171.00–254.00) to the southern edge of the Bois des Essertis. Internal relief's, between the 4th Brigade and the 52nd Brigade continued without incident.[783]

On the 6th, the Germans shot down an American balloon in the Division area. The French activity on Hill 204 had been resumed on the 4th and 5th, without appreciable gains. Except for aerial and artillery activity, the Division front was quiet.[784]

On 7 July the relief was resumed. American aviators appeared for the first time over the 2nd Division. Troops movements continued, uninterrupted, during the night 7–8 July, the 3rd Brigade being relieved by the 51st.[785]

The relief was completed in the night 8–9, the last element of the 2nd Division reporting clear at 3:40 am. At 11:00 pm, Division Headquarters closed at Genevrois Farm and opened at Chamigny.[786]

The 2nd Division settled down in the Army Line, in order, from the right, 5th Marines, 6th Marines, 23rd Infantry, 9th Infantry. The 2nd Field Artillery Brigade disposed its guns to cover the infantry positions. The line ran from Le Barre, at point 171.00–254.00, through the Bois des Essertis, past Bezu, north of Montreuil-aux-Lions, north of La Sablonniere, north of Chambardy, to point 165.00–258.00, and thence to Les Brulis. The troops were everywhere in the woods, and some battalions were billeted, others bivouacked. Under the direction of the Engineers, new field works were laid out and existing works improved, but all organizations had opportunity to rest, clean up, renew equipment, and receive replacements.[787]

On the 10th, General Pershing, the Commander-in-Chief, accompanied by General Degoutte, commanding the French VI Army, General

783   Ibid.
784   *War Diary, 2nd Div.*, 6 July, Vol. 6.
785   *War Diary, 2nd Div.*, 7 July, Vol. 6.
786   *War Diary, 2nd Div.*, 9 July, Vol. 6.
787   *War Diary, 2nd Div.*, 10 July, Vol. 6.

Liggett, commanding the American I Corps, and General Cameron, commanding the 4th Division, visited Division Headquarters at Chamigny. General Pershing decorated, with the Distinguished Service Cross, 17 officers and 17 enlisted men.[788]

Casualties

The available strength of the 2nd Division on 31 May was 1,064 officers and 25,614 men. According to the Journal of Operations, the casualties suffered through the period 1 June–10 July numbered 217 officers and 9,560 men, killed, wounded, gassed, and missing, of which 41 officers and 3,022 men were gas casualties.[789]

Replacements forwarded to the Division, northwest of Chateau Thierry, amounted to 6,200 men.[790] After the total casualties are deducted from the return of 31 May, the addition of the replacement figure shows a strength of 22,254. There were present for duty on 10 July, 963 officers and 23,275 men.[791] The discrepancy, 1,021, probably represents the number of lightly wounded and gassed who returned to duty while the Division was still on the front.

Of these casualties, 194 officers and 8,257 men were killed, wounded, gassed, and captured in the 3rd and 4th Brigades, 16 officers and 953 men in the Engineer regiment, 4 officers and 121 men in the Artillery Brigade, and 1 officer and 38 men in the 4th Machine Gun Battalion. The remaining loss occurred in the special services of the Division.[792]

The 3rd Brigade lost 68 officers and 3,184 men,[793] of which number 18 officers and 722 men were from the 9th Infantry.[794] The losses of the 23rd Infantry and of the 5th Machine Gun Battalion are not listed separately, but

---

788 Ibid.
789 War Diary and Journal of Operations, 2nd Div., 1 June-10 July, Vol. 6.
790 *Folder 1066 weekly report replacements received and required by divisions, GHQ, AEF: Folder 28, Commander-in-Chief report, Part 6, Vol 1: Folder 1057-B replacements required and furnished, GHQ, AEM: Personnel Statistical report, Folders A-9, A-10, A-12, and A-7, GHQ, AEF. AGO file US Army. This figure included Marines, but not the Hospital Corpsmen of the Navy. The 2nd Division War Diary reports replacements received as 119 officers and 4,238 men: whether Marines are included or not, is not specified. [Most likely, not. GBC].*
791 *The missing numbered 2 officers and 286 men. A careful check of the records of the opposing German divisions shows that they claimed less than 100 prisoners, including no officers. Most of the men listed as missing were killed, and their bodies lost sight of.*
792 War Diary and Journal of Operations, 2nd Div., 1 June-10 July, Vol. 6.
793 Journal of Operations, 2nd Division-Chateau Thierry-Vol. 8.
794 Regimental History 9th Inf.

casualties in the 23rd were heavier than in the 9th.[795] Perhaps 1200 officers and men were killed, wounded, gassed, or captured in the movements of 6 June, in the gas attacks about the middle of June, and in the Vaux operation: the remaining casualties occurred in the course of routine sector wastage. The lines held by the 3rd Brigade were everywhere exposed to German observation from the dominating slopes of Hill 204, and the Brigade front was subjected at all times to steady and well directed harassing fire of artillery and machine guns.[796] There exists the report of an inspection of the 3/23, Major Elliott, on 29 June. Three/23 had, on 31 May, 34 officers and 945 men The battalion was more heavily engaged than any other unit of the 3rd Brigade. Its casualties, up to 29 June, numbered 13 officers and 507 men, but 4 officers and 524 men were received as replacements, and on the eve of the Vaux attack there were present for duty 20 officers and 996 men.[797]

The 4th Brigade casualties are given, in the War Diary and Journal of Operations of the Division, as 126 officers and 5,057 men.[798]

The final figures given by the Major General Commandant, USMC, under date of July 7, 1922, total 4,175, the report being compiled from individual records.[799] There are available inspection reports on 5 of the 6 rifle battalions which made up the Marine Brigade, entered in the Division War Diary during June. Two/6, Major Holcomb, was inspected on 19 June. On 31 May, the battalion strength was 31 officers and 941 men. From 1 June to 12 June, it lost 31 officers and 836 men, receiving 4 officers and 331 men as replacements, and on 19 June it mustered 14 officers and 466 men. It sustained the heaviest casualties suffered by any Marine battalion on the Chateau Thierry front, although it was the only unit of the 4th Brigade which did not deliver a formal attack. The weight of its loss came in the gas concentration laid by the Germans on the right of the Brigade sector the night of 13–14 June.[800]

Three/5, commanded successively by Major Berry and by Major Shearer, delivered 3 attacks on and within the Bois de Belleau, including the first assault on 6 June and the final assault on 25 June. On 31 May it had present 34 officers and 1007 men. Between 1 June and 29 June it lost 13

---

795 *World War Division AGO gives the following losses for 3rd Brigade, 4 June to 14 July: 9th Inf, 995; 23rd Inf, 1467; 5th Mg Bn, 147; miscellaneous, 2; total, 3rd Brigade 2,611.*
796 *Journal of Operations, 2nd Division-Chateau Thierry-Vol. 6.*
797 *Report Inspection 3/23, War Diary, 2nd Div, 29 June, Vol. 6.*
798 *Journal of Operations, 2nd Division-Chateau Thierry-Vol. 6.*
799 *Casualties of the 4th Brigade, MGC, USMC, July 7, 1922, 2nd Div. File.*
800 *Report Inspection 2/6, 19 June, War Diary, 2nd Div., 19 June, Vol. 6.*

officers and 776 men, receiving 7 officers and 207 men by way of replacement. On 29 June it had 23 officers and 438 men available for duty.[801]

Two/5, entering the sector with 36 officers and 1,051 men, lost by 18 June, 18 officers and 556 men, most of them on 11 June and 12 June.[802] One/5, with 27 officers and 1,040 men, lost 16 officers and 544 men by 19 June.[803] The casualties of 3/6 were 14 officers and 388 men.[804] There is no report on 1/6, which appears to have been less heavily engaged than any other unit of the Brigade.

The casualties of the 6th Machine Gun Battalion, included in the total for the Marine Brigade, are given in the Battalion History as 12 officers and 195 men. The loss included 2 battalion commanders, Major Edward B. Cole, died of wounds, 10 June, and Capt Harlan F. Major, killed, 15 June.[805]

In the foregoing accounts of operations, authoritative figures for the Marine Battalions have been given as they occurred. No such tabulation has been made from the Army records in the AGO, and the figures which accompany the operations reports in the war diaries are admittedly incomplete. It is evident, however, for all sources, that the Division's loss in rifle strength was well over 50 per cent during the month of June, and the loss, in numbers if not in quality was largely made good by replacements.

The replacements for the 2nd Division, exclusive of the Marine Corps and Naval Medical units, came from depot formations in the rear areas, and from formations newly landed in France. The Marine Corps formed, at Quantico, Virginia, replacement battalions and casual detachments, which were sent over seas and held under training in the vicinity of St Aignon (Loire et Cher) until they were requisitioned by the 4th Brigade. Four Marine replacement battalions of war-strength were in France by the middle of June.

Replacements were ordered up as needed by GHQ, coming as far forward as conditions permitted by train and truck, and marching into the regimental areas at night. At regimental Headquarters, they were apportioned to the decimated battalions, and conducted to their units, wherever they might be, in the line or out of it. Unless a battalion was gravely shattered, as 3/5 and 3/23 on 6 June, it was not withdrawn from the line, but received its replacements and incorporated them into its organization in the presence of the enemy. Men who, in the 4th Brigade, were sent to 1/5,

---

801 Report Inspection 3/5, 29 June, War Diary, 2nd Div., 29 June, Vol. 6.
802 Report Inspection 2/5, 18 June, War Diary, 2nd Div., 18 June, Vol. 6.
803 Report Inspection 1/5, 18 June, War Diary, 2nd Div., 18 June, Vol. 6.
804 History 3/6 Marines.
805 History 6th Machine Gun Battalion. Major L[ittleton].W.T. Waller, Jr., USMC., succeeded to the command of the 6th M.G. Bn.

on Hill 142, the night of 8–9 June, and to 2/6, in the Bouresches-Triangle position, and to 2/5, in the midst of the heaviest fighting in the Bois de Belleau, were plunged into combat under the most trying conditions in most cases, their training was incomplete, and they were unfamiliar with the grenades and auxiliary weapons used by the Division. Reorganization within the battalions proceeded more effectively when replacements were received out of the line.

He Takes the War Too Seriously

The conduct of the green men received by all units during this period was so meritorious as to draw comment, of which the following communication of the 6th Marines is typical:

> 9 June 1918
> Headquarters 6th Regiment, 9 June
>
> From: Regimental Commander.
> To: Major General Commandant, U.S. Marine Corps,
> via Brigade Commander.
>
> Subject: Conduct of Replacement troops.
>
> 1. The remarkable conduct of raw replacement troops which joined this organization on the night of June 8 when thrown into the line is transmitted for the information of the Major General Commandant. The replacement detail of 213 included among it a large majority who were enlisted two months before their reporting to this organization. It was necessary to replace immediately losses sustained in the 2nd Battalion which was holding the right flank of our operations and the stronghold of the town of Bouresches, a line vitally important to the success of the present operations. The detail arrived at Headquarters at 6:30 pm and were placed in the woods and organized for relief. It was necessary to detail the five officers accompanying them to the 3rd Battalion for the purpose of reorganizing that battalion upon its relief that night. These troops were marched past the lines at 10:50 pm under detail from Regimental Headquarters to the point where they were met by platoon guides and conducted to their station. The Regimental Sergeant Major reports that the men obeyed orders without a word, moved in splendid order and across a terrain that was shelled by the enemy by high explosives and lighted up by flares. Their arrival in the lines of the 2nd Battalion relieved a pressing need for men at a vital point. The remarkable steadiness of these men, many of whom had not had more than two months service, under conditions that would have been trying to

A nice day for a hike

veteran troops, is eloquent evidence of the fine material from which the Marine Corps is drawing its men in a critical hour of the Nation's history.

                F.E. Evans,
                Major, USMC
                Adjutant

1st Ind.

From: CG 4th Brigade, to Major General Commandant

1. Forwarded
2. The statements made by the Regimental Commander, 6th Marines, apply

with equal force to the conduct of the replacements which joined other battalions under the same trying circumstances. To say that these men showed themselves of the same fine material as that already composing the 4th Brigade is extremely high praise, but in this case deserved.

J G Harbord,
Brigadier General N A
Commanding

Command and Administrative, 2nd Division

The 2nd Division was detached from the French Group of Reserve Armies of the North on 30 May, and ordered to the French 6th Army, General Duchêsne, Colonel Preston Brown, Chief of Staff, reporting to General Duchêsne at Trilport on 31 May. The 2nd Division was first assigned, by the VI Army, to the French V Corps, and then to the French XXI Corps, General Dagoutte, the latter assignment becoming effective the night 31 May–1 June.

On 14 June General Degoutte was advanced to the command of the 6th Army, General Naulin taking command of the French XXI Corps. About 21 June, the XXI Corps was withdrawn from the sector northwest of Chateau Thierry, for duty in the Champagne, and was replaced by the French III Corps, General Lebrun. The 2nd Division continued under the orders of the French III Corps until 4 July, on which date it was assigned to the new American I Corps, General Hunter Liggett. It remained in the American I Corps for the rest of its service in the Marne region.

Headquarters of the 2nd Division were established in Montreuil-aux-Lions on 1 June. On 10 June, Headquarters were moved to Genevrois Farm, about 3 kilometres southeast of Montreuil, where it remained until the sector was turned over to the 26th Division, at 11:00 pm, 9 July. At the same hour, 2nd Division Headquarters opened at Chamigny.[806]

---

806 *War Diary and Journal of Operations, 2nd Div., 30 May–10 July. Vol. 8.*

APPENDIX I

Biography of John W. Thomason, Jr.

First and foremost, JWT always considered himself a Marine. He decided, following service in France with the 4th Marine Brigade, to remain a "sea-soldier." That certainly was beneficial to the Corps and to him as well. Unlike some of his colleagues, the decision wasn't made out of necessity. His prosperous family wanted him to return home and engage in a career in medicine, like so many of his illustrious forebears, and his father; or enter the field of law. He remained in the Marine Corps because he liked being a member of that small, rather active, military service he had grown to love, as would and had so many others before him.

What made him different from his colleagues was that he had several other very marketable skills. He wrote and he illustrated numerous books, each of which was exceptionally well received. Additionally, he also illustrated many books for other authors. If that didn't keep him busy enough, he wrote and illustrated numerous short-stories for various popular magazines including the *Saturday Evening Post* and *Liberty*, among others; he edited and wrote book reviews for the *American Mercury* magazine; all this while being a full-time active and efficient Marine officer. Thomason was exceptionally busy while engaged in writing the history of the 2nd Division Northwest of Chateau Thierry; two of his books were published during that time period and another conceived and begun.

John William Thomason, Jr., was born on 28 February 1893, in the then small city of Huntsville, Texas, which is located in the southeastern part of the state. His family was and is highly regarded. His maternal grandfather, Major Thomas Jewett Goree, born in Texas, had nobly served the cause of the Confederacy as a staff officer for General Longstreet. Thomason's paternal grandfather, Joshua Allen Thomason, a doctor, was born in Alabama. His father, John William Thomason, was born on a plantation at Oakland, Texas, fifteen miles removed from Huntsville, and his mother, Sue Hayes Goree, was born at Midway, Texas. Consequently, JWT Jr. was all Texan. He never forgot his roots and, while a Marine, returned to his home state frequently.

After serving in a few schools as a teacher, JWT decided he really wanted to be an artist/illustrator and, somehow, managed to convince his father to support him while he attended art school. In May 1914, he traveled to New York City and entered the Art Student's League to begin classes. That sojourn lasted for one year, then he went back to teaching in 1915. In 1916 he was caught up in the military activity along the border with Mexico when he enrolled in a training program at Fort Sam Houston. This was also very brief and in July 1916 he secured a trial position with the *Houston Chronicle* as a reporter. He enjoyed being a newspaperman and seriously considered that as a career. However, events outside Texas conspired against this plan.

He had already made plans to leave the paper when, on 5 April, the announcement appeared that the National Naval Volunteers were seeking recruits. War against Germany was declared by the Congress on 6 April 1917. On that same date JWT enlisted as a private in the Marine Corps' branch of the Texas Naval Militia and was assigned to Company A. His company was transferred to New Orleans and the Marine Barracks at the Naval Station, where he remained two weeks. During this period he applied for a commission. He and his comrades were further transferred to the Marine Barracks, Navy Yard, Charleston, South Carolina where they engaged in further training. It was at that post that he received his commission as a second lieutenant, back-dated to 10 April 1917. Thomason applied for, and in August, was granted a regular commission (temporary) in the U.S. Marine Corps. Because he was a successful officer this commission enabled him to be one of those selected to remain a Marine following the disbandment of the 4th Brigade at Quantico in mid–August 1919.

After a lengthy courtship Thomason married Leda Bass on 24 August 1917, just before his anticipated reassignment to overseas duty as a replacement with the 5th Regiment of Marines. Notwithstanding expectations, JWT had to go through a modicum of further training which began in November when he was assigned to Quantico, Virginia. Schooling was completed in mid–February 1918 and he was assigned to the Third Replacement Battalion. They boarded the USN transport *Henderson* in mid–April for transfer to France, arriving at St. Nazaire in early May. He soon after received his appointment as a platoon leader in the 5th Regiment, then in training north of Paris. His unit was the 49th Company of the 1st Battalion. There seems to be a slight difference of opinion as to when he actually began service with that company.[807] Nonetheless, he soon took his place in the lineup and certainly, based upon all information, was a valuable member of the company.

He fought through the month of June at the Wood and its environs. In mid–July the 2nd Division, 4th Brigade, and 5th Regiment were shipped less than fifty miles north to fight another bloody battle: Soissons. On 18 July the 5th "went over" and advanced deeply into the German lines against strong opposition. Thomason was later awarded a Navy Cross and Silver Star but was wounded that day. He and seven enlisted men destroyed a machine gun nest impeding the advance of the 49th and in so doing, killed thirteen Germans and captured two machine guns.

Following the action at Soissons and rest period at Marbache, he was transferred to the U.S. Army Infantry school at Andilly. Then after a month be returned to the regiment just in time for the rather easy time at St. Mihiel in mid–September. The next engagement would make up for the easy period. In early October the division was once again assigned to duty with the French; this time in another effort to take the strongly held German position on the Blanc Mont Massif. In what turned out to be a mainly American effort, the 2nd Division again paid for their previous successes. The 5th Regiment was shot to pieces and JWT's 1/5 was at the very center of that destruction. The regiment was no longer a viable military organization after 4 October, and for that matter neither was the division. It would require many replacements to refill the numerous holes in their regimental formation.

Like many of his fellows, JWT was stricken with influenza and managed, some might say luckily, to avoid the campaign to cross the Meuse River. The illness was ravaging the entire world and the soldiers of all armies engaged in the war were hit very hard. After being hospitalized for two weeks, but surviving, JWT and the rest of the A.E.F. commenced their march into Germany. During the occupation period, as senior captain JWT commanded the 49th Company, the 66th Company briefly and also the 17th Company before sailing for home in late July 1919. Needless to state, he was very happy to have come through safely and was back with his wife and family.

807 *Thomason never establishes the exact date of his arrival for duty with his company. However, it is a fact that when the 49th Company, as part of the 1st Bn., entered combat on 6 June, the only officer to survive the attack that morning was the skipper, Captain George W. Hamilton. All others were either dead or wounded. Thomason was wounded, but at Soissons in July. Therefore I have deduced that he was a member of the first replacements to arrive at the Bois de Belleau on 7 June (some records state the 8th of June).*

After some soul searching, JWT decided to make the Marine Corps his career. For the next few years he served in Cuba, as skipper of the 37th Company, 7th Marines. This was a mounted unit which patrolled and protected several American owned sugar mills. While based at Camagüey, a son was born to he and Leda, and was named John William Thomason, III. After a short period at the Naval Operating Base, Hampton Roads, Virginia as the base legal officer, JWT was detailed to the Naval Ammunition Depot at Dover, New Jersey. There he had the providential chance, while in New York City, to meet a war-time comrade, Laurence T. Stallings, Jr., now a successful author, playwright, and literary editor of the *New York World*. With this connection, Stallings managed to bring together JWT and the foremost editor of American letters, Maxwell Perkins of Charles Scribner's Sons, then and always the leading American publisher of prestigious literature.

Thomason showed his drawings and discussed his potential articles for the house magazine and soon he was contracted for both. The first manuscript to come out of his short stories became the world renowned *Fix Bayonets*. The man was on his way. After the success of that 1926 book he was encouraged to provide more material and soon came up with a series of collected short stories which became *Red Pants*, mostly about Marines. That imprint was dated 1927. Meanwhile, the Marine Corps had need for this captain of Marines and in May 1925 he was assigned to duty aboard the *Rochester*, flagship of the Special Service Squadron. The duty was mainly plying the waters off the east coast of Latin America, searching for anything that might upset the U.S. State Department.

Meanwhile, the 2nd Division leadership decided to publish a history of their division during the war in France. The Major General Commandant, John A. Lejeune, was approached for Marines to contribute and he in turn convinced JWT to take the responsibility. This was in 1927. Thomason requested special unpaid leave to travel to Europe in order to research in German archives for matters relating to those units which faced the 2nd Division in the sector of Chateau Thierry, and near the Bois de Belleau, later known, after the French fashion, as the Bois de la Brigade de Marine. Upon his return, he was assigned duties at Fort Humphrey (now Fort McNair) in Washington, D.C. The story of this enterprise is interesting, what little is known about it. Essentially, it lasted until 1929 and what you have in the present text was produced by JWT and any others that were working with him. At first, he loved the duty and association with fellow veterans of the war. Soon enough the factual material required him to write the history as it was relayed in records. Battlefield errors had been made, both by senior Marine and U.S. Army officers. He wrote the history as he read it and as it was, and incurred several instances of rebuttal and demands for recantation. That he refused to do. His portion, in draft form, was completed in 1930. Matters became quite heated and he was reassigned to duties elsewhere. The history went nowhere after that. Possibly other writers were being subjected to harassment and no officer wanted his career to end because of major disagreement with then serving general officers. However, in the meantime he wrote and saw published another series of short stories entitled *Marines and Others*.

Thomason was assigned to the esteemed Peiping, China, American Legation Marine Guard post and, with his family, reported there for duty in September 1930. This period would be the most pleasant of JWT's career. He and his family had the time of their lives, as did most other "China Marines." He assumed duties as the skipper of the famed Mounted Marine patrol unit. This allowed him to get back to riding, albeit on small Mongolian ponies. While in China his well-received biography, *Jeb Stuart*, was breaking sales records. It was indicative of his innate ability to write history and biography. His rating by his colleagues was still high and soon he was generally known by the sobriquet the "Kipling of the Corps." While in China he managed to continue his writing and illustrations. He even wrote several accounts of the engagements between Chinese and Japanese soldiers during the 1932 invasion. His series of short stories continued being published; some in the *Scribner's* magazine but he had branched out to selling stories to *Liberty*, the *Saturday Evening Post*, and also to the *New Yorker*. In 1934 his highly regarded collection of short stories, many about service in China, *Salt Winds and Gobi Dust*, appeared. The ongoing depression had slowed down buying of any but essentials so it failed to reached the sales set by his previous books.

As delightful as was China, for "wealthy" foreigners especially, it had its drawbacks. One of these was being very unhealthy for those same foreigners, and JWT, plus his young son Jack, were both stricken; the elder with malaria and the son with a severe attack of scarlet fever and then a double mastoid. The son was well cared for at the Peking Union Medical College and soon after JWT made a point to write a thank-you letter to John D. Rockefeller and the Rockefeller Foundation who funded the school. While physically capable, JWT wrote articles for newspapers, describing the incursion of the Japanese military forces in Shanghai in 1932. During this period, the 2nd Division historical section was dissatisfied with what had been collected and written and requested JWT's return. In fact it was at the personal request of an officer who had complained about material JWT had already written. Nevertheless, Thomason declined and was supported in that respect by the Commandant of the Marine Corps. In August 1933 he and his family boarded the *Chaumont* for the return voyage to the United States.

Upon return, his first assignment was as an aide to the Assistant Secretary of the Navy, Colonel Henry L. Roosevelt, a retired Marine. This position kept him moving about, inspecting naval bases: their training facilities, ship building and repair yards, and supply bases among many other things. Thomason and Roosevelt were both busy and yet JWT managed to continue his writing, illustrations, and now, editing and writing, at H.L. Mencken's personal request for the premier magazine of that period, the *American Mercury*.

Now a major, JWT finished his commitment to Roosevelt's office, as the man had died in February 1936. He was appointed to the Army War College at Fort Humphrey in August of that year. This was the first opportunity he had to further his military education and he made the most of it. Nonetheless, nothing interfered with his continued literary efforts. He was still going great guns with short stories and he even managed his first book of fiction, *Gone to Texas*, which was well received. When the AWC course terminated, he was then assigned to the Naval War College in Newport, Rhode Island, for the class beginning in early July 1937. He not only attended to his duties, continued writing and illustrating, but also had time to find Newport, summer home to the very rich, even during the on-going depression, a "very gay place." While at the NWC he was also the recipient of a long-overdue Navy Cross and promotion to lieutenant colonel.

After graduation in May 1938, he was posted to the 2nd Marine Brigade at San Diego, California. This was his choice; he wanted to return to his roots, with the troops. This time he was placed in command of the West Coast Platoon Leader's Class. That, however, lasted only six weeks, at the end of which he assumed command of the Second Battalion, Sixth Marines. This was what he really wanted to do and, as always, performed at his highest level. While so engaged in training he developed some ideas that were radical to a war the Marine Corps, and the U.S. Army, were still at that time prepared to fight. He wrote to the Commandant outlining those ideas, which passed through one of the aides, a popular and very heroic veteran of World War I, Colonel Clifton B. Cates. Cates replied with a letter lauding JWT's concepts and adding his "cheers" to the forwarded letter.

Still, JWT's work on his books and illustrations continued without letup. The only time when JWT was unable to perform was in the times, now increasing, that he was hospitalized for numerous reasons, some of which were for sheer exhaustion. This only slowed him down. During this period he had, arguably, his greatest success with the publication of another book of fiction, *Lone Star Preacher*. This was the fictionalized story of a man of the cloth JWT knew back home who had served in the Civil War with Hood's Texas forces. Meanwhile Pearl Harbor was attacked and the U.S. prepared for war.

In 1940 Thomason was not assigned to field duty, mainly because his health precluded that. He was instead assigned to the Office of Naval Operations for duty with the Office of Naval Intelligence. His short stories, written while with the Special Squadron in the early 1920's marked him as a man who was familiar with Latin America. No more, perhaps, than any other Marine with brief service there, but that was considered to be where his "expertise" was, so he was assigned to investigations of Nazi activities in the Caribbean. From this point on he would fly over the sea and land at various ports, make his salutations, then fly off to another "hot spot." He worked hard, never giving an inch to any of the younger men, and always reported early and left his office late. Regardless of his commitment to his post, he was not happy being kept off the firing line. One more tome — *And a Few Marines* came off the Scribner plates and presses and it was, like so many other war oriented material, exceptionally well received. This would be his final book. A few more short stories were published, but he wasn't strong enough to illustrate them and they were finished by a Mr. H. von Schmidt.

He was finally relieved from the ONI and proceeded to several duties on the west coast. His final duty was as a staff officer to Brigadier General Harry K. Pickett at Camp Pendleton, California. For foreign duty he had failed recent obligatory physicals and was certified as capable of state-side duty only. His monotony in the training program was briefly interrupted when his son Jack and his wife, returned from overseas, spent the Thanksgiving holiday with JWT and Leda at San Diego. Following that JWT was compelled to enter the Naval Hospital at San Diego. Released in January 1944 he returned to duty. The following month, declining in health, he re-entered the hospital, remaining until the 12th day of March when he succumbed to his many diseases. This was a sad day for the Corps and most if not all Marine bases in the continental U.S. mourned the passing of a Giant of the Corps.

The U.S. Navy destroyer USS *Thomason* (DD 760) was launched in San Francisco, California, on 30 September 1944; the Marine Corps named a plot of ground Thomason Park at Quantico, and Texas installed a portrait painted by his niece, Mrs. Charles H. Atkinson III, in its Hall of Heroes at the State Capitol Building in Austin. Thomason has been dead for nearly sixty years, but even today, he is well remembered by his many fans. His stories still please and thrill a multitude of *Marines and Others*; this final Thomason product will add to their pleasure.— *GBC.*

APPENDIX II

Brief History of the 2nd Division, 1917–1919

Organization

The 2nd Division, Regular Army was officially authorized by the U.S. Army War Department Chief of Staff, Major General Tasker H. Bliss on 22 September 1917. The order further stated:

> ... the War Department directs the organization of the 2d Div, Regular Army. The Div includes troops of the United States Marine Corps which are at Quantico or already in France, and units of the Regular Army stationed at Chickamauga Park, El Paso, Gettysburg, Governors Island, Philadelphia, Syracuse, Fts Benjamin Harrison, Ethan Allen, Myer, Oglethorpe, Riley, Sam Houston, and Camps Robinson and Vail as well as others en route to, or already in, Europe.[808]

Upon completion, the 2nd Division, Regular, would be composed of:

Division Headquarters and Headquarters Troop.
Third Brigade: 9th and 23rd Infantry, 5th Machine Gun Battalion.
Fourth Brigade: 5th and 6th Marines, 6th Machine Gun Battalion (Marines).
Second Field Artillery Brigade: 12th and 15th Field Artillery (75 mm. guns), 17th Field Artillery (155 mm. howitzers), 2nd Trench Mortar Battery.
Divisional Troops: 4th Machine Gun Battalion, 2nd Engineers, 1st Field Signal Battalion.
Trains: 2nd Train Headquarters and Military Polite, 2nd Ammunition Train,

---

[808] *Order of Battle of the United States Land Forces in the World War. American Expeditionary Forces: Divisions. Volume 2*, Washington, D.C.: Center of Military History, United States Army, 1988. p. 25.

2nd Supply Train, 2nd Engineer Train, 2nd Sanitary Train (Ambulance Companies and Field Hospitals 1, 15, 16, and 23).

Other Units: 2nd Mobile Ordnance Repair Unit, Mobile Veterinary Section No. 2, Motor Transport Corps Service Park Units 303–363, Salvage Squad No. 2, Sales Commissary Unit No. 1, Detachment Postal Service A.P.O. 710, Railhead Detachment, Clothing and Bath Unit 320-17, Laundry Unit 326, and Bakery Unit 319.

Sailing Schedule

The 5th Marine Regiment was the first organized unit of the 2nd Division to arrive in France. It had sailed at the same time as the 1st Division in June 1917. Next to sail was the 9th Infantry which arrived in September 1917. They were followed by the 23rd Infantry, which also sailed in September and arrived on 20 September.

Third Brigade's 5th Machine Gun Battalion (formed in August 1917 as a Provisional MG Bn) sailed on 18 September from New York and arrived on 5 October at Le Havre. As early as 11 August, the brigade had already been officially assigned as part of the 2nd Division. In fact, the War Department had considered the idea of assembling infantry from army units around the eastern part of the nation as the division's second brigade, but decided to utilize U.S. Marines instead. This resulted in the Ninth Infantry, the 23rd Infantry, the 5th Machine Gun Battalion and the 2nd Engineers, all arriving in France during the month of September.

The Sixth Marine Regiment had a very complicated schedule. The 1st Battalion sailed earliest, under Major John A. Hughes' command, and arrived at St. Nazaire on 5 October 1917. They too became laborers, much like the other Marines already in France. The 3rd Battalion, 6th Marines under the command of Major Berton W. Sibley was next to arrive on 12 November at Brest. The same thing happened to that battalion as to its predecessors. Major Thomas Holcomb in command of 2/6, managed to avoid the unpleasant duties inflicted upon their Marine comrades. When they arrived and debarked at St. Nazaire on 8 February 1918, they were at once shipped east to a training camp to join the balance of their brigade now in training.

The 1st Machine Gun Battalion, of two companies, arrived at St. Nazaire on 28 December 1917, later becoming the 6th Machine Gun Battalion.

The balance of the division, sailed from different ports at different times. The 2nd Engineers sailed on 10 September, from Hoboken, New Jersey, via Glasgow, Scotland, and arrived at Le Havre, France, on 6 October.

Three field hospitals and ambulance companies moved across in November and December as follows: on 24 November 1917, Field Hospital

1 and Ambulance Company 1 left El Paso, Texas, and sailed on 5 December from Hoboken, landing on 22 December at St. Nazaire; on 1 December, Field Hospital 15 and Ambulance Company 15 left Fort Benjamin Harrison, Indianapolis, sailed on 4 December from Hoboken, and arrived at Brest on 21 December; Field Hospital 23 and Ambulance Company 23 moved from Ft Oglethorpe, Georgia, sailed on 5 December from Hoboken, and arrived at St. Nazaire on 22 December.

On 12 December the enlisted personnel for Divisional Headquarters and Headquarters, 2nd FA Brigade, sailed from Hoboken and arrived at Brest on 27 December; the 15th FA sailed from New York and arrived on 25 December at Liverpool, England. On 13 December the 17th FA sailed from Hoboken and arrived at Brest on 28 December. Both the 4th Machine Gun Battalion (Divisional) and the newly organized 2nd Trench Mortar Battery moved from Gettysburg on 15 December to Camp Merritt, New Jersey. From there they embarked from Portland, Maine on 24 December, arriving at Liverpool on 8 January. Only the 12th FA was delayed in sailing for France until January.

Other organizations of the division left the U.S. in late December and arrived in Europe during January 1918. Principally they were the various trains: 2nd Ammunition Train, 2nd Supply Train, First Field Battalion, Signal Corps, 2nd Military Police, and Motor Transport Corps all arriving, usually, late in January. The 12th FA finally assembled in France on 31 January 1918, the last major arrival.

NAMES OF THE COMMANDING OFFICERS
(Division, Brigades and Regiments: up until and during the period)

2nd Division
Brig Gen Charles A. Doyen, USMC, 26 October 1917 (temporary)
Maj Gen Omar Bundy, 8 November 1917 (designated)

3rd Brigade
Col Harry R. Lee, 21 September 1917
Col Walter K. Wright, 10 October 1917
Brig Gen Peter Murray, 16 February 1918
Brig Gen Edward M. Lewis, 7 May 1918

9th Infantry
Col Harry R. Lee, September 1917
Col Leroy S. Upton, 24 February 1918

23rd Infantry
Col Walter K. Wright, 15 March 1917
Col Paul B. Malone, 15 February 1918

Fifth Machine Gun Battalion
Maj Shelby C. Leasure, 14 August 1917
Capt d'Alary Fechet, 10 January 1918
Maj Harry T. Lewis, 29 May 1918

4th Brigade
Brig Gen Charles A. Doyen, 23 October 1917
Brig Gen James G. Harbord, 6 May 1918

5th Marine Regiment
Col Charles A. Doyen, June 1917
Lt Col Hiram I. Bearss, 24 October 1917
Col Wendell C. Neville, 1 January 1918

6th Marine Regiment
Col Albertus W. Catlin, 17 August 1917
Lt Col Harry Lee, 7 June 1918

6th Machine Gun Battalion
Capt Edward B. Cole, 17 August 1917
Capt Harlan E. Major, 10 June 1918
Capt George H. Osterhaut, 12 June 1918
Maj Littleton W.T. Waller, Jr., 20 June 1918

2nd Artillery Brigade
Brig Gen William L. Kenly, 1 January 1918
Brig Gen George LeRoy Irwin, 1 February 1918
Col William J. Cruikshank, 5 May 1918
Brig Gen William Chamberlaine, 11 May 1918
Brig Gen Albert J. Bowley, 21 June 1918

12th Field Artillery
Col Manus McCloskey, 12 January 1918

15th Field Artillery
Lt Col Thomas E. Merrill, 1 June 1917
Col John R. Davis, 5 May 1918

17th Field Artillery
Col Albert J. Bowley, 17 June 1917
Col John R. Kelly, 26 June 1918

2nd Engineers
Col James F. McIndoe, 1 June 1917
Lt Col Carey H. Brown, 28 June 1918

Training

The 2nd Division was officially organized at Bourmont, France, on 26 October 1917. Brig Gen Charles A. Doyen, USMC, assumed command of the Division and Lt Col Logan Feland, USMC was appointed his Chief of Staff on that same date.[809] The divisional commander designate, Maj Gen Omar Bundy, arrived and assumed command on 8 November. He would retain command until, following the Battle of Belleau Wood in the Chateau Thierry Sector, he was reassigned to command a corps. Upon Bundy's arrival, Doyen would revert to command of the 4th Brigade.

Bourmont, the 3rd Training Area, became the 2nd Division's area when a detachment of the 5th Marines arrived at Damblain on 24 September 1917. Within a few days the 23rd Infantry and elements of the 9th arrived from St. Nazaire. Although the infantry went directly to the training area, unfortunately for the Marine units, they were still scattered throughout the AEF area protecting and unloading. As an example, the 8th Machine Gun Company of the 5th Marines was sent to protect AEF Headquarters at Chaumont. Another company of the regiment, the 67th, was sent to England to provide service for the incoming American troops there. They would return to the division in late March 1918. Consequently, they all lost many hours of training, if, like the 67th, they had any.

The Marines weren't alone in their diversion from the training required. The 2nd Engineers had been engaged in construction work in divisional areas and it wasn't until 10 December 1917 that they took up their official duties. Later, in March, the 2nd and 3rd battalions of the 9th Infantry were sent to do guard duty and railroad construction. So they, like the 5th Marines, lost valuable training time. Both battalions would return in time for their assignment to the Toulon front later in the month. Essentially it was the 23rd Infantry units and most of the machine gunners that were engaged in training.

Chaumont (A.E.F. Headquarters) made the decision that each of the divisions would undergo a three month training period in the art of war. Training commenced with small unit problems; beginning with platoons and up to company level. Many of the lieutenants and captains were new at the job. Some were derived from newly promoted sergeants, especially in the Marine units; others were recent volunteers whose only qualifications were three or four years of college. Consequently, they too were learning. For the most part, they learned extremely well.

After the low level training it was decided that battalions then would interact with French divisions in a quiet sector. During late January and the month of February the concentration of the 2nd Division, less artillery, was completed. By 13 March the division, still less artillery, moved to the area of the French Second Army, near Sommedieue, perhaps a dozen miles

---

809 *This was the first U.S. Marine officer to command a division in any war.*

southeast of Verdun-sur-Meuse. That devastated city was still a bastion of French determination and courage. This was the area in which the division would begin and end its trench experiences.

One of the primary problems of the trench mentality was the difficulty in getting men to move out when they were under modest protection. Getting them "Over the Top" was difficult, but getting them to move as far forward as desired, under terrible fire, was dismaying. With maneuver warfare they frequently would find cover but that might be illusory and subjected to concentration of fire anyway. Consequently, they would move, perhaps hoping for better cover. No matter, the idea of digging in was alien to Americans; Pershing was right; the end of the war came because everyone got up and went forward when the Germans began to fall back.

Unlike the infantry, the U.S. Marines were having little problem with their men in France. Even their relative newcomers, all of whom had gone through boot camp, had been exposed to Marine discipline and *esprit*, and that effectively eliminated difficulty. There were the occasional troublemakers but, as a whole, the preparations before going to France had sufficiently instilled in the men what was expected of them. Not so with the infantry. Many, even those so-called "regulars," had little discipline instilled in their basic training. Partly it was the lack of experienced trainers and partly the inexpert system used in the rapidly expanding army. Whatever the problem, the 2nd Division infantry units were experiencing growth pains before going and especially after arrival in France. The draftees in the 9th Infantry were especially troublesome but with some changes in the command structure they soon became well-disciplined and very effective. The Marines in France were top heavy in field ranks. Majors were plentiful and commands were scarce. There were several experienced Marine majors who had managed to make it over the pond without combat commands. Several were appointed to the 9th Infantry. One, Hiram Bearss, managed to make the 3rd Bn., 9th Infantry, a first-class unit in several weeks of his own special training.

Like most of the Division, the engineers were basically constructed from new men, including numerous draftees. This was brought about primarily because the companies expanded from about 160 men each to the required 250 men. Most of this happened after arrival in France The 2nd Engineers later complained that their training in France was pretty much limited to the post-construction period beginning in mid–January 1918. From 14 January, when the entire regiment was assembled at Bourmont until they left for the Toulon Sector, it was five weeks of infantry training and little else. That was a good thing too, because they would become important helpmates to all the infantry regiments during the bad times ahead.

The first frontline experience of the entire division was with the French at Toulon from mid–March to mid–May, 1918. The infantry/Marines had several contacts with the enemy, the artillery was allowed some firing and the engineers dug and strengthened trenches. The other support units were all allowed to participate and in May the French decided the 2nd Division would do. That was followed by a very brief rest and recuperation in an area northwest of Paris.

On 31 May 1918 the division was transferred to the French command and directed east toward the advancing, victorious German Army. The Boche, as the French poilu had named them, was storming over the Chemin des Dames, driving French armies before them and progressing farther into France than anytime since 1914. By 1 June the 2nd Division was in place west and north of the town of Chateau Thierry. It was in this sector that they would stand and turn aside the enemy, a mere 40 miles or less from France's sacred Paris. The Marine Brigade was assigned to the northern portion of the defensive line, and the 3rd Infantry Brigade, to the south. The present text describes the ordeal, courage, and victory of the American troops in their first major encounter with the German Army.[810]

Following this defense, the 2nd Division would fight fifty miles north of Chateau Thierry, at Soissons on 18–19 July, another very bloody encounter. That was the beginning of the end for the German Army. From that date, the "Boche" were on their way back to Germany. Following Soissons the division would rest, merge replacements, and refit at Marbache during August. Mid-September would find the division at the destruction of the St. Mihiel Salient. In early October the division was once again assigned to the French Army, in yet another one of their efforts to take the powerful enemy positions on Blanc Mont Massif. After succeeding where the French had failed several times in the past years, and once again suffering enormous casualties, the division refitted, replaced, and barely rested. Finally came the Meuse-Argonne campaign. This would be more lengthy than most of the other efforts, and unlike some other AEF divisions, not so destructive to the Second. Not at least until the last night of the war when the venerable 5th Marine Regiment was selected to cross the Meuse River against strong, well-entrenched, German elements. They went and, though suffering intense casualties once again, made it and at 11:00 am when the war ceased, the AEF had a foothold on the east bank of the river.

---

810 *The 26th Division had fought a brief defensive battle (identified as a "local action" by AEF Headquarters) against German raiders at Seicheprey on 20–21 April, and on 28 May, the 28th Infantry, 1st Division had taken Cantigny, but neither was on the order of this fight near Chateau Thierry, both in length of time and extent of fighting. Both divisions, however, would do much more as the war continued.*

Then into Germany as an occupation force in the zone assigned to the Americans. Finally, in July 1919, they packed up, most of them, to head home and in August began the break-up of the 2nd Division as formed in France. The U.S. Army continued the 2nd Division but without Marines. It would earn a fine reputation in more wars to come. Regardless, their finest moments were in France in 1917–1918.— *GBC*.

Suggested Reading

Published material about the American battles in France during World War I are few and far between. The battle for the Bois de Belleau (Belleau Wood) was the major part of the 2nd Division's effort Northwest of Chateau Thierry, this book's primary subject matter. And that was mainly a battle between U.S. Marines and German soldiers, though some French and some American soldiers were, mainly, in a support function during the period. To the best of my knowledge, unfortunately, no one has written a special book about the U.S. Army's Third Brigade during this period. Consequently, most of what has been published will be by or about Marines. The best, but generally unavailable, American source, is the multi-volume publication *The Records of the Second Division* (Washington, D.C.: The Army War College, 1927). Generally a complete record of all documents relating to the division and its various major units. Otherwise, listed below is what is generally available in English about this subject matter. Most have at least some value.

Unpublished Memoirs, Letters and Manuscripts

Barnett, George. *Soldier and Sailor Too*. Unpublished, c. 1925. (The wartime commandant covers his entire career as a Marine, including the war, in this self-oriented memoir.)

Bellamy, David. Untitled memoir. Begins with date October 23, 1917, page 1 through page 137; last entry dated August 22nd [1919] "On Leave."

Cordes, Onnie J. *The Immortal Division*. N.p., n.d., about 57 pages typewritten, a few photos.

Draucker, James H. *Telling it like it was*. N.p., n.d. about 50 typewritten pages. Begins c. 6 April 1917; ends August 1919.

Moore, William B. *Letters to his mother*. Begins 31 March 1918 and goes through August 1919, about 35 pages.

Soares, Denzil I. *Diary of Pvt. Denzil I. Soares. April 1918–April 1919 U.S.M.C.* N.p., n.d., with approximately 20 pages in diary form chronologic entries.

Thomas, Eugene R. *Letters to his mother.* Begins with a letter dated "Mother's Day" 1918. (He was a Marine corporal clerk at division headquarters.)

Zischke, Peter H. *Recollections of my father Herman A. Zischke, etc.* Orinda, CA, 2004. Includes memoirs and additional material put together by his son; c. 100 pages.

Thompson, Troy T. *Private Edward Clyde Thompson — A Marine's Accounting of World War I.* N.p., n.d. c. 2003, mostly diary entry style with added material. Entries are substantial and begin 11 April 1917.

Selected Articles

Clark, George B. "Leatherneck Magazine." *Medal of Honor Marine: John Joseph Kelly.* November 1998, pages 40–47.

Hillman, Col Rolfe L., U.S. Army (Retired) "Proceedings" *Second to None: The Indianheads.* Annapolis: U.S. Naval Institute, November 1987. Pages 57–61. Author's usual excellent research produced outstanding article on the division in the war. Actually, Hillman, a retired U.S. Army officer, was better known for first-rate articles on the Marine 4th Brigade.

Series in the "Marine Corps Gazette" entitled *Lest We Forget ... Infantry battalion commanders in World War I.*

Daugherty, Leo J., III. *General Thomas Holcomb (1879–1965).* Page 88, August 1997

Thomas, Col Gerald C. *Battalion Command 'Over There' The Fifth Marines, 1917–1918.* Pages 112 & 106 (correct). Brief biographical sketches of each of twenty different officers.

_____. *The Sixth Marines, 1917–1918.* Same as above but only nine officers. Pages 88 & 78.

_____. *The Sixth Machinegun Battalion.* Same but with three officers. Pages 96 & 82.

_____. *Regimental Command 'Over There' 1917–1918.* Same with six officers. Pages 87 & 81.

Paris, Gus E. *Hold Every Inch of Ground.* N.d. [c. 1985], Owensboro, KY, 18 page typewritten biographical sketch (unpublished as far as I know) of then Logan Feland by the registrar and professor of history of Wesleyan College, Owensboro. About 18 pages.

Selected Books

Asprey, Robert B. *At Belleau Wood.* New York: G.P. Putnam and Sons, 1965. (The first book published primarily about the battle. Still useable though with many errors. This has been reprinted.)

Bellamy, David. *History of the Third Battalion, Sixth Regiment, U.S. Marines.* Pike: The Brass Hat, 2000. (Original was published in 1919 for members of the battalion. Many pertinent details not found elsewhere. Covers the entire period. Author was adjutant of the battalion.)

Boyd, Thomas. *Through the Wheat.* New York: Charles Scribner's Sons, 1923. (Though considered fiction, the author was a participant and describes from a personal perspective.)

Brannen, Carl A., Rolfe Hillman, Jr., and Peter F. Owens, editors. *Over There. A Marine in the Great War*. College Station: Texas A & M University, 1996. (The work is strengthened greatly by additional material prepared by the two editors, both specialists in World War I USMC history.)

Brown, William. *The Adventures of an American Doughboy*. Tacoma: Smith-Kinney Co, c. 1919. (Member of the 9th Infantry. Well done memoir. Wish there were many more like it.)

Catlin, Albertus W. *With the Help of God and a Few Marines*. New York: Doubleday, 1919. (Author was wounded leading the 6th Marine Regiment on 6 June. This is rather generic history.)

Clark, George B. *Devil Dogs; Fighting Marines of World War One*. Novato: Presidio Press, 1999. (Like most of the books here listed, the subject matter covers the entire period 1917–1919, with heavy emphasis on the battles, especially Belleau Wood.)

_____. *A List of Officers of the 4th Marine Brigade*. Pike: The Brass Hat, 2001 revised. (All active officers, including the U.S. Army officers, during the war with modest biographical details.)

_____. *Heroes of the 4th Brigade. Awards and Citations*. Pike: The Brass Hat, 2002 revised. (Details include awards, where and when, and why.)

_____. *The History of the Third Battalion Fifth Marines 1917–1918*. Pike: The Brass Hat, 1995. (Both the 1st and 2nd Battalions had been published in short, brief, and not very useful histories. This was created to complete the regiment.)

_____, editor. *History of the Fifth Regiment Marines (May 1917–December 31, 1918)*. Pike: The Brass Hat, 1995, reprint. (Original was poorly done requiring massive revisions. Limited value.)

Cooke, Elliott D. *"We Can Take it," with "We Attack."* Pike: The Brass Hat, 1992, reprint. (Excellent personal observations by one of the sixty or so U.S. Army officers leading Marines of the 4th Brigade. The first section deals entirely with Belleau Wood and the latter with Soissons.)

Cowing, Kemper F., and Courtney R. Cooper, editors. *"Dear Folks at Home": The Glorious Story of the U.S. Marines in France as Told by Their Letters Home from the Battlefield*. Boston: Houghton Mifflin, 1919. (Popular propaganda but also with some insightful observations.)

Gordon, George V. *Leathernecks and Doughboys*. Pike: The Brass Hat, 1989, reprint. (U.S. Army officer led a platoon of Marines at Belleau Wood. Good coverage.)

Hamilton, Craig, and Louise Corbin, editors. *Echoes from Over There*. New York: Soldier's Publishing Co., 1919. (More letters, not as solid as Cowing, but lightly useful.)

Harbord, James G. *Leaves from a War Diary*. New York: Dodd Mead and Co., 1925. (Harbord commanded the 4th Brigade at the Battle of Belleau Wood. One chapter devoted to that.)

Hemrick, Levi. *Once a Marine*. New York: Carlton Press, 1968. (Usual vanity press, with modest details by a participant with a memory loss. Could have used an editor. Still, has some value.)

Hunt, George A. *Over and Back*. Battle Creek: 1919. (Soldier with the 23d Infantry. Not seen.)

Mackin, Elton E. *Suddenly, We Didn't Want to Die*. George B. Clark, editor. Novato: Presidio Press, 1993. (Much better than average personal memoir of a private who was there.)

McClellan, Edwin N. *The United States Marine Corps in the World War*. Washington, D.C.: U.S. Government Printing Office, 1920. (The only official publication describing the events and efforts of the Marines in France. Must be used with caution. The author appeared reluctant to touch upon controversial subjects. He was, after all, the Marine Corps' Official Historian reporting directly to John A. Lejeune, MG Commandant and CG of the division after Soissons.)

McCrossen, Bernard J. *Diary of the Machine Gun Company, 23rd Infantry, Second Division, 1917–1919*. Vallender-Rhine: Hartmann Brothers., 1919. (Quite valuable personal memoir of a member of the 23d MG Company, 23d Infantry.)

Millett, Allan R. *In Many a Strife: General Gerald C. Thomas and the United States Marine Corps, 1917–1956*. Annapolis: Naval Institute Press, 1993. (Thomas served at Belleau Wood as an enlisted intelligence man and was later commissioned and went on to become a general.)

Morgan, Daniel E. *When the World Went Mad*. Pike: The Brass Hat, 1992, reprint. (Author served in the 6th Machine Gun Battalion at Belleau Wood. Highly charged memories.)

Morrey, Willard. *History of the 96th Company 6th Regiment in World War I*. Pike: The Brass Hat, 2003, reprint. (Loads of details about individuals, but few about the battles.)

The Ninth U.S. Infantry in the World War. Neuwid am Main: Louis Heusersche Buchdruckerei, 1919. (The regiment deserves much better, though there are some details.)

The Official History of the Second Regiment of Engineers and Second Engineer Train United States Army in the World War. Introduction by [Col] W.[illiam] A. Mitchell. N.p. [San Antonio], n.d. [1920]. (Excellent history, highly detailed with many photos.)

Pattullo, George. *Horrors of Moonlight*. New York: Private Printing, 1939. (Journalistic second-hand story of Belleau Wood.)

Rendinell, Joseph E., and George Pattullo. *One Man's War, the Diary of a Leatherneck*. New York: Sears and Co., 1928. (Author was in 97th Company, same as Scanlon, at Belleau Wood but was wounded in action at Soissons.)

Scanlon, William T. *God Have Mercy on Us!* Boston: Houghton Mifflin, 1929. (The author won a prize for this fictionalized story, but it is more accurate than many other so-called histories of that period. Scanlon was a participant in the 97th Company and describes the fighting better than most anyone else. Highly recommended.)

Sellers, James McB. *World War One Memoirs of....* Pike: The Brass Hat, 1997. (Author was wounded at Belleau Wood. Later commanded the 78th Company at Blanc Mont.)

Thomason, John W., Jr. *Fix Bayonets*. New York: Charles Scribner's Sons, 1927. (Mixture of pseudo fiction and facts, mostly the latter. This book led to JWT's being assigned the duty of writing about the events described for the Official U.S. Army history as titled.)

Wise, Frederick M. *A Marine Tells It to You*. New York: J.H. Sears, Co., 1929. (CO of 2/5 at Belleau Wood. Covers his part at Belleau Wood; used with caution it is excellent.)

The above list does not include a multitude of articles published in both the *Marine Corps Gazette* and the *Leatherneck,* many by the late Colonel Rolfe Hillman, Jr. The list is lengthy and covers nearly all periods since the end of that war to date. The U.S. Army's vaunted units are not as well listed above because, mainly, I do not have a record sufficient to do them justice.— *GBC*.

Index

Adams, LtCol John P. 167, 168, 171–73
Aisne River 19, 23
Anderson, Col Thomas M., Jr. 166–67, 169, 173
Armies *see* individual listings
Arnold, LtCol Alfred C. 112, 118

Bearss, LtCol Hiram I. 157, 187
Beaurepaire Farm 40, 211
Beauvais 23, 24
Belleau (village) 46–47, 49, 58, 61–63, 81, 102, 123, 132, 133, 140, 147, 160, 170, 191, 193
Berry, Maj Benjamin S. 88, 89, 98, 99, 102, 104, 131, 216
Bezu–St. Germain 73, 147, 192, 193, 198, 203–04, 214
Bischoff, Maj von, GA 96, 123, 145
Blake, 1stLt Robert 160
Blanchfield, Capt John 132
Bliss, MG Tasker H. (CoS, USA) 5
Boehn, Col Gen Max von, GA 15, 23
Bois de Baron 75
Bois de Belleau (Belleau Woods) 45, 50, 58, 61, 63, 66, 67, 70, 75, 91–105, 144, 108, 208, 209, 211, 216, 218
Bois de Bocage 100
Bois de Bourbetin (village) 111–20, 193, 194, 195, 196, 197, 198, 207–08
Bois de Bouresches 117
Bois de Bussiares 49
Bois de Champillon 41, 48, 59, 70, 74, 89, 91, 95, 98, 131, 133, 154, 160, 183, 211
Bois de Clerembauts 35, 38, 58, 106, 112–19, 195, 208, 209
Bois de Fond Jars 39, 42, 55

Bois de la Cote 192, 112, 116, 119, 192, 194, 208, 210
Bois de la Marette 36, 73, 111, 120, 193, 196–98, 202, 208
Bois de la Roche 112, 116, 192–94, 200, 201, 204, 210
Bois de Rochets 53, 62, 192, 206
Bois de Triangle 38–39, 54, 100, 106, 107, 114
Bois de Vaurichart 49, 55, 56, 57
Bois de Veuilly 49–50, 55, 56, 82
Bois du Chatel 131
Bois les Mares 75, 82
Bonneil 36, 38, 40, 41, 45, 208
Bouresches 40, 45, 46, 48, 144, 165, 184, 189, 191, 193, 196, 208, 209, 211, 218
Bouton, Maj Arthur E. 36, 195, 199
Bridges, Col Charles H. 26
British Army 16; Fifth Army (Gough's) 16; IX Corps 16, 19
Brockmüller, Colonel, GA 15
Brown, Col Preston 25, 26, 28, 30–36, 43, 44, 80, 103, 165, 166, 220
Brumetz 50, 55, 57
Buford, GySgt David L. 71
Bundy, MG Omar 25, 37, 40, 43, 44, 66, 69, 165, 166, 177, 186
Burnes, Capt John F. 155
Bussiares 46, 48, 49, 50, 58, 61, 65, 66, 73–75, 79, 81, 82, 85, 87, 90, 93, 94

Cantigny 23, 24
Carrières 39, 60
Cates, 1stLt Clifton B. 106, 107
Catlin, Col Albertus 39, 94, 96, 98, 100–02, 104, 106, 184, 185

Chamberlaine, Col William 38, 41, 177
Champillon (brook) 49, 56, 65, 73, 74, 79, 81, 82, 83, 85, 88, 89, 159, 184, 185
Chateau de Belleau 40, 47, 104, 133
Chateau Thierry 19, 21, 22, 24, 27, 30, 34, 35, 40, 41, 44–46, 51–54, 65, 71, 122, 147, 191–94, 207, 210, 216, 220
Chaumont-en-Vixen 11–13, 23, 24, 26, 27, 33, 37, 68, 142
Chemin des Dames 14–18, 23, 52, 76, 122
Clignon Brook (valley) 22, 29, 30, 35, 38, 44–46, 49, 50–57, 61, 62–65, 68, 74, 75, 79, 90, 93, 102, 190, 193
Cocheral 30, 38, 40, 41, 42, 66, 67
Coffenberg, Capt Baily M. 110
Cole, Maj Edward B. 39, 103, 104, 128–29, 217
Conachy, Capt Peter 88, 89, 91–92, 98, 132
Conger, Col Arthur L. 190, 193
Conroy, 2dLt Edward E. 98
Cooke, 1sLt Elliott D. 132, 133, 139, 150
Corbin, Capt William O. 69
Coupru 30, 35, 42, 44, 45, 67, 73, 113, 118, 210, 211
Craig, Col Malin 15, 25
Crouy-sur-Ourcq 26, 28, 29, 30, 32, 33, 34, 37, 38
Crowther, 1stLt Orlando C. 83

De Carre, Capt Alphonse 138
Degoutte, Gen Jean M.J. FA 34, 40, 43, 44, 93, 164, 165, 189, 214, 220
Domptin 44, 67, 211, 212
Dormans 19
Duchêsne, Gen Denis, FA 15, 25, 26, 29, 30, 34, 37, 220
Dunbeck, Capt Charley 133, 139, 151
Duncan, Capt Donald F. 106

Eaton, Capt Starr S. 200
Elliott, Maj Charles B. 112, 113, 114–16, 118, 119, 196, 200–01, 216
Epernay 19, 21
Etrépilly 21, 22, 52, 53, 150
Evans, LtCol Frank E. 103

Fay, Capt John 87
Feland, LtCol Logan 56, 88, 91, 94, 98, 102, 105, 131, 159, 160, 169, 171, 175, 185
Fere-en-Tardenois 19
Foch, Mar Ferdinand, FA 17, 43
Foret de Retz 17, 19
Fox, Maj Milo P. 110
French Army 17–19, 220; 6th Army 15–18, 24, 25, 28, 29, 31, 32, 33, 34, 44, 189, 211, 214, 220; 2d Cavalry Corps 57, 120; 2d Colonial Corps 11; III Corps 190, 194, 211, 220; IV Reserve Corps 19; V Corps 220; VII Corps 29, 42; XXI Corps 17, 21, 22, 104, 120, 133, 166, 189, 190, 208, 220; XXXVIII Corps 42, 73, 120, 166, 190, 193, 208; 7th DI 27; 10th Colonial DI 73, 120–21, 189; 22d DI 15, 44; 39th DI 190, 194, 197, 201; 43d DI 17, 40, 42, 44, 46, 55, 56, 59, 60, 66, 208; 73d DI 29; 164th DI 40, 42, 44, 190, 197; 167th DI 73, 79, 80, 82, 83, 93, 102, 122, 128, 131, 166, 168, 189; 187th DI 79; 53d Colonial RI 120; 116th RI 83, 131; 147th RI 177; 153d RI 198, 199, 202; 7th FA R 195; 37th FA R 67, 195; 232d FA R 67; 236th FA R 67; 333d FA R 179
Fuller, Capt Edward C. 129, 155
Furbush 1stLt George W., Jr. 200

Gallieni, Gen Joseph S., FA 27
Gandelu 29, 32, 37, 40, 46, 50, 54, 55, 56
Gaston, Maj Jesse 169, 170, 172, 173
German Army 14, 42, 216; Bavarian Crown Prince's Army 14, 16; German Crown Prince's Army Group 14, 18; 1st Army 14, 18; 7th Army 14–19, 21, 51, 54, 78, 153; 18th Army 18, 19; IV Reserve Corps 15, 18, 19, 22, 109, 122, 149, 153, 191; VII Reserve Corps 15–16; VIII Reserve Corps 15–16; XIII Reserve Corps 191; XVII Reserve Corps 16; XXV Reserve Corps 16, 18, 22, 51–52, 78, 165; 54th Corps 15–16; 65th Corps 15–16; Conta Corps 52, 54, 70, 78, 164; 1st Guards DI 18, 22, 78; 5th Guards DI 18, 51, 78, 90, 122, 128, 149, 153, 154, 164; 10th DI 51, 52, 54, 164, 191, 192, 197; 25th DI 147; 26th DI 51; 28th DI 18, 51, 52, 78, 164, 182, 191, 192, 197, 203; 33d DI 22, 52, 78; 36th DI 51, 52, 54, 65, 75; 87th DI 170, 171, 182; 197th DI 15, 51, 109, 122, 128, 131; 201st DI 191, 192, 197, 198, 202, 203, 206; 231st DI 21, 35, 51, 52, 53, 54, 63, 75, 78, 112, 121, 122, 191; 237th DI 47, 51, 109, 122, 123, 163, 171, 181, 182, 191; 244th Brigade 147; Queen Elizabeth Grenadier Guard RI 18; 3d RI, Foot Guards DI 90; 3d Reserve Ersatz RI 178, 179, 182; 1/3 178; 2/3 179; 5th Co. 179; 6th Grenadier RI 62, 76, 115, 119; 7th Saxon RI 90; 7th RI 71; 40th RI 123, 129, 130, 135, 137, 138, 141, 142, 145, 146, 147,

148; 1st Co. 146; 2d Co. 123, 148; 3d Co. 138; 5th Co. 123, 146; 6th Co. 123; 7th Co. 123, 146; 8th Co. 138; 47th RI 61, 62, 76, 112, 115, 116, 119; 2/47 76; 109th Body Grenadier RI 18, 155; 1st Co. 155–56; 4th Co. 155; 110th RI 141, 147, 148, 150, 151–52, 193; 273d RI 74, 84, 89, 90; 2/273 84, 90; 345th RI 182; 347th RI 173, 177, 178, 180, 182; 1/347th 177, 178, 179, 181; 1st Co. 178; 2d Co. 177, 178, 179; 3d Co. 177, 178, 179; 4th Co. 177, 178, 179; 2/347th 177, 178, 183; 5th Co. 178; 3/347th 178, 181, 182, 183; 398th RI 62, 63, 76, 107, 112, 115, 123; 401st RI 152, 198, 203, 204, 206; 10th Co. 203; 402d RI 192, 197, 203, 206; 1/402 192, 203; 2/402 192, 194, 203; 3/402 193, 198, 203, 204; 9th Co. 204; 10th Co. 204, 206; 11th Co. 204; 403d RI 192, 206; 431st RI 150; 444th RI 122; 460th RI 84, 85, 91, 96, 109, 145; 9th Co. 84, 85; 10th Co. 84, 85, 92; 11th Co. 84, 85, 92; 12th Co. 84, 87; 3/460 Bn. 84; 461st RI 63, 70, 100, 123, 126, 137, 138, 145, 147, 151, 152, 154, 175, 182; 1/461 Bn. 146; 1st Co. 145, 146; 2d Co. 145, 146; 3d Co. 146; 4th Co. 146; 2/461 Bn. 146; 5th Co. 146; 7th Co. 146; 8th Co. 145, 146; 462d RI 63, 84, 96, 145, 147; 25th Jager Bn. 90; 26th Jager Bn. 71, 90; 28th Jager Bn. 131
Green, Capt James O., Jr. 115, 201

Hall, Maj Charles B. 113
Hamilton, Capt George W. 83
Hamilton-Gordon, Gen Alexander, BA 16
Harbord, BG James G. 38, 56, 58, 80, 144, 149, 155, 180, 186, 220
Hartlieb, Maj von, GA 96, 134, 138, 141, 145, 146, 181
Helm, 1stLt 171
Herrington, Capt William G. 116
Herrinshaw, LtCol William F. 30
Hill 126 49, 63, 74, 82, 85, 93, 94, 96, 103
Hill 133 93, 94, 104, 105, 144, 145, 150
Hill 142 39, 130, 133, 166, 177, 183, 185, 211
Hill 153 132
Hill 161 48, 141
Hill 165 65, 67, 74, 75, 93
Hill 169 96, 99, 132, 133, 160–61, 173
Hill 175 200
Hill 181 48, 96, 100, 104, 110, 123, 159, 160, 162
Hill 182 189

Hill 187 193, 194
Hill 192 63, 112, 114–15, 116, 117, 189, 190, 194, 195, 201
Hill 193 53
Hill 201 36, 39, 41, 61, 65, 68, 211
Hill 204 21, 31, 35, 45, 120–21, 216
Hoffman, GySgt Charles F. 85
Holcomb, Maj Thomas 38, 39, 94, 98, 103–08, 125, 155, 157
Hope, 1stLt Edward B. 89
Hughes, Maj John A. 39, 95, 126, 127, 128, 129, 132, 136, 144, 151, 155, 157
Hurley, Capt P. J. 169

Issonge Farm 40, 70

Kaemmerling, 1stLt Gordon 116
Kaulbars, Capt von, GA 178
Keyser, Maj Ralph S. 159, 174, 177, 180

La Cense ravine 106–07, 114
La Loge Farm 60, 67, 70
Larsen, Capt Henry L. 99, 102, 104
La Voie du Chatel 39, 41, 54, 60, 65, 87, 131, 184
Lee, LtCol Harry 103–05, 126–29, 135, 151, 157, 159, 169, 184, 185
Lejeune, MG John A. 5, 6
Le Mares Farm 49, 57, 63, 65, 68, 69, 70, 71, 74, 83, 84, 131
Lenert, Pvt Henry P. 180
Le Thiolet 35–41, 57, 68, 70, 71, 183, 189, 195, 208, 211
Lewis, BG Edward M. 28, 29, 38, 113, 120, 135
Liggert, Maj Gen Hunter 211–15
Lizy-sur-Ourcq (Lizy) 22, 26, 29, 32, 36, 40, 41, 46, 49, 53, 54
Loconville 12, 35
Lucy-le-Bocage 39, 40, 183, 184
Ludendorff, Gen Erich Friedrich Wilhelm 14–15, 18

MacNider, 1stLt Hanford 198
Major, Capt Harlan F. 217
Malone, Col Paul B. 36, 37, 55, 56, 58, 66, 71, 113, 114–17, 118, 119
Marchand, Gen Jean Baptiste, FA 120
Marigny-en-Orxois 34, 38, 39, 49, 54, 60, 67, 184, 211
Marne River (valley) 21–28, 36, 43, 45, 46, 51, 54, 214
Mathews, 1stLt William R. 139–40
Mattfeldt, Capt Clyburn O. 34

May-en-Multien 16, 26, 56, 67
McFarland, 1stLt Hugh 110
McIndoe, Col James F. 39
Meaux 22–28, 36, 37, 38, 41, 54, 73
Messersmith, Maj Robert E. 108, 112
Milner, 2dLt Drinkard B. 150, 151
Monneaux 45, 120, 189, 194–99, 200, 207–08, 209
Montgivarault-le-Grande 39, 96, 106
Montigny d'Allier 32, 37
Montreuil-aux-Lions 30, 32–40, 43, 44, 54, 66, 67, 167, 214
Moore, Capt Charles E. 200

Naulin, Gen Stanislaus, FA 165, 166, 189, 220
Neufchateau 25, 31
Neufchelles 32, 34
Neville, Col Wendell C. 7, 39, 56, 60, 87–89, 104, 180, 184, 185, 213

Oise River 16, 19
Osborne, Lieut (jg), Weedon E. 107
Ourcq River (valley) 22, 26, 30, 31, 32, 45, 46, 52, 63, 78, 165, 213
Overton, 1stLt Macon C. 142

Paris 12, 24, 25, 27, 37, 39, 42, 45, 188
Paris-Metz Highway 26, 27, 158, 166, 183, 184, 193, 194, 195, 208, 214
Pavillon (Belleau Wood) 150–51
Pershing, Maj Gen John J. 214–15
Pétain, Mar Henri Philippe, FA 17, 43
Platt, Capt Richard N. 133, 176
Pyramide Farm 39, 40, 42, 55, 57

Quigley, Capt Thomas 162

Reims 14, 16, 17, 18, 19, 27
Robert d'Espagne 11, 12
Robertson, 1stLt James F. 107
Robinson, 1stLt Fielding S. 105
Rue Gobert 128, 157, 159

Sector Pas Fini 211–12, 214
Shearer, Maj Maurice E. 128, 135, 155, 156, 176–77, 179–80, 216
Sibley, Maj Berton W. 94, 98, 125–27, 132, 156, 174, 180
Sissler, 1stSgt Joseph A. 107
Soissons 16, 17, 18, 19, 21, 22, 27, 36, 54
Stone, LtCol Edward R. 28, 34
Sub-sector Marine 211–12, 213
Sub-sector Regular 211–12

Torcy 46, 49, 54, 122, 123, 131, 133, 140, 153–56, 169, 170, 171
Triangle (farm) 38, 54, 157, 158, 183, 185, 189, 195, 208, 209
Trilport 25, 30, 33
Turrill, Maj Julius S. 83, 87, 88, 89, 95, 98, 131, 160

United States Army: I Corps 213; Second Division (2nd Division) 5, 6, 9, 11, 17, 22, 23–25, 215, 220; Division casualties 215–18; Division Trains 13, 30, 37; 2d Mobile Ordnance Repair 196, 202; 1st Field Signal Battalion 13, 40, 42; Medical Detachment (ambulance) 13, 40; Field Hospitals 1, 15, 16, 23, 73; Military Police 13; Army Field Post Office 7, 10 13; Postal Detachment 13; 2d Engineers 12, 39–41, 59, 66, 68, 98, 105, 110, 125, 136, 152, 212, 213, 215; 1/2 40, 111; A Co. 195, 196; C Co. 55, 195, 196; D Co. 87; 2/2 40; 4th Machine Gun Battalion 12, 25, 26, 40, 41, 56, 73, 187, 207, 212, 215; B Co. 207; 2d FA Brigade 12, 26, 30, 60, 67, 81, 94, 98, 133, 154, 207, 213; 12th FA 11, 67, 131, 134, 149, 178; 15th FA 12, 67, 111, 195; 17th FA 12, 67, 111, 134, 178, 179, 195; 2d Trench Mortar Battery 73, 206; *3d Brigade* 12, 23, 30, 39, 98, 105, 111, 113, 118, 120, 157, 183, 190, 214, 215–16; 9th Infantry 12, 29, 33, 73, 105, 111, 112, 120, 121, 158, 159, 183, 208, 209–210, 214, 215–16; Machine Gun Co. 195; 1/9, 12, 33, 34, 41, 73, 112, 201; A Co. 201; B Co. 159, 210; 2/9 13, 33, 34, 41, 112, 195, 198, 200, 201, 204, 209; E Co. 199; F Co. 199; G Co. 195; H Co. 199, 200; 3/9 12, 33, 41, 60, 112; 23d Infantry 12, 36, 73, 95, 105, 106, 111–14, 119, 155, 157, 169, 214, 215–16; Hdqs. Co. 13; Supply Co. 13; Machine Gun Co. 12, 116; 1/23 12, 55, 56, 71, 112, 114, 155; A Co. 117; B Co. 117, 159; D Co. 117; 2/23 12, 40, 55, 56, 57, 71, 73, 112; E Co. 159, 209; H Co. 159; 3/23 12, 55, 71, 112, 156, 159, 195, 196, 198, 200–01, 204, 209, 216, 217; I Co. 112, 116, 200–01; K Co. 112, 115, 116, 117, 119, 159, 200, 201; L Co. 112, 115, 200; M Co. 112, 115, 116, 119, 159, 200, 201; 5th Machine Gun Battalion 12, 25, 38, 39, 42, 55, 56, 68, 111, 183, 208, 210, 215; A Co. 111, 195, 196, 197, 198, 201–02; B Co. 111, 200, 201; C Co. 111, 112, 195, 202; D

Co. 111, 195, 196; *4th Marine Brigade* 6, 8, 23, 31, 213–14, 215, 216, 219; 5th Marines 6, 37, 38, 42, 59, 60, 73, 88, 89, 122, 128, 142, 208, 214; Hdqs. Co. 12, 70, 130, 131, 138; 8th MG Co. 12, 80, 83, 87, 89, 91, 95; 1/5 12, 40, 153, 154, 160, 168, 186, 187, 195, 208, 217; 17th Co. 83, 87, 89, 92, 160–62, 168; 49th Co. 83, 85, 87, 89, 91, 162; 66th Co. 83, 87, 162; 67th Co. 83, 85, 87, 89, 91, 187; 2/5 12, 56, 108, 131–33, 180, 186, 217, 218; 18th Co. 133, 134, 141, 150, 151, 152; 43d Co. 133, 138, 150, 151, 152; 51st Co. 69, 70, 88, 89, 91, 94, 131–34, 135, 137, 138, 150, 151, 152; 55th Co. 71, 92, 131–34, 136, 137, 138, 140, 150, 151, 152; 3/5 12, 57, 60, 154, 156, 158, 159, 195, 207, 216, 217; 16th Co. 91, 102, 176, 178, 179, 180; 20th Co. 99, 133, 158, 162, 178, 180; 45th Co. 88, 91, 92, 96, 98, 99, 102, 132, 176, 178; 47th Co. 99, 104, 105, 173, 176, 178, 179, 182; 6th Marines 13, 37, 38, 41, 42, 94, 96, 98, 102, 109, 125, 128, 135, 159, 183, 184, 185, 214, 218, 219; Hdqs. Co. 100, 101, 126; Supply Co. 13; Stokes Mortar Platoon 125–26, 129; 1/6 39, 41, 58, 59, 95, 177, 182, 186, 217; 75th Co. 129; 76th Co. 142; 2/6 38, 39, 41, 58, 186, 187, 208, 216, 218; 78th Co. 106, 108, 114, 157; 79th Co. 103, 106, 107, 108, 155; 80th Co. 106, 110, 125, 155, 157; 96th Co. 103, 104, 106, 107, 108, 114, 157; 3/6 41, 60, 144, 153, 154, 160, 166, 168, 171, 180, 186, 187; 82d Co. 100, 110, 126, 127; 83d Co. 100, 110, 125, 127, 176; 84th Co. 100, 108, 125, 127; 97th Co. 100, 108, 125, 127; 6th Machine Gun Bn. 12, 13, 25, 56, 68, 103, 112, 128–29, 130, 132, 159, 187, 207, 217; 15th Co. 83, 84, 87, 94; 23d Co. 89, 128, 207; 77th Co. 80, 94, 207; 81st Co. 89, 94, 95; *3d Division* 11, 21, 120, 166; 7th Infantry 166–67, 169–70, 174, 185, 207; 1/7 166–67, 170, 171, 172, 173, 175, 180; A Co. 167, 170, 171, 172, 173; B Co. 167, 170, 172, 173; C Co. 167, 170, 172, 173; D Co. 167, 170, 172; 2/7 169, 174; E Co. 169; F Co. 169; G Co. 169; H Co. 169, 173, 174; 3/7 169, 170, 172, 174, 177; I Co. 169, 171; K Co. 169; L Co. 169, 174; 30th Infantry 120; *26th Division* 47, 188, 210, 213, 214, 220; 51st FA Brigade 213–14; 51st Infantry Brigade 210, 214; 52d Infantry Brigade 188, 213–14; 101st Engineers 213; 103d MG Bn. 207, 210

Upton, Col Leroy S. 28, 29, 33, 34, 35, 36, 120

Valentine, Capt Frank C. 115, 200
Vaux (Vaux-la Roche) 21, 48, 96, 112, 115, 119, 120–21, 165, 212, 213
Ventelet Farm 40, 41, 42, 57, 60, 216
Verdun 11, 46
Verneuil 19, 21
Vesle River 18, 19
Veuilly 49, 57, 65, 67, 70, 74, 75, 79, 89, 93, 95, 105, 130
Vierzy 19, 21
Villers Cotterets (and forest) 19, 21, 54
von Conta, Gen, GA 51, 52, 191

Waddill, Maj Edmund C. 112, 114–15, 117
Wass, Capt Lester S. 133, 139, 151
Whitley, Maj Franklin L. 35
Williams, Capt Lloyd R. 69, 88, 133, 138
Winans, Capt Roswell 87, 160–61
Wise, LtCol Frederick M. 69, 92, 105, 144, 160, 162
Wodarczyk, MarGun Michael 137

Yowell, Capt Robert 176

Zane, Maj Edmund L. 207
Zane, Capt Randolph T. 106–08, 126
Zone of Principal Resistance 211–12
Zone of the Advance Posts 211–12
Zone of the Reserves 211–12

www.ingramcontent.com/pod-product-compliance
Ingram Content Group UK Ltd.
Pitfield, Milton Keynes, MK11 3LW, UK
UKHW041938140426
5217IPUK00014B/550